Ain't you got a right to the tree of life?

Ain't you got a right

THE PEOPLE OF JOHNS ISLAND, SOUTH CAROLINA—THEIR FACES, THEIR WORDS, AND THEIR SONGS

Revised and Expanded Edition

Photographs by Robert Yellin
New Photographs by Ida Berman, Gary Hamilton, and Others
Music Transcribed by Ethel Raim
Preface by Charles Joyner
Afterword by Bernice Johnson Reagon

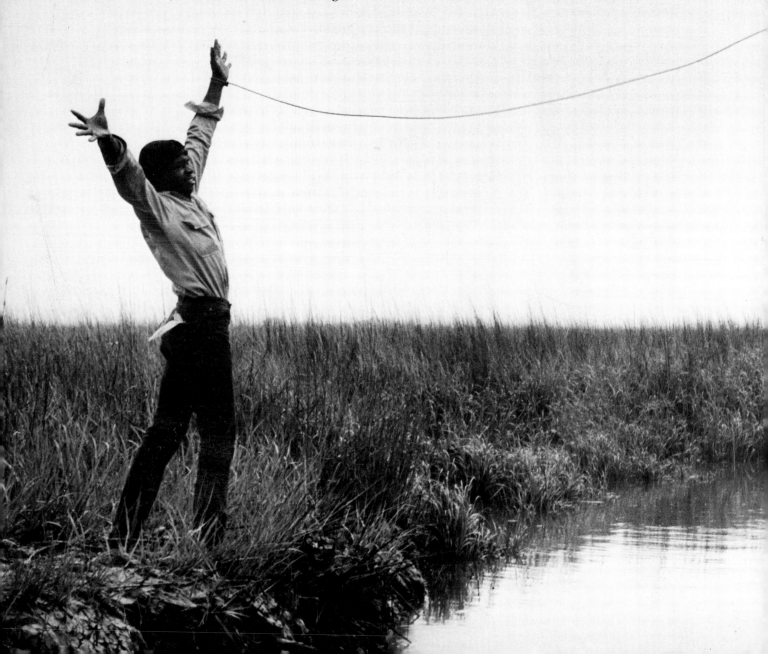

to the tree of life?

Recorded and Edited by

Guy and Candie Carawan

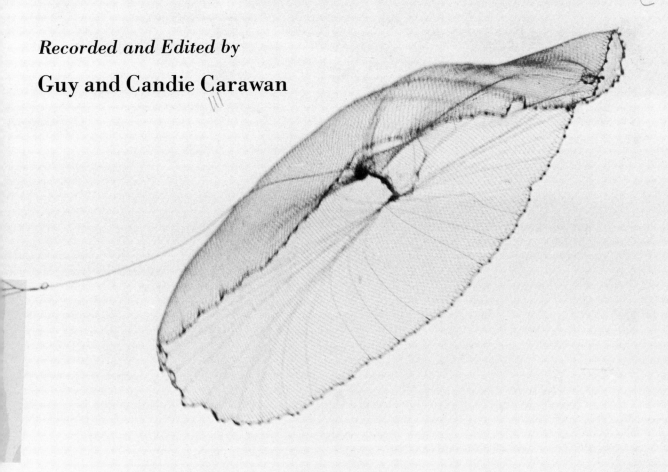

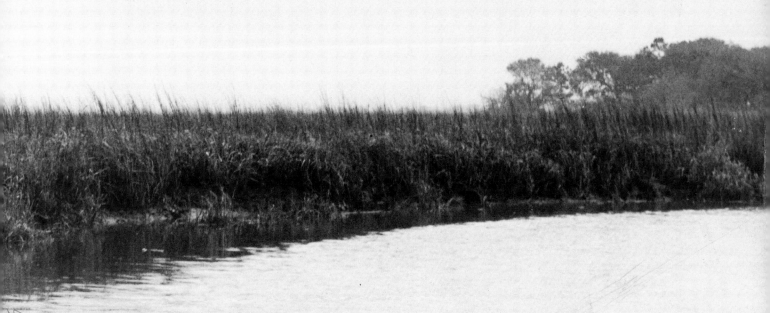

Brown Thrasher Books

THE UNIVERSITY OF GEORGIA PRESS

Athens and London

Text © 1966, 1989 by Guy and Candie Carawan

Words and Music © 1966, 1989 by the Class Meeting of Moving Star Hall

New Words and Music © 1989 by Alice Wine and the Moving Star Society

Photographs © 1966, 1989 by Robert Yellin

New photographs to the Brown Thrasher Edition are copyrighted in the names of the individual photographers.

Preface and Afterword to the Brown Thrasher Edition © 1989 by the University of Georgia Press, Athens, Georgia 30602

The paper in this book meets the guidelines for permanence and durability of the Committee on Production Guidelines for Book Longevity of the Council on Library Resources.

Printed in the United States of America

93 92 91 90   C 5 4 3 2

98 97 96 95 94 P 5 4 3 2 1

Library of Congress Cataloging in Publication Data

Carawan, Guy.
  Ain't you got a right to the tree of life? : the people of Johns Island, South Carolina—their faces, their words, and their songs / recorded and edited by Guy and Candie Carawan ; photographs by Robert Yellin ; music transcribed by Ethel Raim. — Rev. and expanded ed. / new photographs by Ida Berman, Gary Hamilton, and others ; preface by Charles Joyner ; afterword by Bernice Johnson Reagon.
      p. cm.
  "Brown Thrasher books."
  Bibliography: p.
  ISBN 0-8203-1132-4 (alk. paper)
  ISBN 0-8203-1643-1 (pbk.: alk. paper)
  1. Afro-Americans—South Carolina—Johns Island—Social life and customs.   2. Johns Island (S.C.)—Social life and customs.   3. Afro-Americans—South Carolina—Johns Island—Music.   4. Folk music—South Carolina—Johns Island.   5. Folk-songs, English—South Carolina—Johns Island.   I. Carawan, Candie.   II. Title.
E185.93.S7C3   1989
975.7'915—dc20   89-4846
                                     CIP

British Library Cataloging in Publication Data available

Ain't You Got a Right to the Tree of Life? was first published in 1966 by Simon and Schuster.

CONTENTS

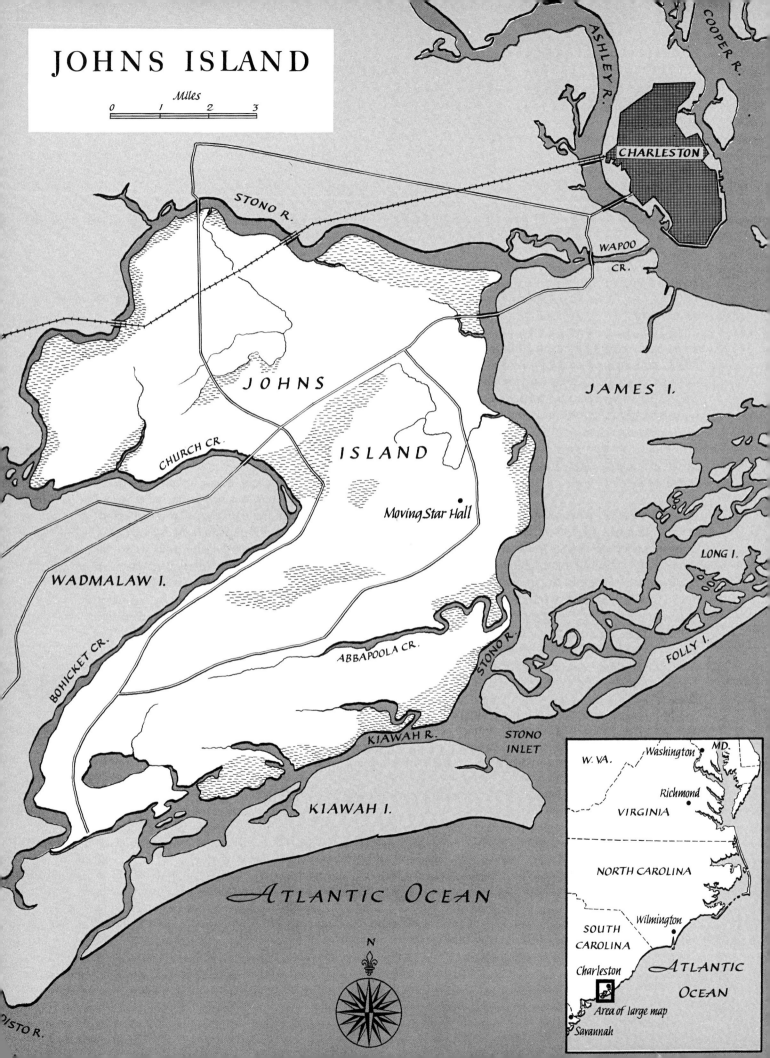

PREFACE

The future of American Negroes is in the South. Here they have made their greatest contribution to American culture; and here they have suffered the damnation of slavery, the frustration of reconstruction and the lynching of emancipation. . . . Here is the magnificent climate; here is the fruitful earth under the beauty of the Southern sun; and here, if anywhere on earth, is the need of the thinker, the worker, and the dreamer. This is the firing line.

W. E. B. DuBois, speech at Benedict College, Columbia, South Carolina, October 20, 1946

THE TRAFFIC on River Road is heavy. When I first came to this part of Johns Island in 1964, it was a quiet rural black community. Now expensive cars cruise past on their way to Kiawah and Seabrook islands. These resort islands can only be reached by driving across Johns Island and meeting the approval of a guard at a security gate. Beyond the guarded gates are plush hotels and upscale shopping facilities, beachfront houses and condominiums. Those who are waved through the checkpoint are mainly affluent visitors from afar.

The traditional and the modern coexist eerily on Johns Island now. I notice the incongruity at once in Wesley United Methodist Church. I sit in its elegant pews and listen to the organist and the robed choir perform staid hymns from the Methodist hymnal. But the congregation sings out in the old African polyrhythmic style of the sea islands, almost as though the hymns were ancient spirituals. The present organist accompanies the hymns in a jazz-influenced modern gospel style that dominates the singers and sometimes drowns them out. The result is exciting, but I miss the special kind of excitement of the old *a capella* shouting style for which Johns Island is famous.

I have come to Johns Island with Candie Carawan, historian Albert Raboteau, and filmmaker Louise Cox. Candie's husband, Guy, is flying in from a folk song concert and is to join us this afternoon at Janie Hunter's house. In the 1960s Guy and Candie lived and worked among these black people on Johns Island for two years. They wrote a book about the people of Johns Island—*Ain't You Got a Right to the Tree of Life?* But they are more than just the chroniclers of this story. They are part of the story too. They came to Johns Island to learn about Gullah culture; but they also made a great contribution to the people of Johns Island, and through them, to the civil rights movement and to all of us.

The story of Johns Island is one of a community's efforts to develop its economic and social resources in accordance with its own needs while at the same time preserving its incredibly rich folk heritage. Balancing development and preservation is a difficult task under any circumstances. When one considers the formidable obstacles against which the people of Johns Island had to contend—the legacy of slavery and segregation, the burdens of poverty and lack of education, the pressures of economic survival—that they have maintained that precarious balance for more than a generation seems little short of miraculous. It is not a story of inevitable or easy success, and it is not over yet. But enough has happened to command our attention. And enough remains in doubt to command our sympathy.

SKIN AND HAIR. Skin and hair. They seemed to matter more than anything else when Guy first came to Johns Island in 1959. The statute books in South Carolina were filled with laws based on differences in skin and hair. It seems unbelievable in retrospect, but it was the official policy of my native state to separate South Carolinians from one another on the basis of skin and hair. Blacks and whites could not legally associate except in the sanctioned roles of subordinate and superior. Not only were most black citizens disfranchised at the polls, blacks were systematically separated from whites in schools, in jobs, and in public accommodations. The policy was called segregation, or Jim Crow, and it was very thoroughgoing. Behind the mask of civility, our harsh racial caste system branded all black South Carolinians as inferior.

Segregation was characterized by two sets of almost everything: there was one set of churches, stores, funeral homes, and drinking fountains for black Carolinians and another for white Carolinians. Black students were relegated to Jim Crow schools, black travelers to the back of the Jim Crow bus, and black moviegoers to the Jim Crow balcony. And there were separate neighborhoods for blacks and whites. It was not difficult to tell which were which: the pavement ended where the black neighborhoods began. But not everything came in pairs. Some things, such as parks, libraries, and swimming pools, were rarely available to black Carolinians at all.

Anyone could tell that the segregation laws were unconstitutional on their face: they violated the constitutional requirement that states not deny the equal protection of the laws to any citizen. But the system of segregation was even more subtly entrenched in South Carolina law and practice than that. It was also characterized by discriminatory enforcement of other laws that were not in themselves discriminatory. And social services were administered on a discriminatory basis. As a result, black Carolinians had less than half the chance of finishing high school as white Carolinians and less than a third the chance of finishing college or entering a profession. Moreover, black Carolinians had the prospect of earning less than half as much as white Carolinians, were twice as likely to be unemployed or imprisoned, and could expect a shorter life span.

Until the mid-twentieth century the only organization in South Carolina explicitly dedicated to racial advancement was the National Association for the Advancement of Colored People (the NAACP). At the time Septima Clark began teaching on Johns Island, the first chapters of the NAACP were being organized in South Carolina. By 1920 there were more than a thousand members in chapters around the state.

But the NAACP was an extremely cautious organization in those early decades. It took as its mission the improvement of black life within the segregated system rather than challenging the state's official racism. Unfortunately, its cautious approach enhanced the white stereotype that blacks were "contented." When the South Carolina Conference of the NAACP was formed in 1929, however, a shift occurred from "uplift" to a quest for equality. Three major legal cases—the teachers' salary equalization suit, the challenge to the all-white Democratic primary, and the suit for admission to the law school of the University of South Carolina—advanced the cause in the 1940s. When *Briggs v. Elliott*, the Clarendon County school case, was filed in 1950, the NAACP legal staff decided to launch a direct attack against public school segregation. *Briggs v. Elliott* was the only case from the Deep South in the package of cases upon which the United States Supreme Court, in a historic decision on May 17, 1954, declared segregated public schools inherently unequal. After the NAACP's aggressive legal action, the South Carolina legislature passed a law in 1955 forbidding any city or state employee to belong to the NAACP. Septima Clark, a long-time member of the organization, was dismissed from her elementary school teaching position. Although she had taught in the Charleston County school system for almost forty years, the Charleston County School Board denied her retirement pay when she was fired. She then took a job with Highlander Folk School.

In 1957, with training and assistance from Highlander Folk School, Septima Clark and Esau Jenkins began the first citizenship education school on Johns Island. They chose Bernice Robinson to be the first teacher. The classes did not merely stick to reading and writing for voter registration but also discussed the power that people could have if they know how government is organized. The islanders became aware of their rights as citizens and learned ways to achieve them. By 1960 nearly six hundred registered black voters were added to the rolls in Charleston County through the efforts of the citizenship school.

Guy Carawan first arrived on Johns Island on Christmas eve of 1959, and Esau Jenkins took him to the all-night Christmas Watch Meeting in Moving Star Hall. There Guy encountered African cultural survivals and what he called "the oldest form of Negro folk life still alive today in the United States." He had come to Johns Island from Highlander Folk School to learn about sea island culture and to serve as a chauffeur for Septima Clark, who did not drive. A native Californian with family roots in South Carolina, he had a master's degree in sociology and some training in folklore when he came to live with Esau Jenkins on Johns Island. Septima Clark and Esau Jenkins took Guy to community meetings and church services, where he met and sang with various members of the black community. "With these two beloved leaders to vouch for me," he noted at the time, "I've had the inside track in getting to know people who under different circumstances might be suspicious and unfriendly." He was inspired by the islanders' Afro-Christianity and their "praise house" form of worship. He thrilled to the old sea island spirituals and the islanders' "shouting" style of singing them. He fell in love with the sea island folktales and folk beliefs. He immediately recognized the importance of the rich folk culture he encountered on Johns Island, which would bring him back to the island year after year.

During his first winter on Johns Island, Guy developed a singing program as a new feature of the citizenship schools. The singing program had two purposes. One was to help keep alive the islanders' beautiful singing traditions. The other was to build group consciousness and boost morale by singing the old spirituals, protest songs, and other folk songs. The singing program proved to have profound inspirational value for everyone who participated.

One day Guy sang a version of "Keep Your Hand on the Plow." He had learned the song in the 1950s as part of the Peoples' Songs Movement. Alice Wine told him she knew "a different echo to that" and sang a sea island version. Guy passed on her version, "Keep Your Eyes on the Prize," to young civil rights workers at conferences in 1960. Thus it was that the Johns Island version of this spiritual became one of the great inspirational theme songs of the civil rights movement.

In 1961, prompted by the rapid growth of citizenship schools to other islands and the Charleston area, Septima Clark and Bernice Robinson developed the first program to train citizenship school teachers. This curriculum spread throughout the South as participants came from the Carolinas, Georgia, Alabama, Mississippi, and Tennessee. Thousands of teachers were trained. Such community leaders as Fannie Lou Hamer in Mississippi and Hosea Williams in Georgia went home to teach and to organize voter registration campaigns. They simply refused to put up with segregation anymore. By 1962, when the major civil rights groups turned their attention to voter registration, they were able to use the approach pioneered in the citizenship schools between 1957 and 1961 because by then it was clear that the approach worked. Thus the citizenship schools on Johns Island were the foundation for the voting rights movement and played a major role in the overthrow of Jim Crow.

SINCE 1959 Guy had spent part of each year working with the citizenship school on Johns Island. In 1961 Guy married Candie Anderson; and in 1963 they moved to Johns Island with their small son, Evan. During the next two years they shared in the life and fellowship of the black community around Moving Star Hall. Their purpose was to help preserve some of the older black folk culture on the island by bringing honor and recognition to it. As Guy wrote to Pete Seeger in 1965, "These days, you can go to any one of the major folk festivals at Berkeley, UCLA, Chicago, Philadelphia, or Newport and see some of the finest folk talent in the country. But the communities from which these people come have been neglected. Leadbelly and his music are forgotten in Shreveport, Louisiana. I'm hoping our work on Johns Island (South Carolina) will provide an example of what can be done in other areas. It would be a shame to let this music die at the roots." To that end Guy and Candie arranged for the Moving Star Hall Singers to perform their spirituals, folktales, and children's game songs across the country, from the Newport Folk Festival to UCLA. The Carawans produced recordings of the Moving Star Hall Singers, and Guy told of them and sang their songs in his own performances. As a result of Guy and Candie's efforts, the Moving Star Hall Singers became widely recognized across the country as perhaps the preeminent tradition bearers of the oldest layer of African-American cultural expression in living American tradition.

During this period Guy and Candie organized a number of "Sing for Freedom" workshops around the South, cosponsored by Highlander, the Southern Christian Leadership Conference, and the Student Non-Violent Coordinating Committee. At a three-day gathering in Edwards, Mississippi, for example, young civil rights workers from all over the region came together. There they exchanged ideas and shared experiences with the Moving Star Hall Singers, the Georgia Sea Island Singers, and traditional singers and instrumentalists from Mississippi. There they swapped songs and learned new verses. Many sea island songs were thus introduced to new areas in the South because of these freedom song gatherings.

Guy and Candie also worked closely with the Johns Island community to produce a series of sea island folk festivals. The folk festivals picked up much of their meaning from the context of all the things that were happening in the sea islands and the South—the citizenship schools, the voter registration drives, the mass demonstrations of the civil rights movement. The festivals did not celebrate a quaint past; they related the past to the present. The festival became the focal point for "pilgrimages" from leading civil rights workers in the South—Vincent Harding, Julius Lester, Bob Moses, Willie Peacock, and Bernice Johnson Reagon. The old songs and stories, the old talk and tales seemed strikingly new and fresh. The traditions of the past had a power to move a generation, a power to call the youth to the task of achieving democracy.

MANY CHANGES have come to Johns Island since Guy and Candie first lived and worked there. Some of the changes—low-cost housing, a health care facility, and a home for the elderly—have been initiated by the islanders themselves. But rapid resort development on Kiawah and Seabrook islands have contributed in their own way to the transformation of Johns Island, bringing new pressures and new challenges to the islanders.

One part of Esau Jenkins's legacy is a dedication to progress, to building institutions that enable the people of Johns Island to control their own lives. But another part of his legacy is a dedication to preserving the cultural heritage from which the people of Johns Island draw their strength and their distinctiveness. Not all islanders share both parts of Esau Jenkins's legacy equally. There are some who believe that the cultural heritage created by the ancestors in the bitter days of slavery and segregation is best forgotten. They feel the past as a burden of shame rather than as a source of strength. But without a sense of where they came from, how can the younger generation understand their achievement or comprehend how far they have come?

Whether the next generation will recognize and value the power and beauty of the past is by no means certain. At least some members of the younger generation are drawing strength from the old traditions. They are at home in the present because they are oriented in time as well as in space. Without a sense of where they came from, how else can people know whether they are going forward or backward?

If Esau Jenkins were still alive, I believe he would like this new edition of *Ain't You Got a Right to the Tree of Life?* In it Guy and Candie Carawan have preserved the magnificent heritage of the past in such a way that it can serve as a source of strength for the present. Johns Islanders—and all of us—can use that strength as Esau Jenkins did: to look to the future, to see what contribution we can make, to summon our friends to work together to do what still needs to be done.

Charles Joyner
December 1988

INTRODUCTION

IT HAS BEEN more than twenty years since *Ain't You Got a Right to the Tree of Life?* was first published—twenty-three years since the material was recorded and the original photographs were taken. In some ways the world pictured in those photographs no longer exists. When you visit the island now, you are immediately aware of change. There are many more houses and signs of prosperity. Most of the older, weathered, wooden homes are gone, replaced by brick or newer wood ones. The two main roads are heavily traveled now, primarily by people on their way to the two resort communities adjacent to Johns Island—Kiawah and Seabrook. On the major crossroads there are small shopping centers and in the summer months produce stands to market vegetables to resort-goers.

In the early 1960s the islanders were hard-pressed people—maids, cooks, farmhands, and laborers. The level of education for most was quite low and yet we found an insight and wisdom about life, and particularly a richness of folk expression, that was inspirational. Before Guy came to Johns Island, he had traveled and worked in many parts of the South. A musician with training in folklore, he had a keen appreciation for the depth and variety of southern folk culture. On Johns Island he found something special, a world with a beautiful and flourishing cultural heritage unlike any he had encountered before. He felt it should be shared with many more people and nurtured in a way that would enable it to survive. Yet Johns Island was in the midst of cultural and social transition. How could he, as a visitor, make a contribution to its survival? We would spend the two years we lived on Johns Island in 1963–65 struggling with that question and trying a variety of projects designed to focus attention on the cultural richness of the

area. Visiting the islands year after year since then, we are still concerned with the survival of its culture.

We did not come as traditional academic researchers. We came to work with a literacy and citizenship program developed by the Highlander Folk School to empower people. We knew this program would bring needed change to the islands. In a sense we had to create a role for ourselves which would both encourage that change and nurture those cultural roots. Guy worked during the winters between 1959 and 1961 using his music as part of the literacy classes. He drove Mrs. Septima Clark, the supervisor of the program, throughout the islands. He was introduced to the community by Mrs. Clark and by Esau Jenkins, a long-time fighter for progress and change, and was therefore accepted as a friend.

In 1963 we moved with our small son into the middle of the community around Moving Star Hall, the praise house and gathering place for many of the people Guy had met in the literacy program. During the next two years we gradually got to know our neighbors until finally they were sharing with us many of their real treasures: their warmth, generosity, candor, and humor, their wisdom, their songs and stories, the good times in their homes and fellowship in their social and religious gatherings. We recorded many hours of interview material, life experiences, religious expression—particularly several all-night watch meetings in Moving Star Hall, folktales and remedies, children's game songs. We produced two albums and published the first edition of this book. During this period we worked with Esau Jenkins and others to put on a series of sea island folk festivals for island residents and for visitors from the lowcountry area and elsewhere. We also arranged for a group of singers from Moving

Star Hall to travel to other parts of the country to share their songs, in an effort to keep alive some of the older folk material. Each of these projects brought a complex mixture of success and problems and a renewed determination to keep trying.

For generations the Johns Island people were relatively isolated from mainstream America. The low, flat island, covered with tidal creeks and marshes, farmland, and forests of oaks draped with gray Spanish moss, was accessible only by boat until the early part of the century, when bridges and causeways connecting it with the mainland began to be built. Cut off from the mainland, these descendants of cotton plantation slaves retained many aspects of the old slave culture: a regional dialect, Gullah, still marked by distinctly African and Caribbean traits; a large body of folktales, cures, and supernatural beliefs; and a folk version of Christianity with a "shouting" style of singing old spirituals and hymns and a local "praise house" form of worship.

Old and new institutions existed side by side. For many people, Moving Star Hall—a tiny, battered clapboard building—had been the central meeting place for nearly fifty years. It housed a "tend-the-sick" and burial society, a secret lodge, and a community of worship. Here the members could express themselves freely and fully; in the Sunday night worship service each person took a turn preaching, testifying, praying, and raising a song.

Down the road a mile or so is Wesley Methodist Church, where a number of these same people attended regular Sunday services. Here the old folk ways were gradually being replaced by more formal modern practices. Wesley is a fine church with handsome pews, Methodist hymnals, a robed choir, and an organ. On the first Sunday of the month everyone listened to the Reverend G. C. Brown, who came from the mainland in the 1930s with a college degree, and sang hymns and spirituals led by the choir. But on the three Sundays a month when he preached in other churches, the congregation forgot about the organ and the hymnals and sang older spirituals, hymns, and shouts,

accompanied only by foot and hand rhythms; the service became much more spontaneous, like that in Moving Star Hall.

In the intervening years, this evolution toward more modern forms has continued. Moving Star Hall is no longer being used for the intimate and intense prayer meetings or for the all-night watch meetings attended primarily by the older people. These important gatherings now take place in the larger churches. The Hall is currently home to a younger congregation, a Pentecostal church pastored by David Hunter, a member of one of the families very important to the original book. Here you find, along with more modern gospel songs and sermons, echoes of the old form of worship, but with the accompaniment of snare drum replacing the complex hand and foot rhythms of the shout. In the larger island churches, there is a vigorous contemporary religious culture with gospel choirs, wonderful organ accompaniment, and powerful preachers. But the older, more spontaneous forms of expression—raising a song by the spirit, taking it into a shout, testifying and preaching when moved by feelings—are not so easily integrated into the more formal structure of the service. There is a feeling from some of the younger people that it will be no great loss if this older level of expression dies out completely. One member of Wesley put it most succinctly when he explained, "There is a battle going on in the church now to get rid of all the old-style religion and singing. The battle is going on subconsciously. It's not going on knowingly because if it was put on the table, folk would take another look at it." It is our profound hope that people *will* take another look at it and make sure a place for the older expression remains. For this deepest layer of cultural tradition is marked by great complexity and beauty—the product of generations of community creativity.

In the 1960s the most unusual and modern institution on Johns Island was the Progressive Club, a successful consumers' cooperative owned and operated by some of the poorest people on the island. It contained a large grocery store and the only gym on the island and served as a center for adult education and voter registration. The man who organized the Progressive Club was Esau Jenkins, who was born and raised on Johns Island and became one of the most effective grass roots leaders in the South. It was Esau who first conceived the Citizenship School Program, which the Reverend Martin Luther King's organization later administered throughout the South. The remarkable story of Esau's life and his efforts to bring progress to Johns Island is told in chapter 6. At that time it was not so clear how important the spread of the Citizenship School Program across the South was to be. A chapter has been added to trace the history of the program in the 1950s and its subsequent impact on the civil rights movement.

Esau Jenkins died in 1972, and his wisdom and understanding, his fighting spirit, are missed by all. In December 1987, while we were interviewing people for the update to this book, Septima Clark also died. A teacher all her life, she taught on Johns Island in 1916 as a teenager. She was part of the Charleston County school system until 1956, when she was fired for belonging to the NAACP. She then went to work for the Highlander Folk School and became supervisor of the literacy program in the sea islands. At the time of her death, she was recognized nationally as an educator and civil rights leader.

In 1988 many of the families who told their stories in the early 1960s still live on Johns Island. Most of the older people have passed on, of course, and children have grown and married and have children of their own. The younger generation has received more education, sometimes quite sophisticated skills. Gerald Mackey is a good example. At the end of chapter 6 he can be seen as a teenager riding in the back of a truck on the way to work in the fields. Today he is an evaluator of teachers for the school system and a candidate for his doctorate. Esau's children became teachers, community workers, a lawyer, the administrator of a major health care delivery system on Johns Island.

Bill Saunders told us in 1965 that had he been born white, he might have accomplished something. He nevertheless has gone on to accomplish a good deal. He founded the Committee on Better Racial Assurance (COBRA), a multi-issue community organization in Charleston also serving the sea islands. He has been chairman of the Charleston County Democratic party. He ran for state senate and received support in both the black and white communities. He is the owner of WPAL, a vital radio station in Charleston that consistently addresses social issues as well as responds to the musical tastes of the community. He was the principal mediator in the major civil rights campaign of the Charleston area—a strike of hospital workers in the late 1960s.

The job situation on Johns Island has improved slightly. In the 1960s all young people who finished high school left the area to find work. Now, with improved transportation, it is possible for them to work in Charleston and still live on the island. The resort developments and the new small businesses offer some employment, but farming, long a mainstay in the island economy, is steadily declining. Farmland is now the prime target of developers. But the people who have stayed on Johns Island have held onto a firm determination to live in their traditional community, and many of their hopes and dreams are still in place.

Development on Johns Island has taken two forms. Tourist development, spreading rapidly all along the coastal islands south of Washington, D.C., is a threat to the indigenous population on Johns Island. Kiawah and Seabrook, accessible only by driving across Johns Island, are full-fledged resort communities with condominiums, hotels and inns, shops and boutiques, and large private homes. Both are entered by passing through a security checkpoint. Viewed initially as offering some economic and social benefits to island residents, both have been disappointing, catering to wealthy visitors from outside the region and offering only menial and limited employment. Wadmalaw Island, just across the Esau Jenkins Memorial Bridge from Johns Island, is in the throes of plans for development. An island committee made up of black and white landowners has been meeting regularly to design their own development plan that may counter those of outside interests. The County Commission accepted this new plan for limited and controlled development in early 1988, but the island residents know they must be constantly vigilant to ensure its success.

But another kind of development is here as well. In the 1970s a comprehensive community organization was put in place to address health needs on the island. Beginning first with a small clinic as part of Rural Missions, Inc., a local community improvement association, it grew to include environmental health, housing for the elderly, nutrition, and programs for substance abuse, as well as the development of a full-scale medical clinic and a nursing home. The Sea Island Comprehensive Health Care Corporation is a crucial factor in the present and the future of five sea islands—Johns, James, Wadmalaw, Edisto, and Yonges—and in many ways is a direct outgrowth of the story Esau Jenkins recounts earlier in this book. The Health Care Corporation is also a landowner, but it has utilized the land for the benefit of the indigenous community rather than for wealthy newcomers. It's a model worth looking at.

One of the greatest pressures on Johns Island is land ownership. As the chain of sea islands becomes increasingly valuable for tourist development, the patterns of passing property down through families and the need to know about land and tax laws become crucial to the survival of the community. People on Johns Island are now well aware of the value of their land and are coming together to plan their futures. Further down the coast, on St. Helena Island, Penn Community Center has sponsored a program to guard against the loss of land by blacks. The center's director, Emory Campbell, having seen his home community of Hilton Head undergo drastic change in the 1950s, is an eloquent speaker for the protection of the land for traditional communities. He and a co-worker, Joe McDomick, have come to Johns Island to participate in workshops on land issues.

As in 1965, education is still a major concern on Johns Island. Esau told of the struggle to get a black high school on the island. In the late 1960s the schools were integrated, and St. Johns, previously all white, became the high school for all island youngsters. Many white parents subsequently put their children into a private academy, but for the youth of the black community, St. Johns High offered new hope. Yet today the school system is still lacking. A desegregation suit against the county school system has been in federal court for six years. Brought by the Justice Department with the NAACP, it charges the Charleston County School Board with maintaining segregation and providing inadequate educational opportunities for minority students.

For nearly thirty years two things have greatly impressed us about Johns Island. One is the continuing process of community education and struggle that enables local people to maintain some measure of control over their institutions and their lives. The other is the rich Afro-American cultural life on the islands. Given the pressures of development and economic survival, the need to address contemporary issues with sophisticated tactics, what will survive of the older sea island culture? Public interest has certainly grown in coastal culture, language, and history on both a popular and scholarly level. In addition, there have also been patterns of change in the community and the cultural choices made by island people.

The Moving Star Hall Singers, a family group who began traveling nationally when we lived on Johns Island, continues to travel and to share religious music, folktales, children's game songs, and life experiences in a range of settings. They are widely recognized as outstanding carriers of the oldest layer of Afro-American cultural expression in the United States. In more recent years they have been invited to perform in local situations, including the Spoleto Festival held annually in Charleston. In the summer of 1988 they performed at a national festival of Afro-American arts in Atlanta.

In 1984 Mrs. Janie Hunter received a National Heritage Fellowship from the National Endowment for the Arts. Here is how the NEA described her:

> Sea Island people are noted for their retention of African cultural influences and for their creation of a rich body of game, work and religious songs, stories and craft skills. Janie Hunter is the matriarch of a family notable there for its musical artistry. Her voice is as strong and clear as a clarion bell and she carries in her memory a large repertoire of religious songs. Many of these came from her father, Joe Bligen, a fisherman and part-time farmer. Mrs. Hunter is an artistic decision-maker as well as a singer for the Moving Star Hall Singers, a group named for a Praise House on Johns Island.
>
> The music heard in Moving Star Hall is joyous, a music in celebration of life, freedom, and a deeply felt religious optimism, the dawning of a better world. Mrs. Hunter and her friends and family sing not only with their voices, but with their hands and feet as well.
>
> Like many other folk artists, Janie Hunter is multi-talented. She carries in her memory a collection of animal stories. They are for the amusement of children and adults, but they also show the uses of wit and logic. Mrs. Hunter is a maker of quilts and of dolls, a keeper of folk medicine techniques. She learned and remembered all these skills, and she is also an activist and transmitter. She has trained her children and the children of neighbors to respect and keep the beauty and artistic self-sufficiency of an important American place.

Mrs. Hunter felt she represented the island community when she was recognized for her cultural knowledge. When she traveled to Washington to receive the award, a vanload of family and friends from Johns Island went with her and joined in a jubilant shout as part of the Heritage award concert. When she returned to Johns Island, she was honored by her church, Wesley Methodist, and valued as a teacher in their own series on Afro-American heritage. Also recognized that same year by the NEA was a basketmaker from the Charleston lowcountry, Mrs. Mary Jane Manigault.

The older people will not lose their heritage. It is already too much a part of them. But they have fewer and fewer places to collectively express their wisdom and their traditions. With the testimonial meetings no longer taking place at the small praise houses, they gather in the larger churches or in the senior citizen centers. But as they explain, "You can't feel yourself in such a large place," or, "You can't really shout on a cement floor covered with carpet." And who will help the younger people recognize and value the strength and beauty in the older forms of cultural expression?

When we were on the islands in December 1987, we went to a Christmas party for senior citizens from centers on each of the five islands—about two hundred people, all from the older generation, attended. At each of these centers regular gatherings are held, and singing and sharing stories and remembrances are a vital part of the meetings. For all the interest of a wider public in sea island culture, it would seem that this kind of gathering in the community on a regular basis is the most encouraging thing of all.

Even more important, what these elders know must be readily accessible to the children and the younger people on the island. Surely in some homes and in some churches it is. It would be wonderful if it were also part of the school system. Mrs. Hunter is occasionally invited to a school in the Charleston area to share what she knows, but as she explains, many older people know what she knows if only they were encouraged more actively to pass it on. In the Johns Island senior center Mrs. Maggie McGill has organized a group that includes her mother (Mrs. Maggie Russell) and others, all of whom are wise in the old ways. The Senior Lights have recently begun to give programs of sea island spirituals and shouts in the Charleston area. In February 1989 they represented the coastal region in a conference at the Smithsonian Institution focusing on congregational song and worship traditions in black communities.

One very encouraging development in the Charleston area is the work of the Avery Research Center for African-American History and Culture. One of its goals is to maintain an archive of material from the Afro-American people of the lowcountry.

It houses several collections especially relevant to island residents, including the Esau Jenkins papers. In 1987 we placed more than sixty hours of recorded material, along with prints of Robert Yellin's masterful photographs at the center. We wanted people from the islands, as well as scholars, to have access to this material.

In 1963 Esau Jenkins told us:

Now some of us, because we can read a little bit more, forget about the place we came from and some of the songs which help us go on. And when older folks sang those songs, it helped them realize they're trusting in God and reaching for a better day. We certainly wouldn't want the children to get away from it. We should cherish it, we should preserve it and keep it. . . .

Now if we hide those sweet songs and try to get away from what we came from, what will we tell our children about the achievement we have made and the distance we have come?

In 1988 we noticed a plaque in the office of Bill Jenkins, Esau's oldest son and the administrator of the Sea Island Comprehensive Health Care Corporation:*

A people who have not the pride to record their history will not long have the virtues to make history worth recording: and no people who are indifferent to their past need hope to make their future great.

There really is treasure here—honey in the rock. Our hope is that it will always be a part of the islands and a source of strength to island people as they struggle with the pressures and challenges of the present and the future.

THIS BOOK IS BASED on tape-recorded material. In putting it together we tried to use the strongest photograph to illustrate each text; the person in an accompanying photograph is not necessarily the person speaking. Please see the list of photograph credits at the back of the book for specific information.

We have deliberately refrained from caricaturing the pronunciation of Gullah dialect by distorted spellings. There are a number of scholarly studies of Gullah now available in addition to Lorenzo Turner's classic 1949 book *Africanisms in the Gullah Dialect*.

The songs are sung without instrumental accompaniment. In most of the religious songs, complex hand and foot rhythms are added as the spirit mounts. This particular style is called "shouting." Songs are usually sung with an informal leader in a call and response pattern. The transcriptions are inevitable simplifications of what is sung, for to capture the subtle shadings and minute variations of pitch and rhythm would result in an almost unreadable score. Because the style is highly improvisational, the melody, the words, and the order of the verses vary with every performance and from one singer to another.

We strongly urge the reader to listen to these songs on two Folkways records of Johns Island music that are available: *Been in the Storm So Long: Spirituals and Shouts and Children's Games* and *Moving Star Hall Singers and Alan Lomax: Sea Island Folk Festival*. A new compilation of the best of these recordings is available on Folkways album 40031, *Been in the Storm So Long: Spirituals and Shouts, Folktales and Children's Songs*. An interesting comparison of the particular style in the Johns Island area with that of coastal singers further south can be made by listening to the albums of songs from the Georgia sea islands and from nearby McIntosh County.

*The authors' royalties from the Brown Thrasher edition of *Ain't You Got a Right to the Tree of Life?* are going to the Tree of Life Fund administered by the Comprehensive Health Care Corporation in support of cultural activities in the community.

WE WOULD LIKE TO THANK the following people for help and support in the publication of this book: Alan Lomax for consistent and continuing encouragement over the years; Myles Horton, who with his late wife, Zilphia, laid the groundwork on Johns Island for the citizenship school program and in the early 1960s encouraged us to make our home there; Ethel Raim for sensitive and skillful transcription of the music; Roger Phenix who helped us record and organize the material for the original book; all of the photographers represented here who contributed their photographs to the project; David Richer, a masterful photographer in Knoxville who has made the prints to be used for publication; Myrtle Glascoe-Greene and the Avery Institute for finding a home in the lowcountry for the original tapes and photographs; all the people on Johns and the surrounding islands who spent time with us helping to shape this new edition.

THIS BOOK IS DEDICATED to the people on Johns Island and the surrounding islands. It is their book in the most real sense of the word—they speak for themselves. From them we have learned much and are learning still, and our respect and admiration are very deep. It is dedicated to the memory of Esau Jenkins and of Septima Clark, two pioneering spirits whose vision and determination helped bring about much-needed progress and change. Finally, it is dedicated to the young people coming of age in the sea islands . . . to Gerald Mackey and Elaine Jenkins and others like themselves who have gained professional skills and chosen to plow them back into their home community . . . to the children of the Hunter family and others like themselves who have honed the rich cultural skills of their parents and ancestors and who now contribute these important resources to the islands.

Guy and Candie Carawan

August 1988

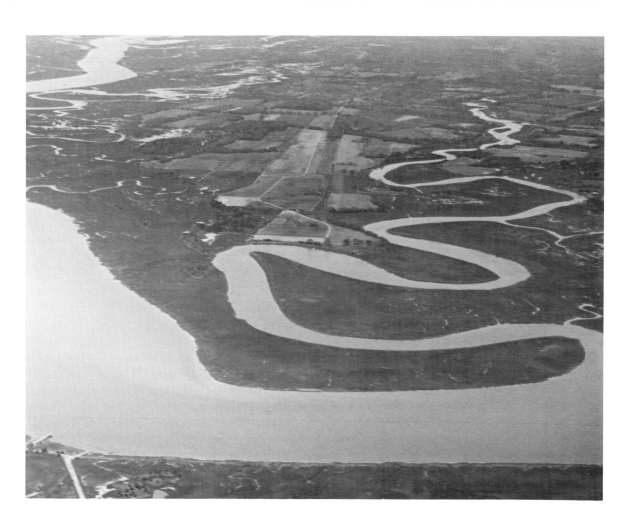

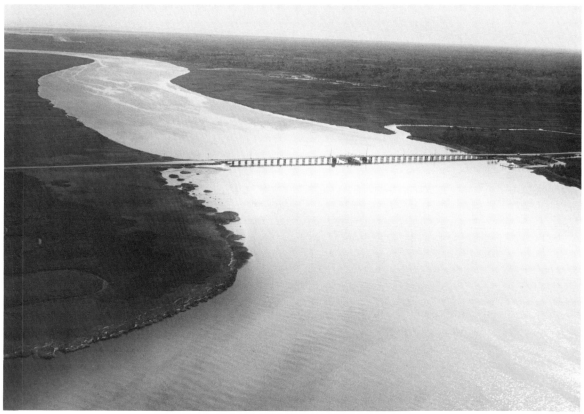

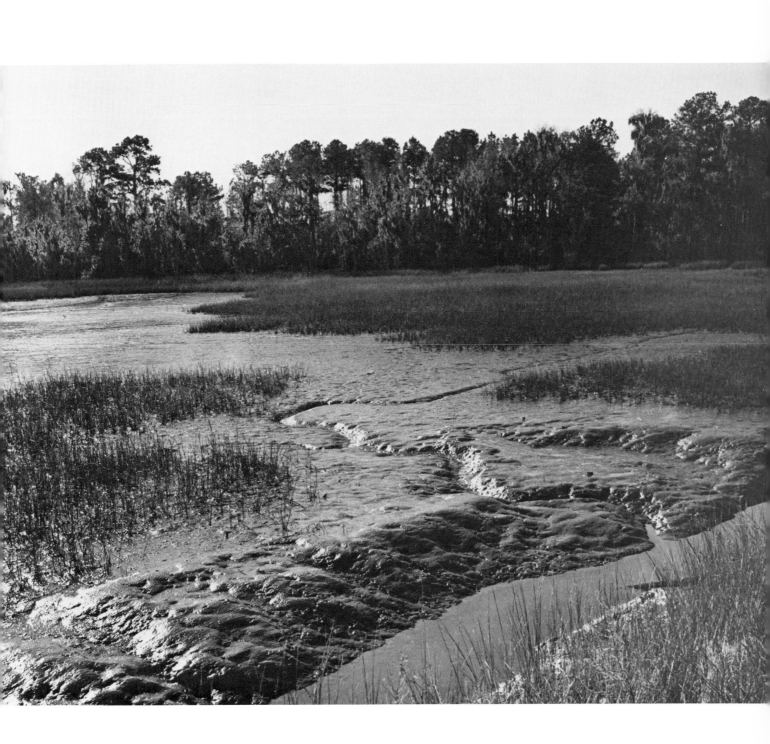

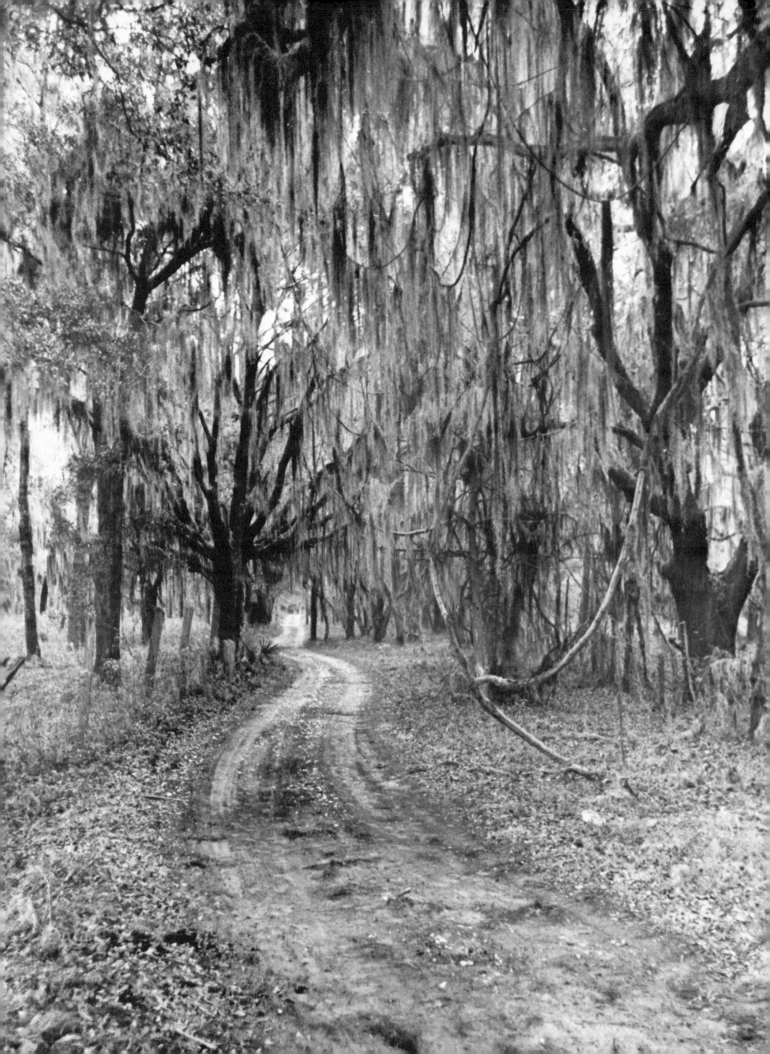

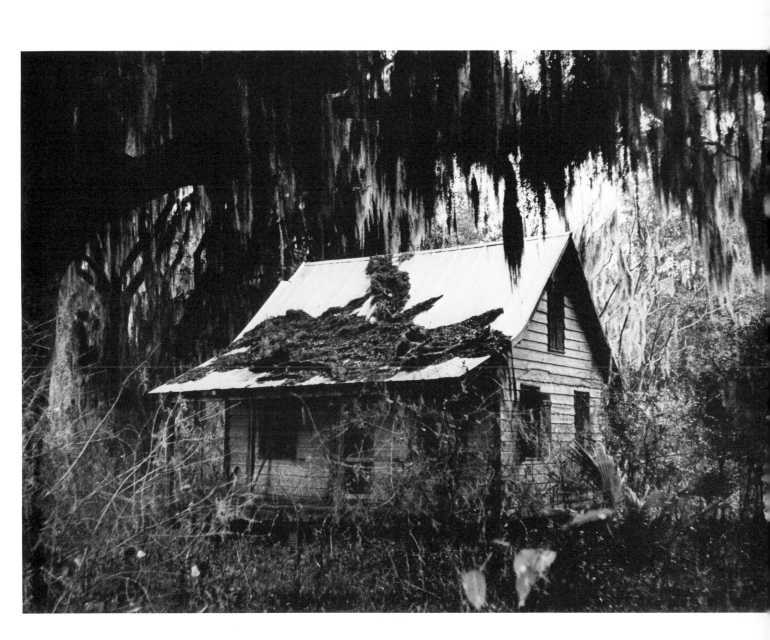

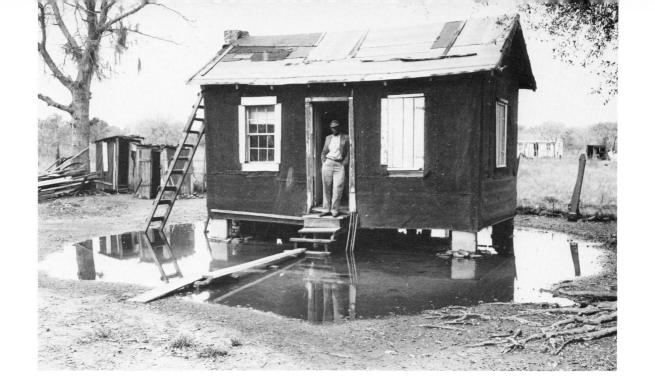

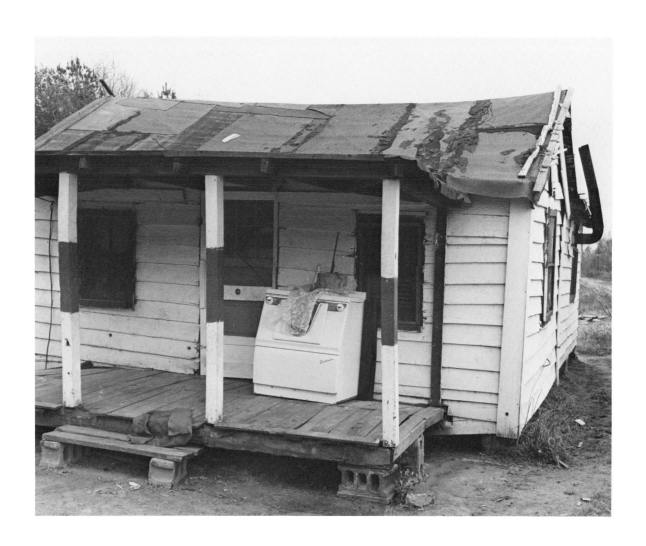

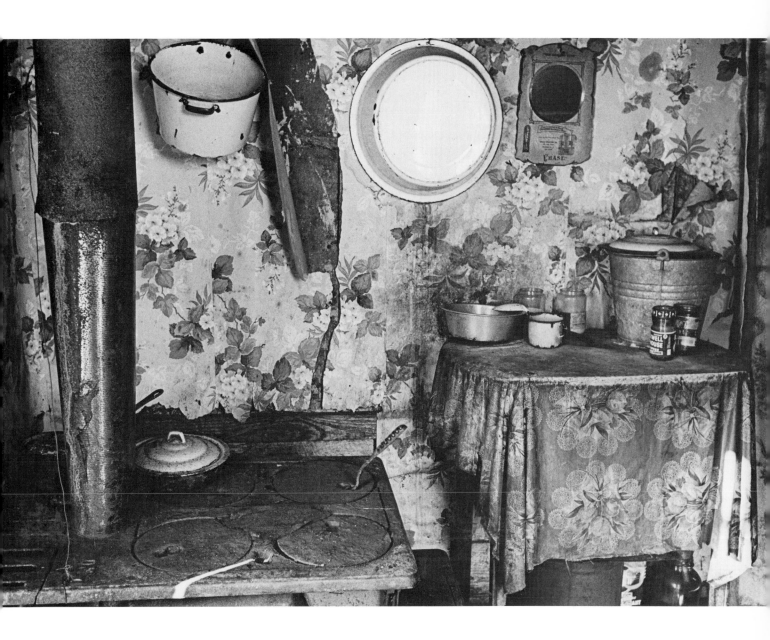

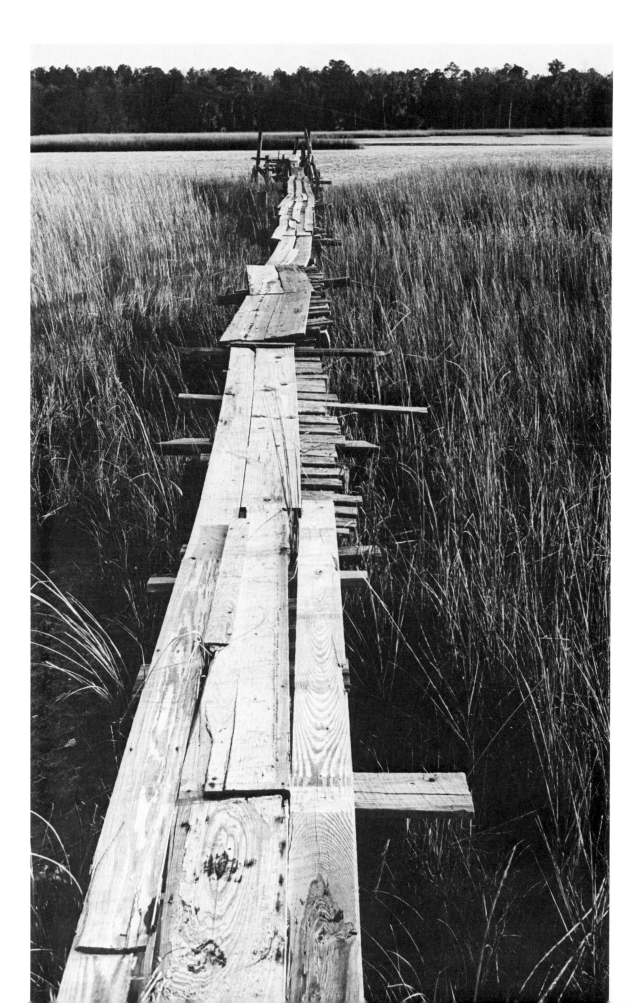

1. BEEN IN THE STORM SO LONG

DAYS PAST

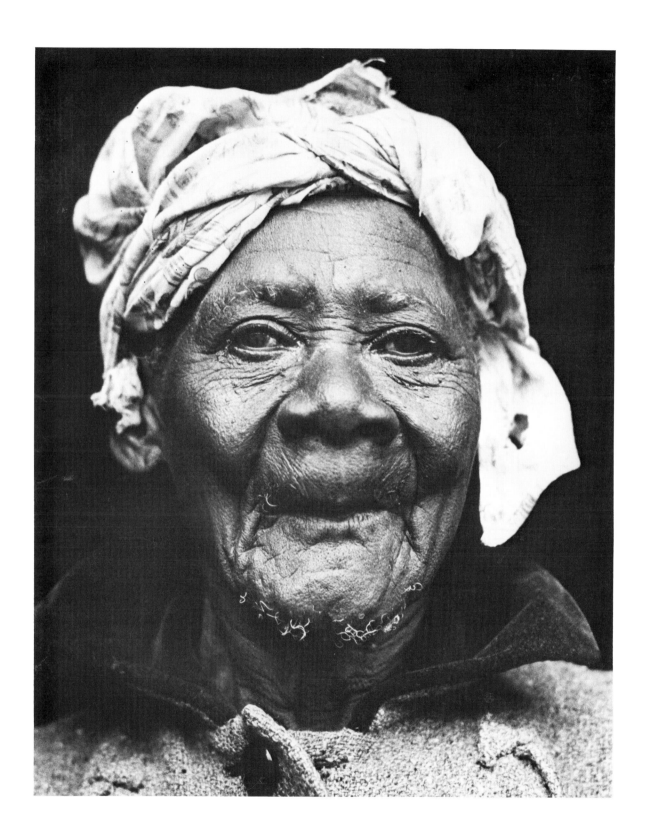

Rev. G. C. Brown
MY FATHER WAS BORN A SLAVE

My father was born a slave. He was fourteen years old before he had a shoe on his foot. And across the hills of South Carolina you could track him. They had big snows in the winter, and he wrapped his feet in gunny sacks. He said you could track him through his blood in the snow as he went out to bring the cows home during those snowy nights. In the morning he'd get up and run the cow up from where he slept all night to warm his feet, warm his hand with the warmth of their bodies. He was fourteen years old before he had his first pair of shoes.

My grandmother was half Indian. 'Course the Indians are stubborn, supposed to be. And being a half Indian and then being a slave also, she was very stubborn. She said that her master was a very cruel man. Since she was stubborn, he'd take her by the ears to the corner of a house, and just bang her head against the corner until she'd bleed. Come out covered in blood.

She died in the insane hospital in Columbia. You couldn't find three square inches on her head where there wasn't a scar when she died. And well, you find naked places all through her head where she was beaten until she be beaten into unconsciousness. Sometime she come to herself under a tree; Master had knocked her out. In her latter years it was discovered that during one of those forays the skull was crushed into her brain. The older she got, the worse it got. So she died at the age of seventy-seven, right there in Columbia Hospital. I knew her. I went to her funeral.

Mrs. Betsy Pinckney

THAT WAS THE TIME WHEN PEACE DIDN'T DECLARE

My grandmother was Hannah Seabrook. She raised me up and told me a lot about Rebel Times. Old Hannah Seabrook was a cooker and a washer. Her first husband got sold. Yes sir! They sell my father's daddy. Sell him for money.

When my father was coming up he used to have to go see what old Master wanted him to do. He was just a boy and couldn't do none of that heavy work. So the old Master would have him shine he shoes. One day he found some finger marks on 'em and knock my father down the stairs. Good thing I wasn't living in those days—you would of had to kill me first. But that was in the time when peace didn't declare.

When the war came through, my daddy, Cyrus Jenkins, was just a young boy. That time he was in the creek—had to dig the mud and mud the field for what they gonna plant that year. My daddy just up and ran off with the Yankees. He followed the Yankee until peace declared. My grandma didn't see him for four years. When he come back Grandma went to the depot. When she see her one son she drop her little bit of clothes and bind the son. That's right, had only one raggedy soldier coat and nothing else but that.

Mrs. Betsy Pinckney

SHE TAKE THE SCRAP AND MAKE
A LITTLE DRESS FOR ME

I born in 1878, the twentieth day of November. I was my ma's seventh child. Everybody run for give me name. I grow up in the white people house. I do the small things—I could thread needle for grandma, man. And they make me a little dress, you know. I even wash the Missus' feet. That's right, sir! That's right! Wash her feet in the basin. And when she was the only dressmaker 'round the village, she take the scrap and make a little dress for me.

My grandma had a scarf handkerchief—a white handkerchief she brought from Rebel Time, and when she died I tie he head with that. That's right. Yes ma'am!

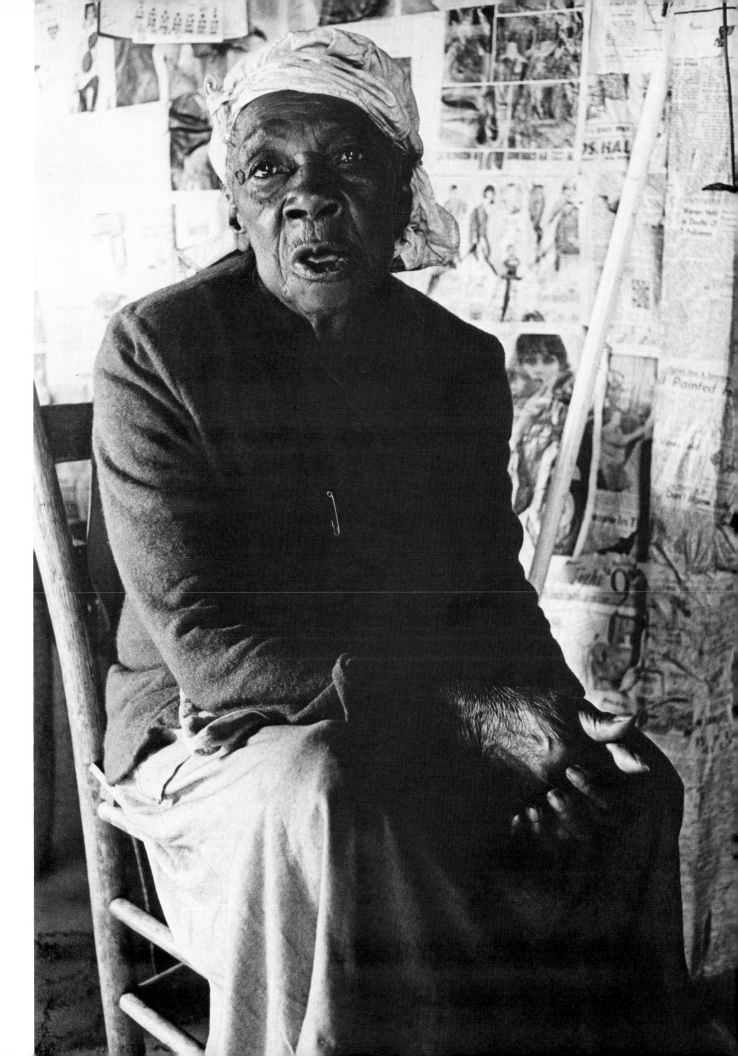

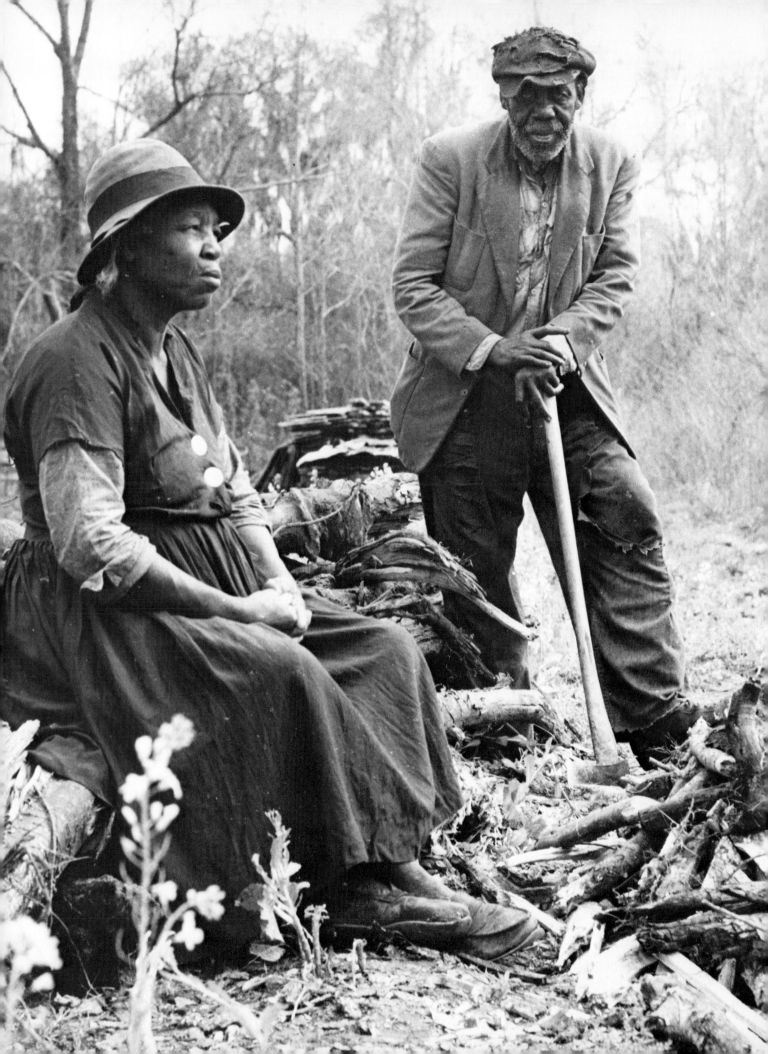

Mrs. Belle Green
WE ALL TWO WORK

I in my seventy-two. Then on the twenty-seven day of next year in August coming, I'll turn seventy-three years old.

When I married to Levy Green I was young. Me and him was married two years when the 1911 storm come. We raised on Johns Island—Levy home at Burden, the Clemmens' plantation, and my home is miles go down on that side. We didn't raise no children. I ain't got anybody. All my people dead out.

We all two work. I does work on the farm, in the field. Hoe work. Cabbage and white potato. We get three dollars a week. After I come down here I start to work with one man, and then I get so unpleasant and unfeeblish, he tell me, "If you can't work, I wouldn't look for you to work." I just give up. So painful old people now.

Levy used to work all about on the farm. He would take care of me if it the last thing he would do. Bus used to carry him all about to work. Then after he couldn't work no more, he give up. They put him on, you know—help. Wasn't much, but yet they put him on and we live by that. All of that done gone through. But I is a person don't complain. If I have anything I don't complain; if I have nothing I don't complain. It's no use. I just go on what God give me.

I thought I would done gone before Levy, 'cause I was the sickest one all the year through, but you see God took him and left me. Levy say, "Anna, don't you worry at all 'cause I going where Jesus is. Don't tell none I going, but I just go walk out."

I say, "Man, walk out where? Where you going?"

"I ain't going stay here no longer. You best try to go to the store and see if you can get something for your Christmas, 'cause I ain't go be here."

I say, "Man, hush your mouth; you talk like you don't know what you say."

He say, "I know what I say. By next Sunday I gone."

I say, "You can't know that. God only one know that."

He say, "All right then, you'll see." And he did so too. He died the fourth Sunday December, 1963.

I didn't know how old he is, but he tell me before he died, "I was born in 1880, December the twelve day." He live to be eighty-three. He was a good little man. Good little man. I have to say so 'cause I know. I sure miss him. He was all I had in the world.

7

Mrs. Janie Hunter
THIS WAS A KINDA POOR COUNTRY

There were ten children in my family. Daddy was a foreman for Mr. Jenkins, and he have his own garden. I work in it. All work in it. Pick lima beans, pick cotton, tie the two cotton pod in the bag, and put a string on 'em, and hang the bag around your neck, and go to each one of those cotton bush, and pick the cotton, and stuff 'em in the bag. They was paying two cents a pound. Make thirty-five or forty cents a day. Man is getting forty cents a day.

We wasn't making enough to afford a good living. My daddy, he make a living out the creek. He catch fish and we go around and sells 'em—a whole string for ten cents. Me and my sister Florence, we goes around with white dishpan on we head and sometime make two dollars. And two dollars would give you a box of food that time, 'cause food was very cheap. You could buy three cent worth of sugar, and you get a whole big piece of fat meat like that for a dime. You get a sack of grits for about fifty cent. Food was much cheaper than it is now. That's how we make living. Plant plenty of sweet potato, plenty peas and corn, and raise hog.

Then we had flat flour. That's when President Hoover had chair. We had to go 'round to Mr. Walpool yard. They used to haul the flour there in one those big van truck, and load up his barn with this flour. Then all the colored and white had to line up and call by name, and they give you a bag of flat flour. 'Til we finally made a song out of it:

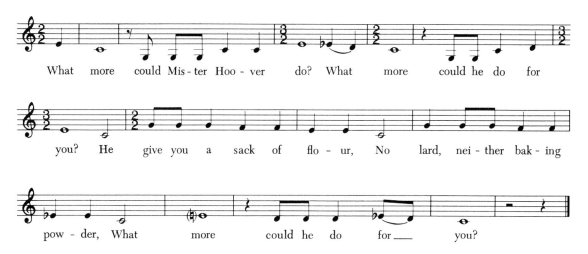

What more could Mister Hoover do? What more could he do for you? He give you a sack of flour, No lard, neither baking powder, What more could he do for ___ you?

Everybody so hungry, so want the flour. We have to mix the flour, didn't have no grease, no lard. Just put 'em in the pan and bake. Some people could afford to buy baking powder and fix it good. But who couldn't, just had to bake it—sprinkle some flour on the bottom of the frying pan so it won't stick.

But after he turned out and President Roosevelt took seat, then we began to live a little better life. I don't think just the Negro was glad; I guess some of the white too was glad when President Roosevelt took the chair. This was a kinda poor country.

8

Rev. G. C. Brown
THOSE WERE ROUGH DAYS

My wife and I've been here since '36. No pastor had lived here the last forty years before we came. And of course by not living with the people, they couldn't know their need and their desire. They wanted somebody to come and live with the people—that's why we came.

The first thing I found here was extreme poverty. That was during the days of the Depression, and there was no work except the WPA project. That white schoolhouse out there was built as a WPA project. The men on the farms were working for seven cents an hour. Oh yeah, seven cents. And the women, five cents.

The men plowed; the women did all the farm work. That time they didn't have planters to plant the potatoes. They cut the potatoes, dropped them in the field, and the men did all the work with the plows. That give pretty good farm employment. You had a number of men running plows, the women go along and drop the potatoes, and that give them a good day's work—several days' work in springtime. That give them employment during the planting season.

And the cabbage plant out by hand. Nowadays some have a planter. Some children worked then, but they didn't have too many children that time. There hadn't been so much marrying and going on.

Those were rough days. Food was short, scarce, didn't have much. The most they ate those days, they ate rice, grits and canned tomatoes. They bought their tomatoes at the store. They were cheap then. They bought the grits. Some made their own grits. They had a few mill. And they used to raise their own rice. There were a lot of rice farms around. They had a way of cleaning it and milling it.

Most of 'em were poor. Had no income. Very little income. They lived out of the creek. In the summertime they had crabs and shrimp, and in the wintertime had oysters. You could buy right at your door about three times a week, undressed shrimp—five cents a plate. In the wintertime we buy

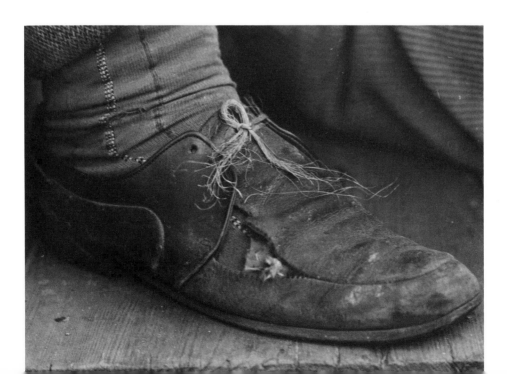

fish. People went into the streams and they hauled out fish trying to make a living. Anything they could do to make a living.

They used to gather moss—this same moss. Every month a man came along with a big truck to pick up this moss for mattress factory. They had pretty good moss business. They had three or four sales a year. They had a special way to cure the moss. Dig a hole in the ground and put hot water on it and that'd make it cure quicker.

The homes were poor. Lots of the homes were built out of logs. They go into the woods and cut a log about six feet, then put another six feet. And the frame was cut out of the woods, most of it. Sills, uprights, everything—cut right out of the natural woods. And for a long time they'd be lined with newspapers and any number of houses burned down during the winter. You know those were hard days.

The chimney was built out of stick and mud. They built the frame from the ground up out of wood, and they took pine straw and mud and daub that inside and out. Kind of clay-like. They build up this fireplace and give it a shape—outside and inside. Then they make a fire and bake it. It get kind of hard like brick-making, and they'd use those for heating. That was a common thing here then. They could put a rock or something down and cook in the fireplace.

Then in the summertime most of 'em cook outdoors. They'd lay two green logs together and make a fire between and put those pots on. That was the cooking utensils.

Sometimes a rain would come, wash out a piece of the chimney in three places. It was dangerous. Sometimes a house catch afire and burn down from the chimney. Pine straw was the binder with the clay. I don't think there's one around this island anywhere now. It's been years since I've seen one.

When I came all these roads were dirt. I think that there were only three cars in my churchyard except mine. That was the general thing all over the island. They used carts and that little tacky—pony, little horse, you know. Almost everybody had a pony, marsh tacky they call it.

Rev. G. C. Brown
WORLD WAR NUMBER TWO IS WHAT CHANGED THIS ISLAND FINANCIALLY

World War Number Two is what changed this island financially. The army came and got the men, carry 'em to war. Well, the farmer had to change his plan of farm. He had to go to tractors—didn't have the manpower, see? That's when the farming situation changed; they built these roads, and they began to produce more food for defense. White farmers. Negroes have come to tractors in later years, after they got on their feet. But they have small farms. No comparison with white farms.

There weren't too many white people here then, but they owned most of the land and they had the farms. The Negroes were little farmers. Many of them had their own lots, but weren't able to build a house. World War II came, they were able to make some money and they moved off the farms and built little homes.

More people work in the city now. Nothing here to do except a few farmers to work for. Few women have employment on the farm. They work in the city as domestics. You find a few on the farm here and there. In the springtime they take trucks around and pick up the hands for the day.

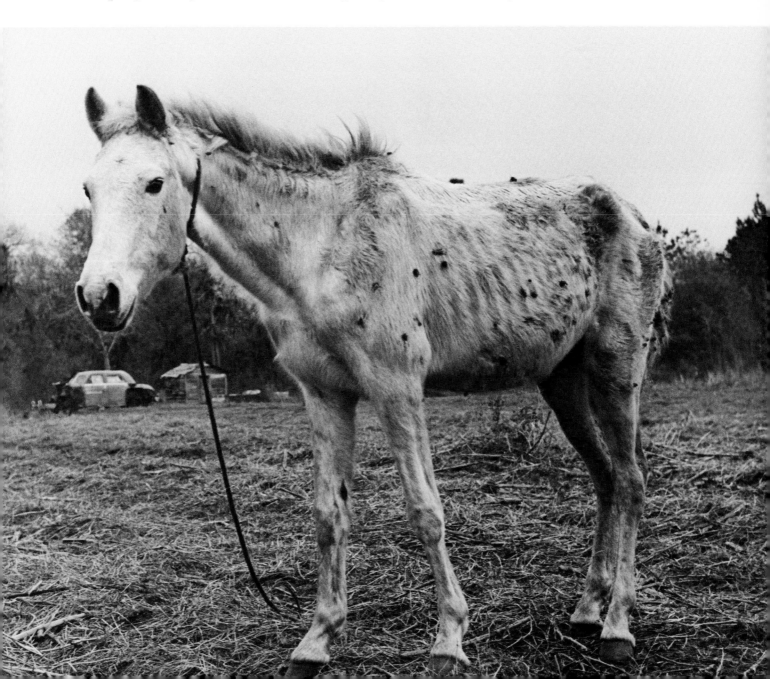

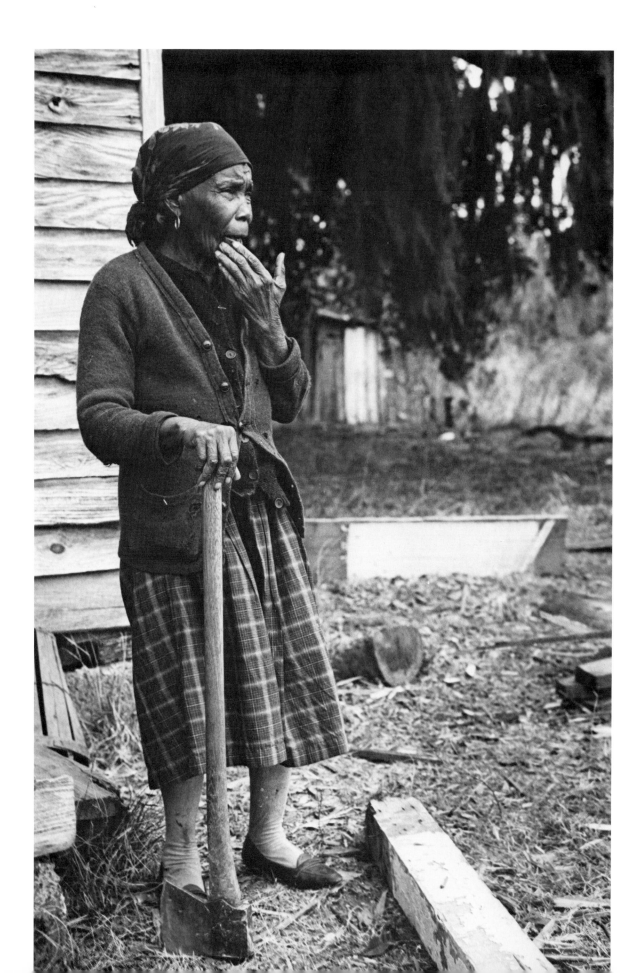

Mrs. Alice Wine

WE DO EVERYTHING FOR WESELF

Old times we never buy food. Man, you *never* used to buy nothing that time. Money use to never worry people but pay church and buy little things what you want or something like that. People raise the apple, they raise the fig tree, raise the plum, all kind of different thing. But now you got to see money. Money! You got to go for make money to buy. Is harder now. You got to work so hard to get a little bit of money. In that time you could get a quart of grits for two cents.

My daddy farm for heself. He raise he own food. We raise all vegetables. Something to keep in the barn in the winter. He plant corn, plant peas. He have sons plow. I do some too. And after we do all that, then they harvest 'em there in the barn. Then you ain't have to work in the winter.

Them times just a couple of stores, but you have to walk over seven miles to it. They sell food, but when you can plant your own, you make your own living. We have plenty chicken and have eggs and have plenty cows and have the milk. And my mother made butter—we own butter. Have we own churn and everything. Do everything for weself. So we never buy.

Those times people raise the tomatoes and the okra and can it. And they do that right now. They can it, they fix the bean, they dry the beans and the peas. They cut up the okra and they dry that.

My mother didn't never buy no kind of food. They make soap. They make plenty soap. But what they make it out, I don't know. They grind corn and make flour and grits. And we have the mortar and beat the rice. And meat, we kill the hog and put 'em in salt. End of the year, they put up hog. Kill the cow and have beef meat.

Daddy go in the creek and get we tub of fish—plenty fish that time. Get the fish out the creek—oshters, crab, mushel. Then we use to get them cookies five for a penny. Now cost penny a piece.

For clothes my daddy and mother they buy the cloth and make it. My mother had a machine and he do all his sewing.

Mr. Joe Deas

WE BEEN CLIMBING ON THE ROUGH SIDE
OF THE MOUNTAIN

From the time I have sense enough to recollect in this world, we have trouble and crosses, ups and downs. We been climbing on the rough side of the mountain—climbing up, falling back, grabbin' bottom.

Way back yonder, in 1893, we had to work for something to eat. Work on the white folks' farm, move from place to place, eat with stick for spoon. Got oshter, fish, crab and 'tato. Get corn meal, carry 'em to the mill and grind 'em and eat corn meal. Sweet potato. All that just to bring us this far. And I say thank God that I live to see light come into the world. Wise man from all part of the world come into *this* world. The world is lifting up more and more.

My old parents didn't see these things—automobile, airplane. We come from rowboat time. Had to row from home to town and back. Sometime I have to stay a whole day; have to wait on the tide, all that to row. And God spare us live to see this day.

We used to drive with ox and cart, haul wood with old oxen, plow with oxen. All that. Today no oxen. Nothing but car and truck and bus and trailer and all kind of thing like that.

Old days you couldn't eat nothing but 'tato and peas and corn and corn flour and crab and all like them. Well these days it's Christmas every day. Anything you want now you get 'em. In them days back, if one somebody kill a hog in the community, you think it was Christmas by the hog only. But now, eat hog meat any day you want. Go from store to store to get the thing you want. It's Christmas every day now for we. Light come into the world. Them times we had to buy, and money was so little, you can't see your way to buy what you need for live. Had to make out 'til we leave the white folks' place and then start to come up.

It's a blessing we see the day. Everybody lifting up. God put a way to your brains to catch on to these things, that you may have bread to carry you 'til He ready for you. The world is comin' up and is wise and wise and wise, until we *all* can get some bread from God. Man ain't able to give 'em, God put 'em into that man that he can share around to the next brother.

The Bligen Family
ROW, MICHAEL, ROW

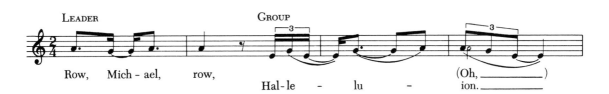

Row, Mich - ael, row, Hal - le - lu - ion. _____ (Oh, _____)

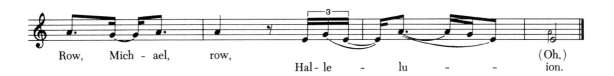

Row, Mich - ael, row, Hal - le - lu - ion. (Oh.)

ALTERNATE VERSION

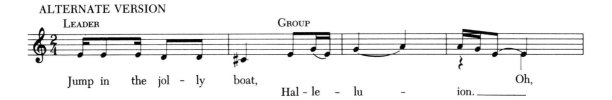

Jump in the jol - ly boat, Hal - le - lu - ion. _____ Oh,

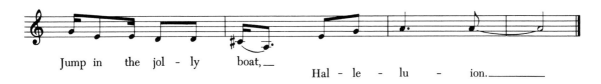

Jump in the jol - ly boat, ___ Hal - le - lu - ion. _____

LEADER: Let's row the boat ashore,
GROUP: Halleluion.
LEADER: Let's row the boat ashore,
GROUP: Halleluion.

Oh see how we do row . . . etc.

Row, Michael, row . . . etc.

Let's row the boat ashore . . . etc.

Just gimme a living chance . . . etc.

Sister Mary, row your boat . . . etc.

Everybody try their chance . . . etc.

Row, Michael, row,
Halleluion.
Row, Michael, row,
Halleluion.

Mrs. Janie Hunter

ASH CAKE IS SOMETHING YOU BAKE
IN THE CHIMBLEY

Way back yonder the old lady and them had some hard times. Had to take water out the creek to cook with. They'd cook ash cake. Ash cake is something you bake in the chimbley—in the fire hearth. You have the fire hot and burn down to ashes. You mix the corn meal and you open the ashes and place the corn meal in the ashes. You haul the coals on it, and it come to a brown. After you take 'em off the hearth, you wash 'em in something call dishpan and you put it on the table and let it cold. Cut it open with the knife, and you call that ash cake.

In the old time you couldn't afford to buy coffee or tea. We'd take the corn off the cob, break the corn off the stalk and put it in the chimbley hearth and let it burn. You have a pot of water on the fire, and when the corn burn you drop it in the pot and that turn coffee. You drink that along with ash cake. For tea, you take grits and put a frying pan on the fire, let the grits parch 'til brown. Then you pour water in the pan and that turn tea. Call 'em grits tea.

Yeah boy, we come through a great tribulation. But there's freedom now. You can get anything you want if you got the money.

Mr. Willie Hunter

WE SEE MEAT, BUT WE DON'T GET IT

My aunty raised me from a little baby, 'cause I ain't know my mother, neither father. He raise me up on his farm, was plant cotton, and peas, potatoes, and all. For dinner we eat peas and some corn grits, little sweet potato, and drink some water. And after that we go back in the field, pick some more cotton, dig some more 'tato. We see meat, but we don't get it. They had little meat in the soup, you know, boil with the peas or turnip, and cook with some meat in it, but you don't get none for we children, 'cause wouldn't have that much meat for give we, understand?

16

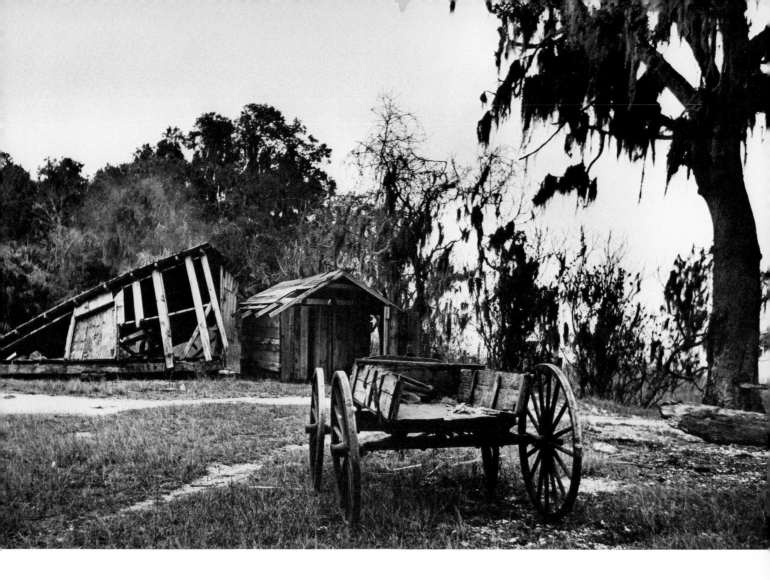

Mrs. Betsy Pinckney
DON'T LET THE RAIN CATCH YOU

I remember in 1907 we had a tornado on Saxby place. I stand in my door, and my grandma say, "I going now." And I say, "Yes'm, Grandma, I see you going. Don't let the rain catch you." And you know, the wind pick up the house, just as natural as that. And it carry 'em about two tasks [a task is twenty-one rows in a field]. And my grandma lay down on the stomach and hold on to the wire fence, to the post. Yessir, I know that! And I there home whooping and hollering, "Oh Lord, that big air cloud carry Grandma!" That's right!

We had another storm in 1911. I cook peas and rice that day. It was a Sunday. Josh was laying 'cross the bed sleeping. I lean against that post and every time I feel that house shake, I say "Josh, get up. You better get up and see he going to storm." You see, I had seen one. Done gone 'cross one in 1886.

Rev. U. L. Brewer
I BEEN SWALLERIN' BITTER PILLS

I been swallerin' bitter pills and chewin' dry bones. In the old days they just give me cornbread and sweet potatoes, but still I could plow the hell out of their mules.

Mrs. Isabel Simmons
THAT'S THE WAY I COME UP IN THIS WORLD

I come up in a hard time, and I still having a hard time. I was the oldest one in the house, and I had all the work to do. When I was small they put me to tend corn—ten cents per task. Some day I do five task, some day I do six. Tend 'em. If there's two stalks in a hill you kill one off. In September we go and pick some weeds we call Morning Glory.

Sometime I use to have time to play on Sunday evening, but I couldn't go no place. I couldn't go no further than the house. I get cornstalk and make corncob dolly and play with dirt and spoon. I never went to no dance. My mother didn't allow us to leave the house. When they do have something like the Fourth of July or Labor Days, a big drum come from the city. Play drums and horn.

That's the way I come up in this world.

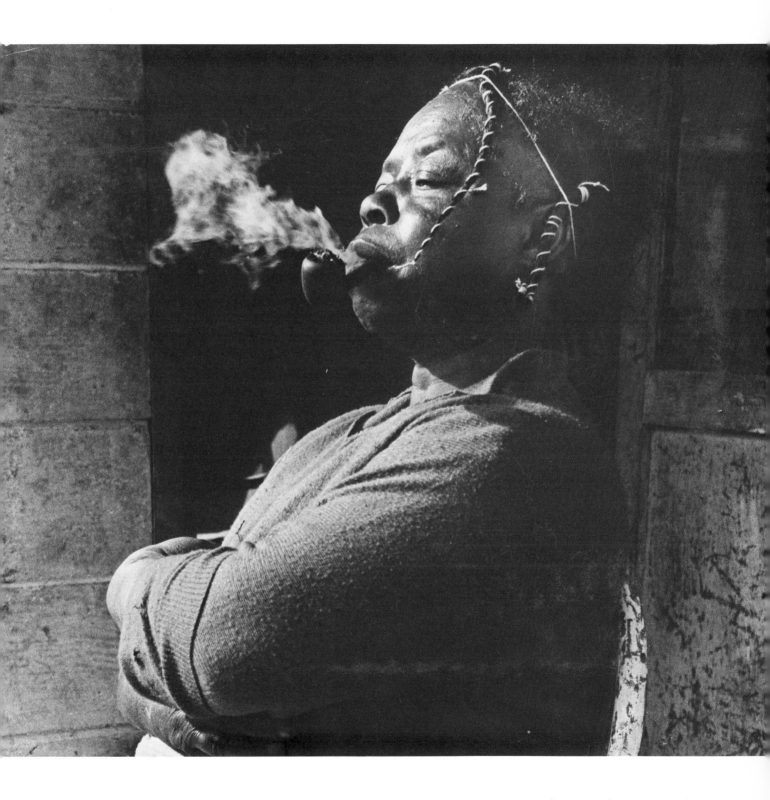

Mr. James Mackey
WE IS HAD A DANCE

Dance! That's my favorite. In certain times of the year like Fourth of July or Labor Days, we is had a dance. Had guitar and all like that. First of all we used something called accordion, and we'd beat stick. Then after that we was enabled enough to buy something call tambourine. A man lived back in the woods used to play guitar. James White used to play fiddle. And another fellow and I used to assist him. When I don't feel like play awhile, I dance in on the set until it broke up. We didn't have this new style they got here now—hug together.

We dance eight in a group. Two on the head this side, two on that side, two on the side like that. The fellow who knock the tambourine, he teach the set. He says "swing to your left," then you come swing that. Then swing your partner, then swing home. Then he say "promenade all," they all hook hands, grab hands together and just soshay all around, 'til they get back to the place what they was.

Later on after these girls used to come from the city, then they used to dance hug together.

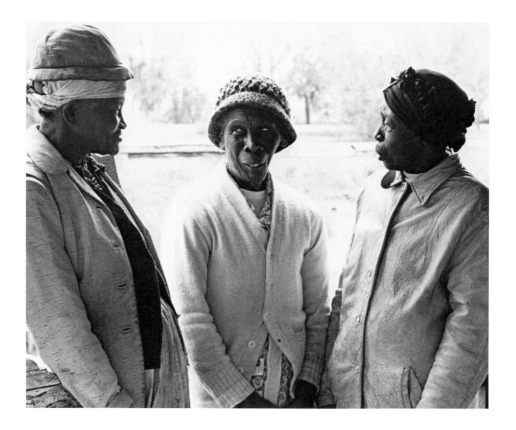

Mrs. Janie Hunter

WE DIDN'T 'LOW TO GO OUT AFTER DARK

When I was a young girl, we just used to go talk with friends, we didn't 'low to go out after dark. So the first time I went to a dance—that was 1932 when I first met my husband which is Willie Hunter—my mother tell 'em to have me back in the house by sundown. He took me to a dance at Miller Hill, right over there where that water hole at. Mr. Charles Clemmens used to have a dance call a trap dance. It be drums and be washboard and all such music like that.

Used to have dances called Charleston, Pick Cherry, Alligator—get down on floor and do 'gator tap-tap, tap on your heel and toe—"One-Cent Herring, Two-Cent Grits." Sometime two hook hand and go around. Call that a waltz dance. Some of these dance now is old-time dance, but they just change and give it a different name.

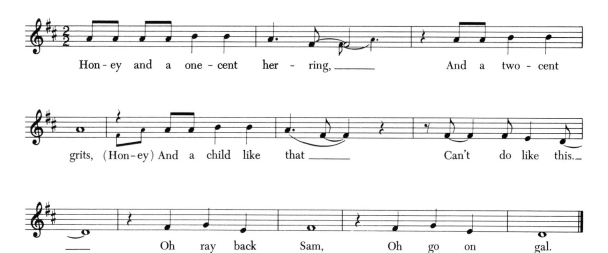

Hon-ey and a one-cent her-ring, _____ And a two-cent grits, (Hon-ey) And a child like that _____ Can't do like this. _____ Oh ray back Sam, Oh go on gal.

So when we get to the dance, the dance music was so good that we stays until about nine-thirty, and the water come across the road. The water come so high and I get scared. He have to put me on his back and tote me across the water. When we get back to the house, my mother smoke a pipe.

I was scared to go in. I said, "Willie, you best go in, 'cause I ain't going get a beating." My mother won't lick you before company.

So he went in, he says, "Mama, I'm sorry because we late. The tide was high across the road."

And my daddy, he is the first one to give in. He said, "Well, I know 'cause I go to the creek, and I know how that tide run."

I didn't say "good night." I sloop right in my bed. I was seventeen then.

Mrs. Betsy Pinckney

YOU GOT TO WORK LIKE THE DEVIL

Oh Jesus, that hoe! When I married to Josh, I couldn't lift the ground. Didn't know nothing 'bout lift ground. Josh, he work in the field. Milk the cow, then plow, man, plow. Sometime he dig the bed so wide if you reach your hoe, you better have a good long hoe stick.

We used to work for our rent and our food. You got to work like the Devil! Plant your cotton. Plant your corn. You have to work five task for that land and that house. Take oxen and plow. You have to work that 'fore you work your crop. That's you house. That's the rent. If he calls every week, you'll have to go.

In 1918 we move to our own place, where I am now. Josh go in the road and cut all them bush. Work with the ax and hoe. Some people carry the ax, some carry the hoe. Chop them bush. Cleared out the way for the cart and buggy come down. Then we had a crowd of children in there. And we had 'tato. When you throw 'em on the ground, just like somebody throwing dice on the floor. I had eleven head of children. And every one of my children had children. With the grands and the great-grands I have a hundred and forty-odd.

Mr. Willie Hunter

WE RAISE GOOD THAT TIME

I was raised right around here. Know the Bligens long before I ever marry they daughter. I know Bligen long time. My wife. All nice people. If they weren't nice people, I don't go in their family, I be in some other family. Nice people, man.

They like me too. 'Cause I have plenty manners to them. Course I raise up that way, 'cause I raise up through the old school. Plenty manners. You had to have manners to them old people that time, 'cause in that time anybody could of lick you, you been sassy with any people. But now, we don't do that.

See if anybody lick me, outside my aunt what raise me, if I go home and tell Auntie that somebody lick me, I get some *more* lick. The best thing I do, keep my mouth shut and take what I get. Oh we raise good that time. Now things changed a whole lot. But I try to raise my children like I was raised.

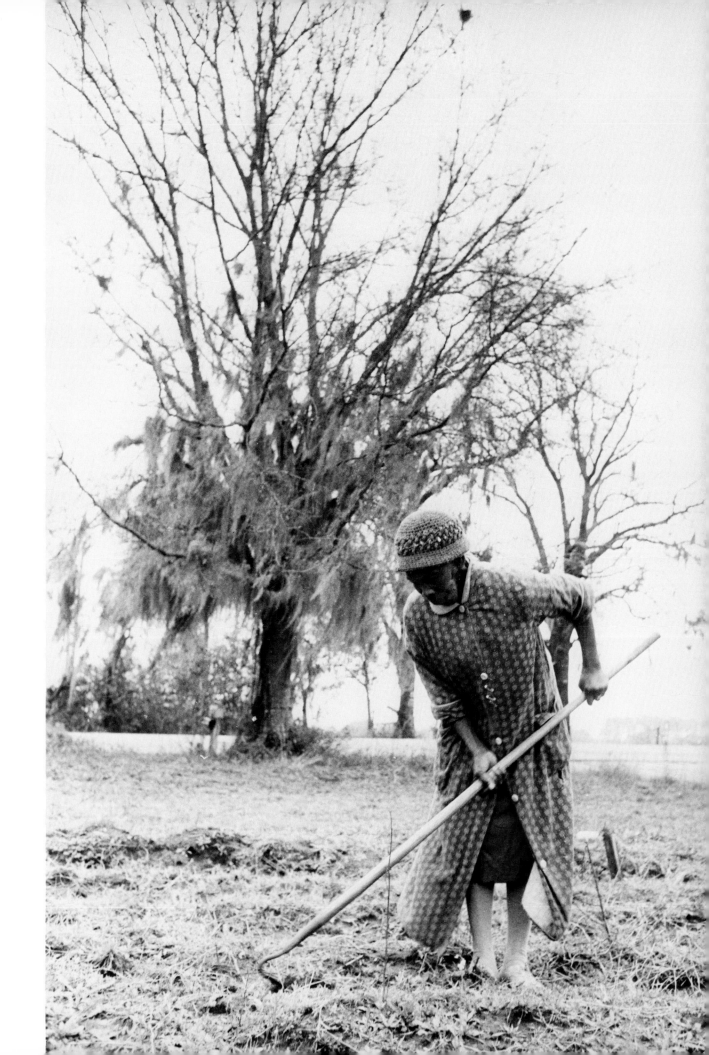

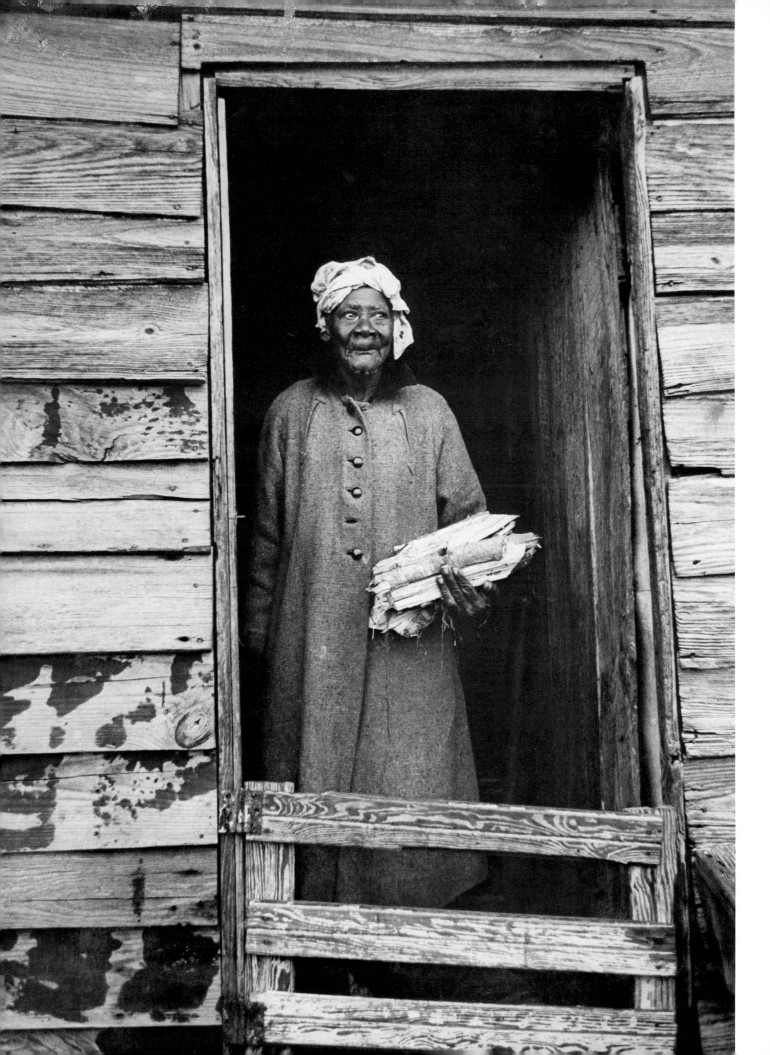

Mrs. Betsy Pinckney

EACH LEAF ON THIS TREE WILL
HEAL A NATION

I sick one time, in 1894. I sick 'til my mother and father give me up. Typhoid fever, gracious God! Oh that's a good God. I can prove it!

I was to go into the hospital the next day. There was a door, just like I looking on it now. I see a white man come through and walk just past my bed. He come and just look at me. Didn't say nothing, then go out. 1894.

And when the day was clean, the white gentleman come through the door again; I didn't know how he come in the house, but there he was. And he had on a blue gown, and hair drop on he shoulder. Yes sir! And he come to my bed, ask me, "What will you have me to do?"

And you know what I tell him? I say, "Please sir, could you read the fifteenth chapter and the psalm, 'The Lord Is My Shepherd'?"

He say, "Have you a prayer book?" Ask me just like I asking you a question!

I say, "Yes, sir."

He read the fifteenth chapter, the first six verse. Then after he done read that, he turn to the Twenty-Third Psalm, and he read it for me.

And he take me and he carry me down to a river. My spirit go on down to the river. Jesus! And when I get there, he said, "This tree bears twelve manna fruit. Every leaf on this tree will heal a nation." Gracious God have mercy!

Well sir, I wake up. I ain't seen when the man gone, but I know he come and carry me to that tree, down to that river side, and he tell me, "Each leaf on this tree will heal a nation."

Never sick so again yet! And that's the truth. Gracious God have mercy! Don't tell me don't serve God, because I going serve God until he say "well done." Yes ma'am, "well done."

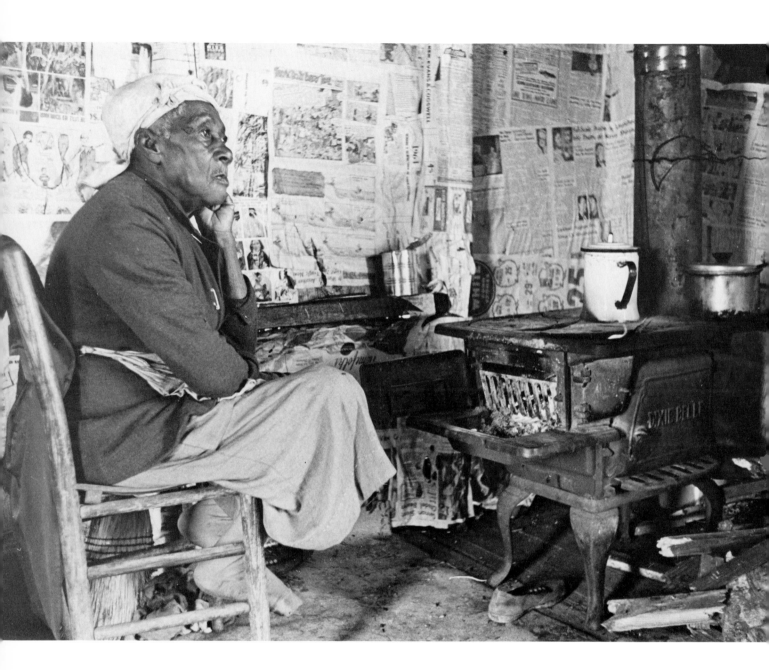

Mrs. Janie Hunter

THEY WORKED THEIR OWN REMEDY

We doesn't go to no doctor. My daddy used to cook medicine—herbs medicine: seamuckle, pine top, life everlasting, shoemaker root, ground moss, peachtree leaf, big-root, bloodroot, red oak bark, terrywuk.

Now when my children have fever I boil life everlasting; squeeze little lemon juice in it. Once they go to bed it strike that fever right away. That something very good.

And you hear about children have worm? We get something call jimsey weed. You put it in a cloth and beat it. And when you done beat it, you squeeze the juice out of it, and you put four, five drop of turpentine in it, give children that to drink. You give a dose of castor oil behind 'em. You don't have to take 'em to no doctor.

If anybody fall down and break bone, my daddy get a towel and pour some water in the basin—put half a bottle of white vinegar in it. He hot the towel and bathe the leg in some mud. Go in the creek and get some mud, band that whole leg up in mud. Couple days you be walking. That knits it right back together.

For a cut, to stop 'em from bleeding, Daddy just get a big spoonful of sugar and throw 'em in there. He say once a cut stop bleeding it's not dangerous. Spider webs grow up in the house and you get that and tie 'em on. Web grow right in there.

If you get sores you get something you call St. John out in the field. And you see those little bump grow on a gum tree; you get them and you burn them two together and just tie 'em right on that wound. That heals right up.

When my little boy got a nail stuck in his feet, I got a basin of hot water with physic salt and let him hold he feet down in that—draw the poison out. Then I tie a piece of butts meat on it. His foot get better.

You hear about some little thing run back in its hole—fiddler crab? We use that for whooping cough. Catch the crab, boil 'em up with something else—I can't 'call the name—and strain 'em through a white cloth. Give that for drink. It'll cure the running whoop.

All this from old people time when they hardly been any doctor. People couldn't afford doctor, so they had to have and guess. Those old people dead out now, but they worked their own remedy and their own remedy come out good.

Mrs. Belle Green
ALL MY OWN GONE

Sometime I stand here in the nighttime, ain't but me in one little room to sing. Then I study, you know, my mind run across, and he run on the old man. I just stop, sit down, and me heart get full. The other day I couldn't eat no supper. Me heart fill, and I feel full up the whole afternoon. Couldn't do nothing. I just maybe could of get a little bit wood then.

Now I can't testify like I used to. 'Cause I ain't able. My heart been bad for so long. I just trying to hold up. But they know me; all they at Moving Star Hall know me. I full of fire too. I been way down, but the Lord lift me up. Make me feel good the week out. I just pray to make my voice come back. Give me my voice back as I does been, one time before I die.

When you get an old woman, and you can't go, the government take care of you. That's what got me today. Government got me.

Threescore and ten, that's seventy years I come to this day, but I ain't got much more. So I'm trying to be as close to the Man as I can now. But thousands and thousands have gone. All my own gone. Just a branch now, like a tree put out branch.

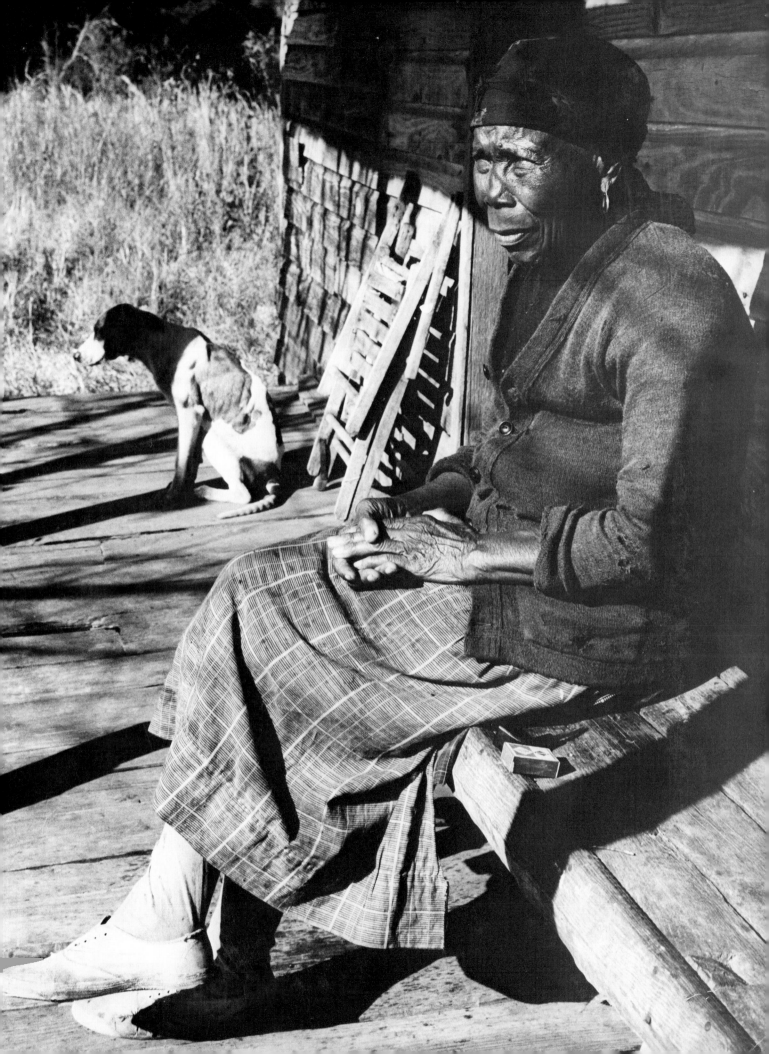

Mrs. Bertha Smith and
the Moving Star Hall congregation
LAY DOWN BODY

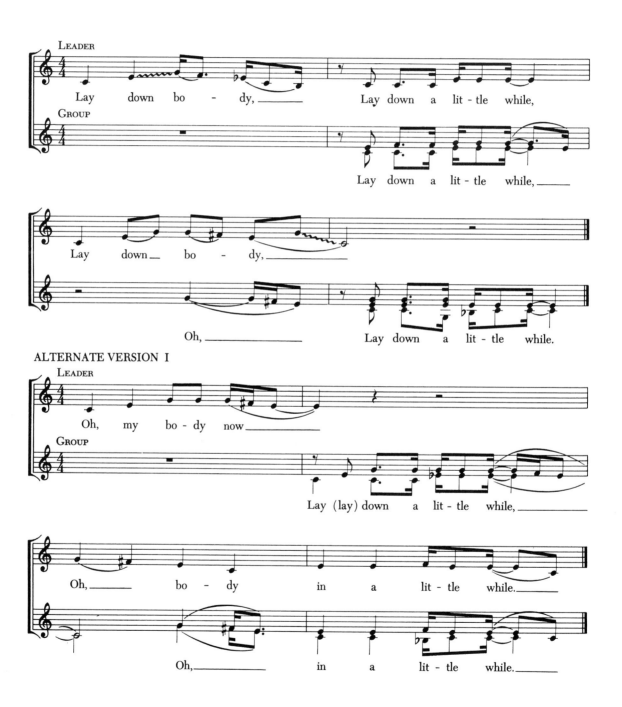

ALTERNATE VERSION I

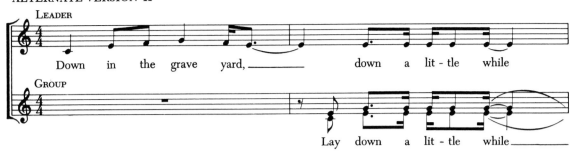

LEADER

Down in the grave yard, _____ down a lit-tle while

GROUP

Lay down a lit-tle while _____

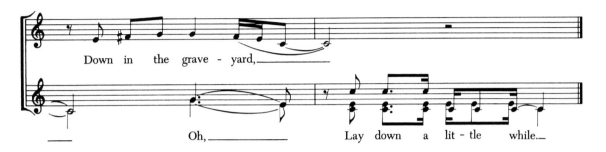

Down in the grave - yard, _____

_____ Oh, _____ Lay down a lit-tle while._

LEADER: I know you tired,
GROUP: Lay down a little while,
LEADER: I know you tired,
GROUP: Lay down a little while.

Come from a distance . . . etc.

Oh body now . . . etc.

Ain't you had a hard time? . . . etc.

Last December . . . etc.

Tedious was my journey . . . etc.

Rocky was my road, Lord . . . etc.

Ain't you got somebody gone? . . . etc.

I got somebody gone . . . etc.

Oh my body now . . . etc.

Just keep a-rollin' . . . etc.

Body, ain't you tired? . . . etc.

Body, ain't you lonesome? . . . etc.

Body, ain't you weary? . . . etc.

Lay down body,
Lay down a little while,
Lay down body,
Lay down a little while.

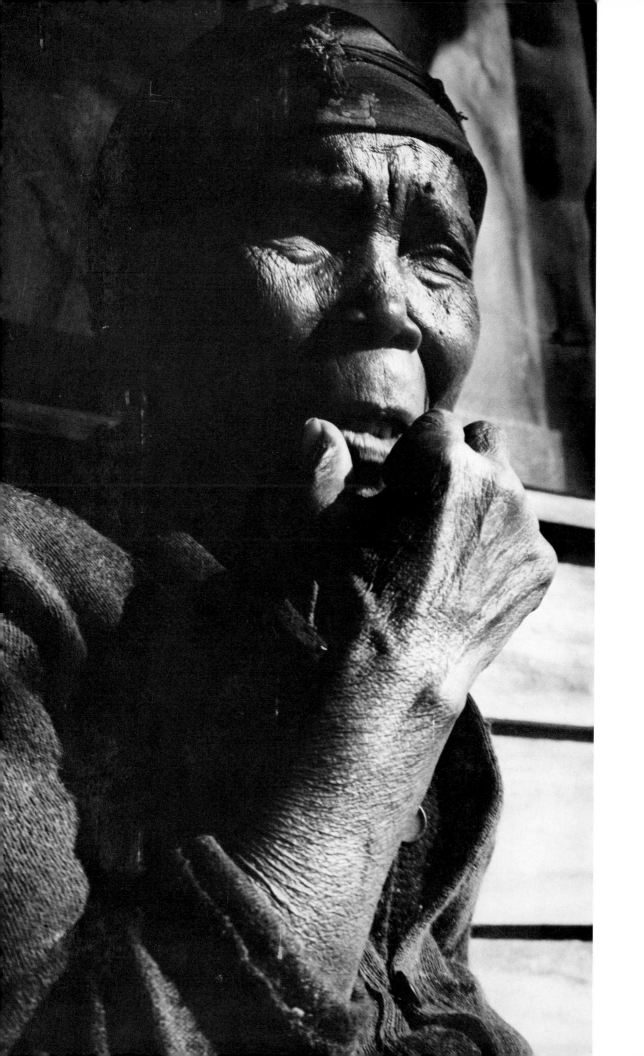

Mrs. Mary Pinckney

BEEN IN THE STORM SO LONG

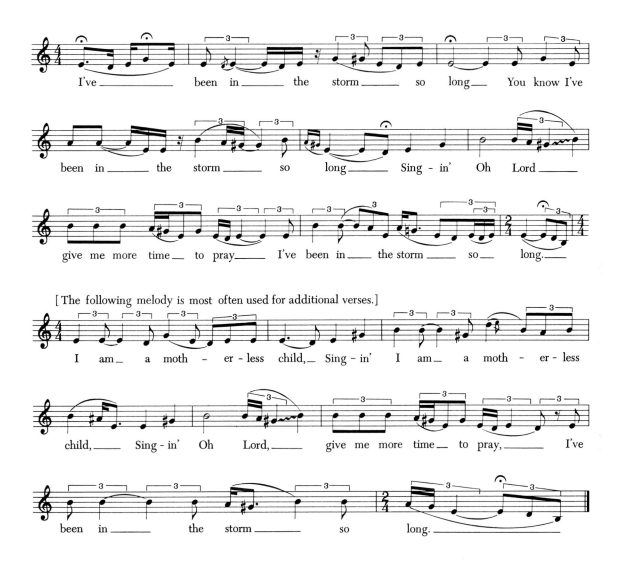

I've _____ been in _____ the storm _____ so long _____ You know I've

been in _____ the storm _____ so long _____ Sing - in' Oh Lord _____

give me more time _ to pray _____ I've been in _____ the storm _____ so _ long. _____

[The following melody is most often used for additional verses.]

I am _ a moth – er - less child, _ Sing - in' I am _ a moth – er - less

child, _____ Sing - in' Oh Lord, _____ give me more time _ to pray, _____ I've

been in _____ the storm _____ so long. _____

This is a needy time,
This is a needy time,
Singin' Oh Lord, give me more time to pray,
I've been in the storm so long.

Lord, I need you now . . . etc.

Lord, I need your prayer . . . etc.

Stop this wicked race . . . etc.

Stop all my wicked ways . . . etc.

Somebody need you now . . . etc.

My neighbors need you now . . . etc.

My children need you now . . . etc.

Just look what a shape I'm in,
Just look what a shape I'm in,
Cryin' Oh Lord, give me more time to pray,
I've been in the storm so long.

33

2. THE STORM

THE PRESENT

IS PASSING OVER

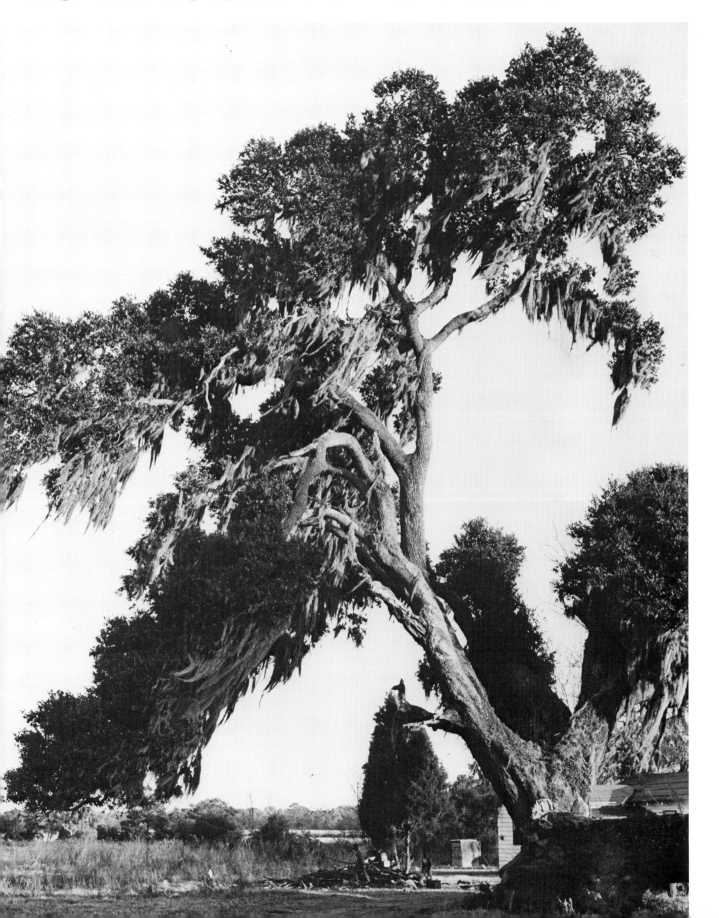

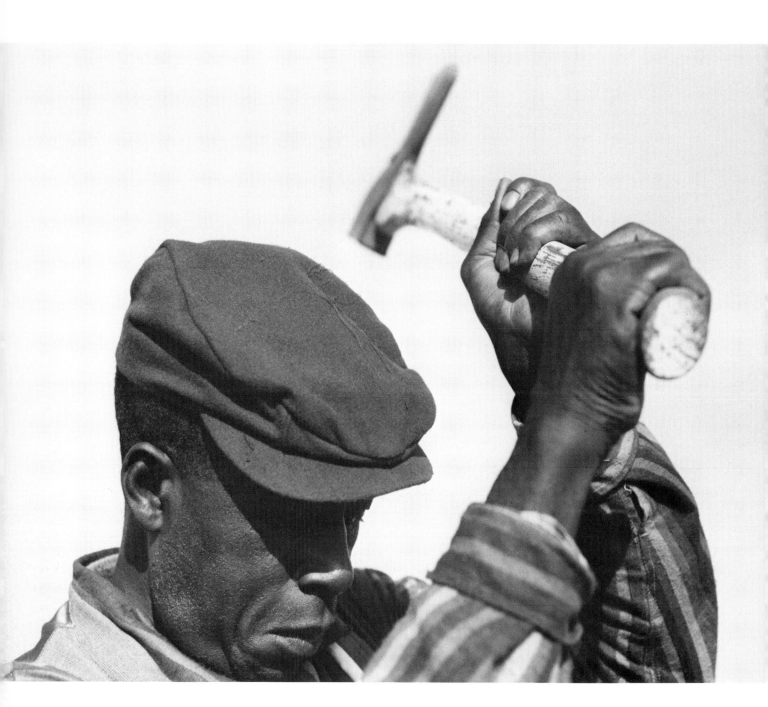

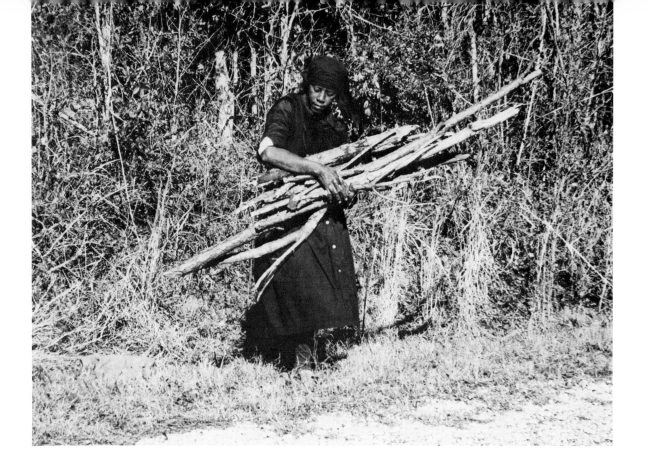
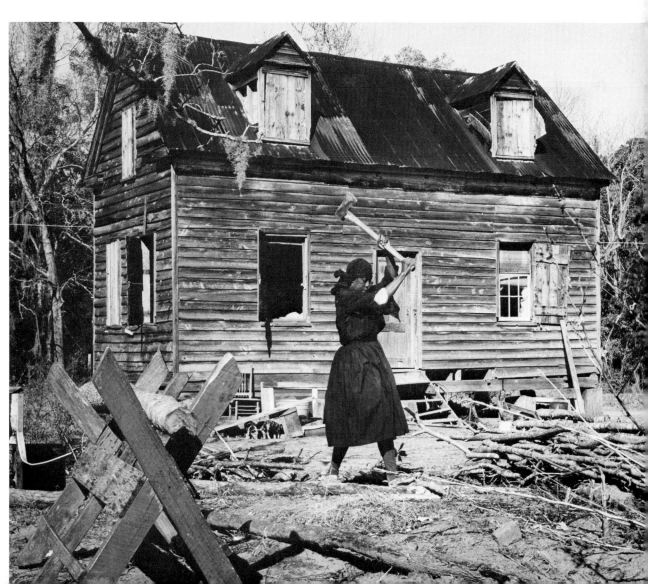

Mr. Esau Jenkins

SOMETIMES WE UNDERESTIMATE THESE PEOPLE

The people on Johns Island, those that are not working in the city or as domestics, most of them make their living off truck farms on the island. Especially the women. They work on the farms of plantation owners. They pick snap beans, they dig white potatoes, they pick tomatoes, pack cabbages, spinach and whatnot. Those are the things that they depend on for a living.

During the winter months they go into a hardship because most of the farms don't have anything to do. That's the hardest time that they have to face.

Sometimes we underestimate these people and forget they have something we really need. These are people who haven't gotten a college education, or even a high school education. But anyone able to raise twelve children—and raise 'em healthy too—must know something good. They were smart enough to plant and to raise the kind of thing the children need. They raised their own hogs, they raised their cows, they had the milk with vitamin D what they need.

Some of these older people thought very deeply. Mother-wit and faith in God helped them to do a lot, and some achieved more than some of the young people who have been able to go to college.

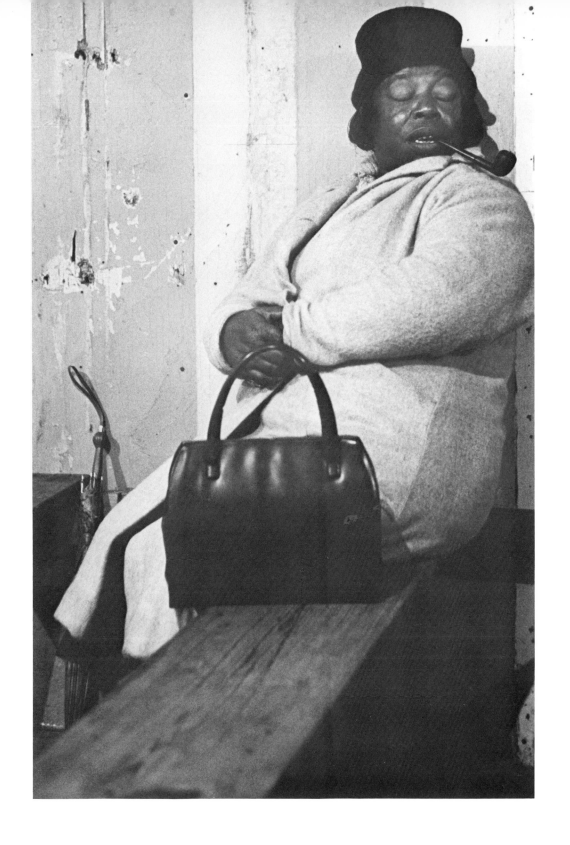

Mrs. Alice Wine
I DON'T HAVE ONE DAY HOME

That's what I'm doing now—working in a kitchen. I get up around five o'clock now, get on my clothes, wash my face and wash up, and I'll go to the back yard and feed chicken. From that I come back and clean up my house, and get out in the road and catch a ride and go to work. And I get to work I take off my coat, my hats, put on a apron and a hat, and go upstairs and get towels, and I wash those towels and put 'em on the line and come back in, start to clean rooms, make up beds. Then after I done do all that, then I come in the kitchen, get something to eat, and home I go. Well sometime I be waiting from three to four hours catching a ride.

I come back do a little work home, and leave from there to go on down to the Progressive Club and stay down there until about nine-thirty, ten o'clock, when it's a clear day. But when they having these party we don't leave 'til two and three in the morning. Get up next morning, go back on the job again. I don't have one day home.

On Sunday, go to church. I get up in the morningtime, get wash up and go outside feed my chicken and water 'em, and take my feet and go on down to the club and open 'em up. I be there around 'bout 'til eleven-thirty, catch a ride and go to church.

Come from church, I'll come back home and get dinner, and from there I go to the society meeting. Then the same Sunday evening we go to the hall to prayer meeting.

I don't have but a couple hours in everything I'm doing. But when I leave from home and come to someone house, like I here with you all now, I'm resting. And when I go home there's no rest. Something there for to do. Ain't nobody pushing me 'round; I'm pushing myself. I see it to do and I got it to do, so I just do it.

I don't care how hard I work in the day, if I get my night rest, it just like I ain't work that day. I get up that next morning, I don't feel it. But what put me down if I don't get my night rest. I get tired and don't feel like going. If I go to bed 'round seven-thirty, eight o'clock, I get up the next morning I don't feel nothing.

The Moving Star Hall congregation

I KNOW YOU'RE TIRED

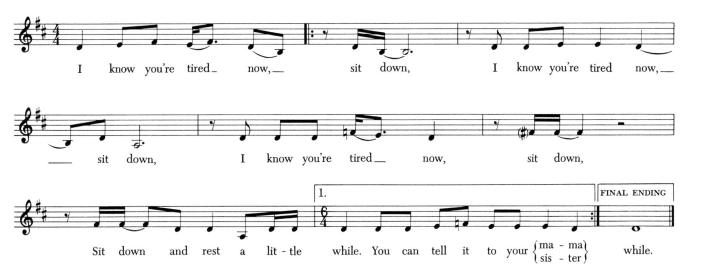

I know you're tired_ now, __ sit down, I know you're tired now, __ ___ sit down, I know you're tired _ now, sit down,

Sit down and rest a lit - tle while. You can tell it to your { ma - ma / sis - ter } while.

You can tell it to your { mama, sit down,
sister,
You can tell it to your { mama, sit down,
sister,
You can tell it to your { mama, sit down,
sister,

Sit down and rest a little while.

You come from a distance, sit down . . . etc.

I know you weary, sit down . . . etc.

Oh sit down servant, sit down . . . etc.

I know you're tired now, sit down,
I know you're tired now, sit down,
I know you're tired now, sit down,
Sit down and rest a little while.

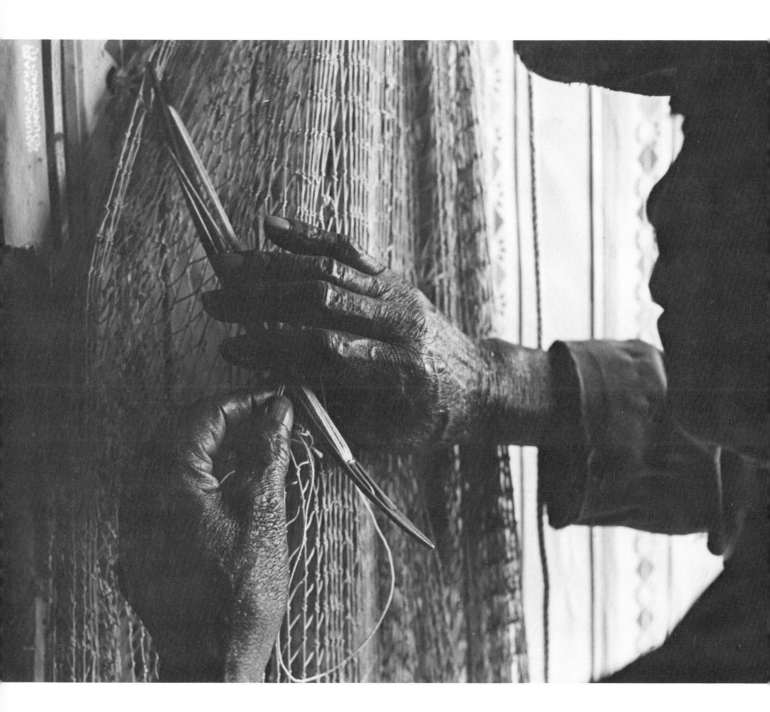

Mr. Joe Deas
I BEEN GOING IN THE CREEK
FOR FORTY-ODD YEARS

Fishing, yeah man, I been doing that for years. Get 'em with net; get 'em with line. Go down and push the boat overboard, go to bail 'em out, and go out casting. We go to Hut Creek, Willis Creek, then out to the sea. Great Lord, that's miles and miles out there—way out past the place they call Kiawah, then go out to the south. Get your whiting and trout. For mullet you go in the night. Course if you got a net, then you can go in the day and catch shrimp.

I make nets—knit 'em with cord and needle. Make my needle out of wood, board, tin. You can make 'em out of palmetto—take a branch of palmetto and cut 'em out of that. I make all most things myself—boat, net, two-wheel cart. If you ain't got that, you have to ride the ox

I do everything from the time I could turn around for myself. I been going in the creek for forty-odd years. Catched a ton of fish. Gone around and sell 'em to different people—make a living. I gone and got a license. Have to go to customs house and get license to go in the creek—get the fingerprint and all. When you come back from the creek, if you don't have enough to sell, you got enough for your family to eat.

That's the way we had to struggle in this world. But thank the Lord, we're here yet.

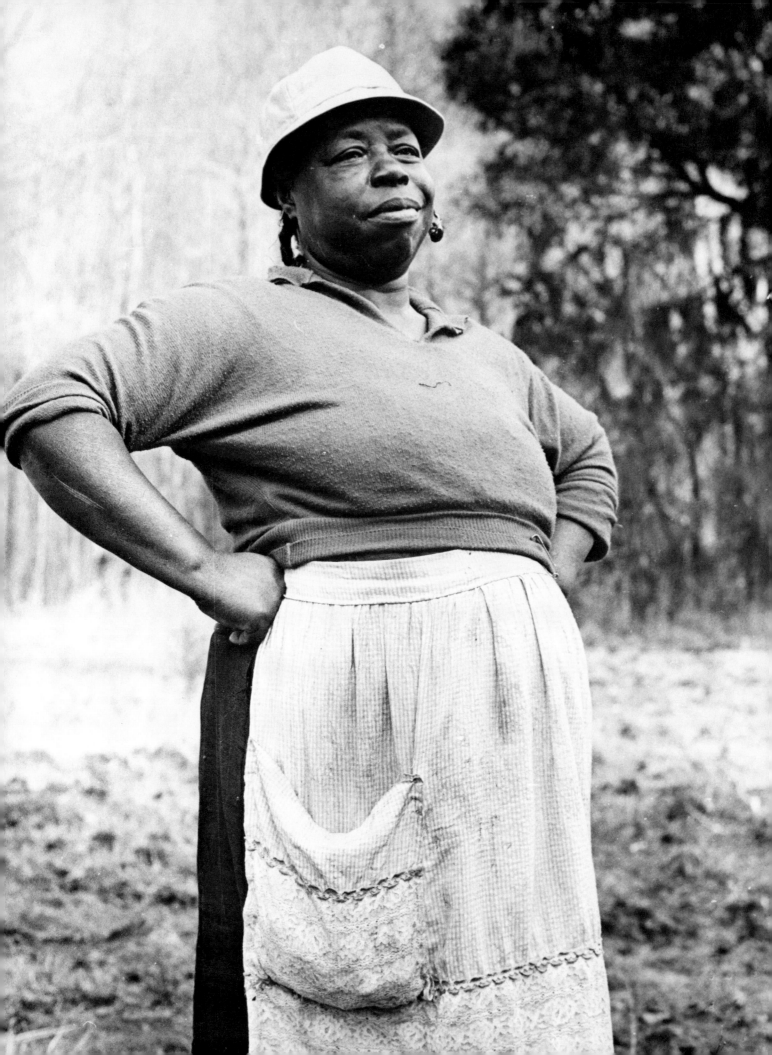

Mrs. Alice Wine

I CAN'T STAND TOO MUCH SITTING DOWN

If I be sitting down and don't have nothing to do, I get stove up. I get painful and lazy. I can't stand too much sitting down. I likes to go. You must be always active. You miss and sit around all day, lay around all night, you're so painful 'til you can't hardly get up. But you be working all the time, get your nerve together, get your vein together, then your muscle won't lock. Lot of people muscles lock by sitting down so much. No sit down for me. I likes to go.

I do any kind of job. I can plow, I can cut wood, I can sew, I can iron, I can scrub, I can do any kind of work in the field.

My husband was a farmer. He was a market man. He run a big farm. We have plenty chickens, plenty cow—two cow, and hogs. He get up and go to the market 'round two-thirty in the morning. Then I get up, put my baby to sleep, and get out there. Sometime we have these Columbia truck come in all time of night. These white people come in and carry these cabbage and thing. I'd be out there with them around four o'clock in the morning. After they go I come back to the house to see about the baby, then get in the tub and wash. Do all my washing, do my house cleaning, cook meals, have meals on time, cut cabbage, crate 'em too, pack 'em too.

I'm gone through a rough deal, but I thank God I'm still living. And I was doing those things in my nineteen and twenties. I'm fifty-nine now. So I'm not no baby!

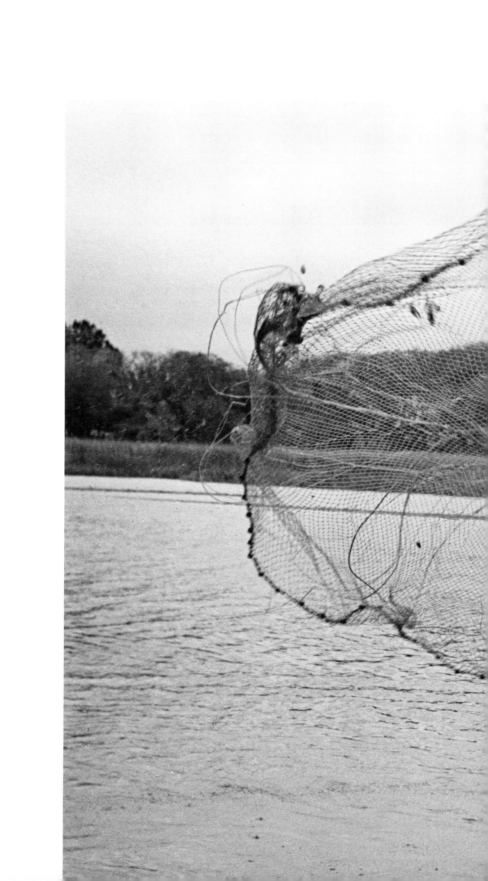

Mr. Benjamin Bligen
I DO MY OWN WORK NOW

The first work I used to do was work on our own farm. I worked to help my father because they really had a hard time to raise us, and we just had to get out and do what we could to help in them days. We had to plant a garden.

Then my daddy was a fisherman, and I began to go in the river along with him and he teach me how to throw net, so I finally learn how to. And

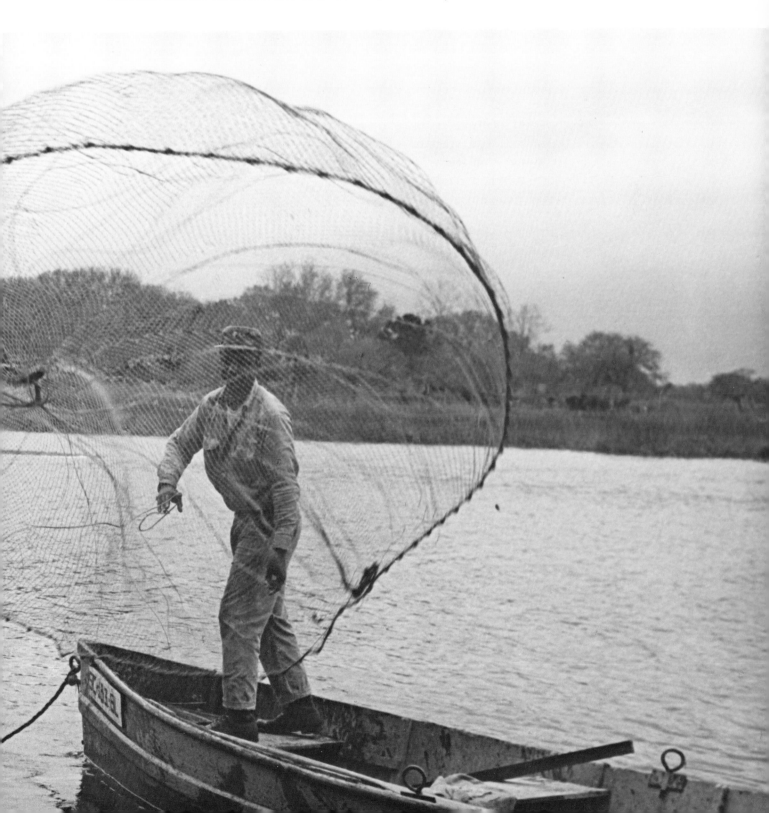

he teach me how to paddle a boat. After he died, I took it up myself. I did the same thing: go in the river and catch some fish and sell it. Most of it is mullet fish, mullet and spots, and some catfish, all different kinds. Cast net. Run from three to four feet deep to maybe sometimes seven to eight feet deep. I go by myself or with my brother.

I began to do some carpenter work too. I was working along with a carpenter, and after a time I began to learn how to do some of the work for myself. So I finally try alone, and I made it all right. I do my own work now. I'm working at a block and pipe company—making door lintels and window lintels, all different kinds of stone.

The best kind of money people can make is on electricity works and 'chanical works and maybe expert carpenters and bricklayers. Harvesting season in the fall, you can't make much because it's only about three or four weeks long. You can do all right for those three or four weeks. You can make it anyhow. But 'round May and June, that's about the best months of the year on the farm. October you start having maybe some string beans. Then you sit 'til next year in May and June.

Mr. Benjamin Bligen
MORE LIGHT IS SHINING

I am forty. The look of the pudding is not the taste all the time. I have two children. I have a better time raising mine than my parents had raising us. Foods went up a lot, but still you can make it a little better now than you is in past time.

More light is shining. Can see more. Likewise you can do more and think more, 'cause I believe that more light is shining now than was shining in the past. And so help me God, I so glad that I can see some light. And I know there's more light for me. There is a bright light somewhere and I'm going to find it.

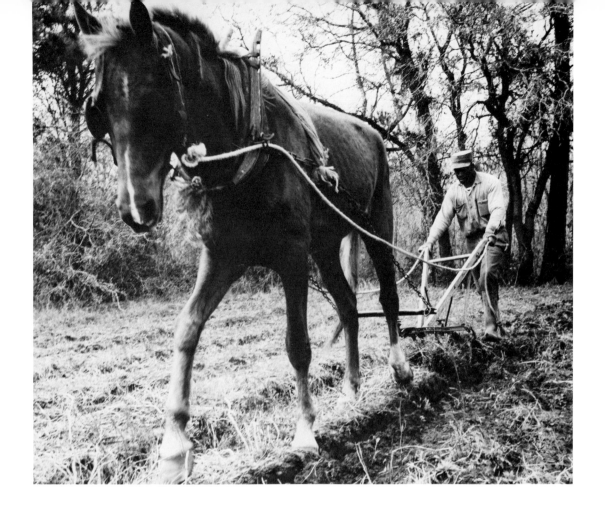

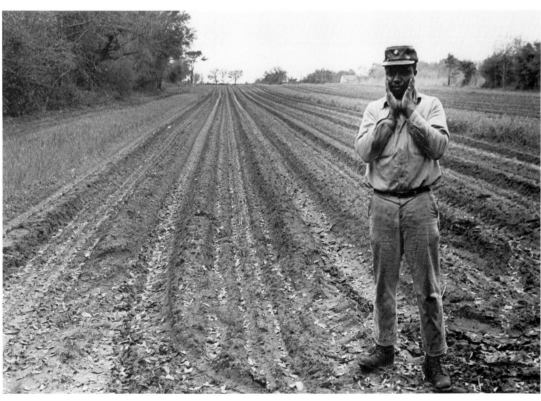

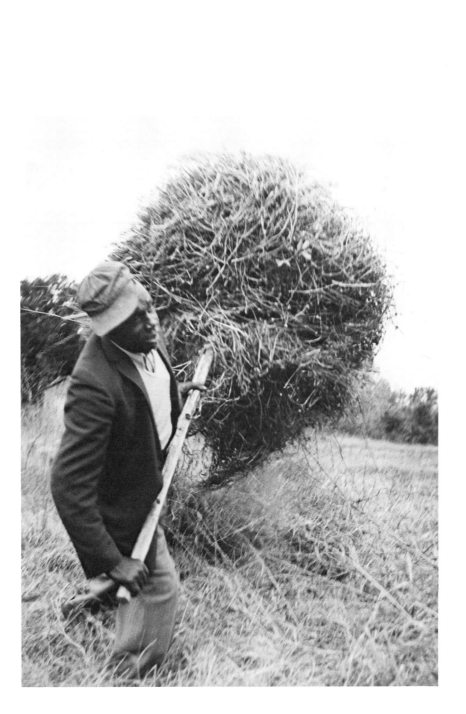
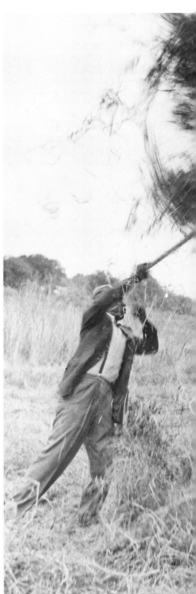

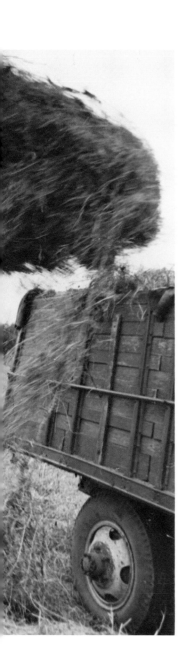

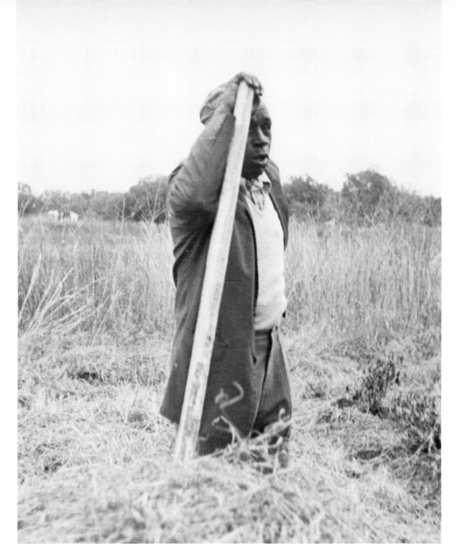

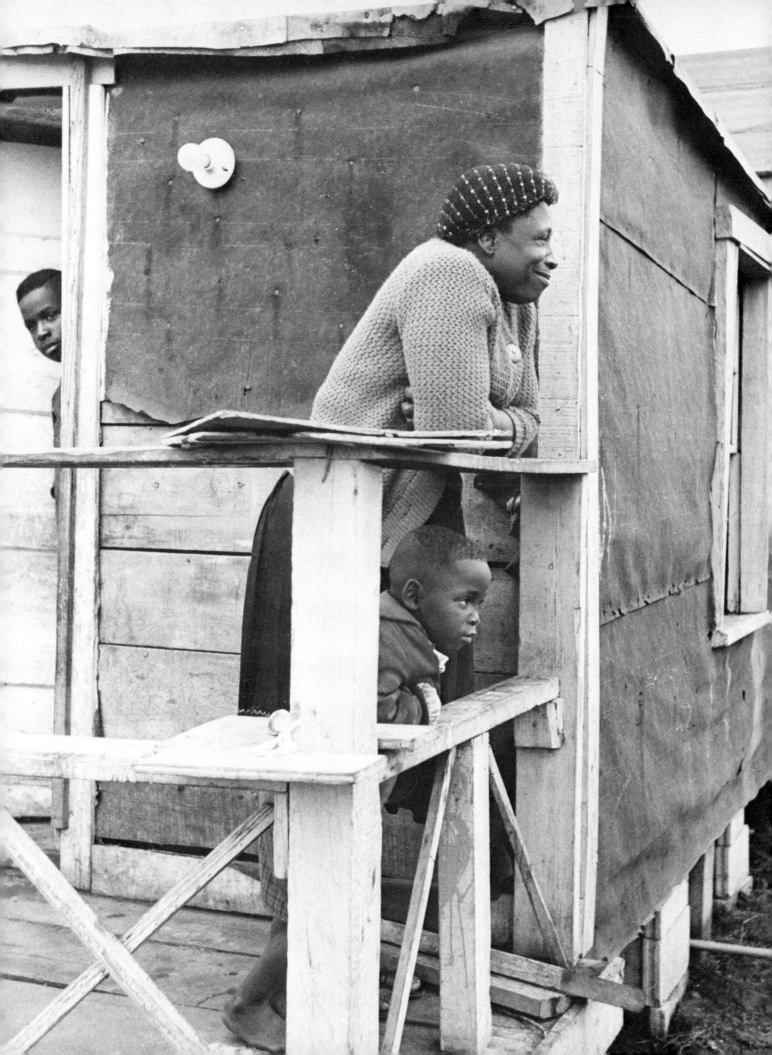

Mrs. Janie Hunter
I SEEM TO MAKE IT ALL RIGHT

When we first bought that piece of land in 1940, my husband was making thirteen dollars a week. I was washing and ironing for two person, and I wasn't making over three dollars a week. And we had to buy the land off that, and build that same house which burn down with that money, plus raise children. But I seem to make it all right. I get used to it. I get four dollars a day now, and it still don't seem much easier. Food cost more, clothes cost more, and the children takes more to go to school.

But the Lord didn't promise no human being to eat grass. Only horse and hogs eat grass. So he have a way paved for all those children, and we's had, if it be just one good meal a day. And I raise all of 'em up—hard time and good time—all is a healthy family. Didn't have no trouble 'til I lose my baby a year ago, and he wasn't sick but two days. But with the Lord, all things possible. And God give and He takes, and He takes nothing but His own. I know all those children belongs to the Lord, and He only give it to me for a special time. And I feel like He wants me to keep them children, He make a way for feed them. As the song say, "feed you when you hungry, and He clothes you when you naked." So up to this present minute I can say I have thirteen children living, and I thank God for all of them, and they is good children.

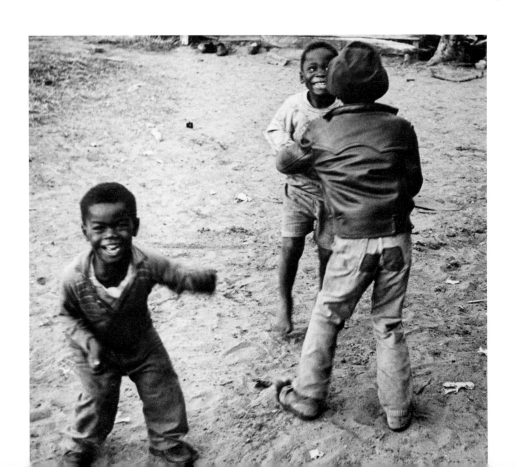

Mrs. Janie Hunter
THEY WANT ME TO TALK ABOUT THE PAST

I tell you, young people got a lot chance to think more in their age than I had to think in my days. 'Cause I couldn't think 'bout nothing but plant peas and corn in my days. But now these children got so much different thing to go through and learn, and they got nice schools. If they don't learn, it's nobody's fault but their own. Then I try to teach them these stories and different song and let them know what blues was like in my days coming up. My children like it. They sit down and they want me to talk about the past. They enjoy hearing it. I want them to know about it, so when I gone there be somebody to carry it on.

Mrs. Isabel Simmons
LIFE IS VERY DIFFERENT NOW

The old times was hard, but we still need religion right now. Life is very different now.

There is so much television here now; you didn't had that. It don't make life easier for me; it make 'em hard 'cause people stay home more. Lot don't go to church and different thing because they stay for see story. In them time only story you would hear tell, you tell your own story. This time, you watch television for story.

And the children now, they watch the TV and they take the thing on the TV to do just what they doing now. They think what is on the TV is real. But them time there doesn't be that kind of killing and shooting and cutting up like what going on now. Once in a while you hear about somebody die, but don't never hear about nobody get killed.

Mrs. Alice Wine
EVERYBODY SITTING ON THEIR OWN STOOPS

'Course that day, coming in 1919, all around like that, people was more friendly to one another. People come and sit with you and read the Bible. But these days you don't find anybody come visit. Everybody sitting on their own stoops. You don't find nobody to my house. When you're sick, people used to go around and have meeting for you and pray for you. Now the people who live in the house with the sick people got to come and ask somebody come pray for them. But before, people know you is sick. Not now. That's done pass.

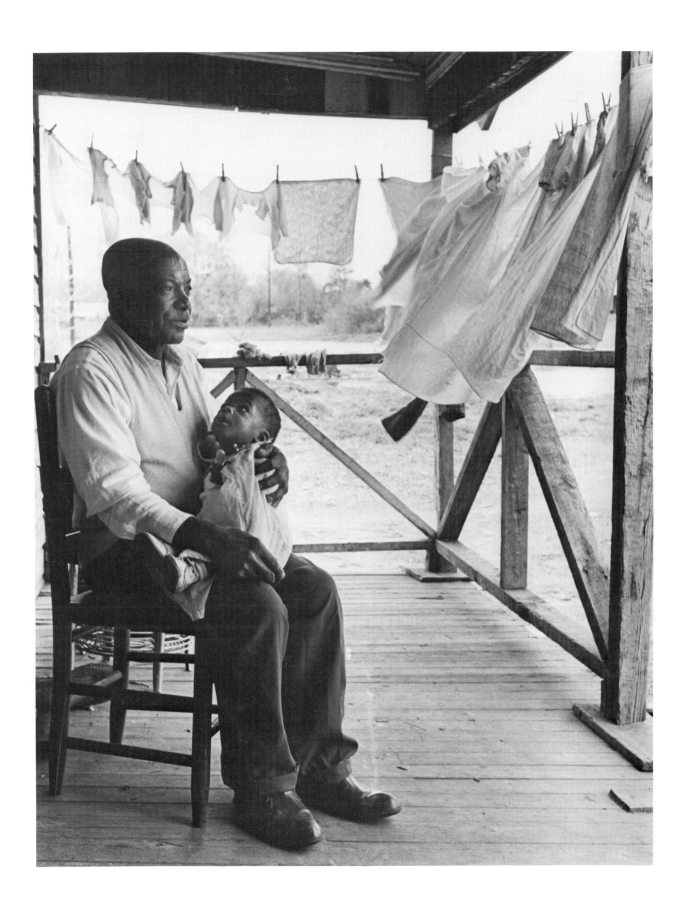

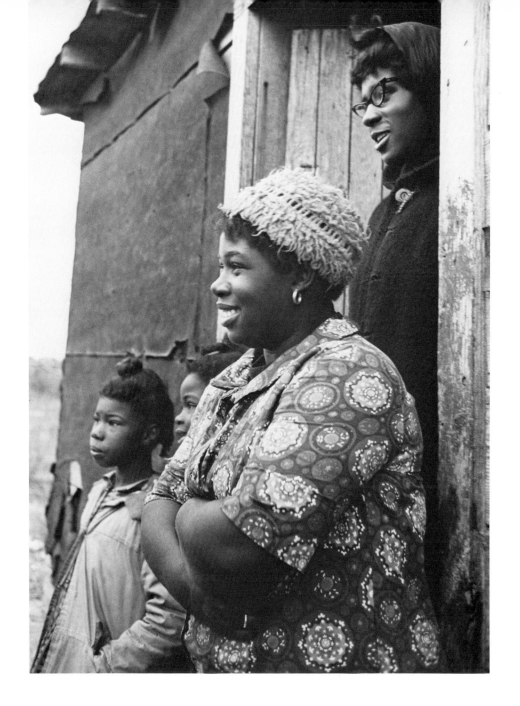

Mrs. Mary Pinckney

IT'S TOUGH TO RAISE FIVE CHILDREN—SURE IS

I get married to the church. And I had the reception in Robbie Fields'
store. They had wine and piccolo playing, and dancing. I danced once. But
I couldn't dance 'cause my dress was too long. Long white dress, white shoes
and white veil 'cross my hair. Lot of people came to the church and lot of
people at the store. They had as much in the yard as was in the store,
couldn't come in. I guess 'round about three hundred head. Big wedding.

We was young children, growing up together. I met him long time ago,
but I didn't realize that was to be my husband today. I remember he was
picking the potato on the farm and I had to go work that morning and he

was there. I didn't have no partner to pick up potato with, so he say, "Come on; I'll be your partner." So we was partner for the day, picking up potato until over with. And when I get 'round about fifteen, sixteen years old, he come to my house and ask my mother can he keep my company. My mother ask me, will I accept it. First I say I don't know. So he come back and come back. And finally he wrote my mother a letter. Mother call me, she ask me, will I accept Arthur Lee company. So I say yes.

Those years keeping company I doesn't go out with no fellas, but I does see other boys, talk to them, go out to a party my brother be along. But I never love but one, and that's the one I get married to.

Now I'm twenty-five. I have five children. I work from seven in the morning 'til five-thirty in the evening—five days a week doing kitchen work. I mind five children, and when I get home I got to take care of five of my own.

My husband leave home 'bout six in the morning for he to wait on the road for a ride to go to work. He don't have he own transportation. He works out on contractor job, 'round about four years now.

It's tough to raise five children—sure is. My husband make 'round thirty, sometime forty dollars a week. And if it rain he don't bring in that because he don't work. I get paid for holiday when I'm off, but my husband don't get paid. He just have to wait it out. My mother used to take care of the children that aren't in school before the house burn down, but now I don't have anyone to take care of them. I have to stay off from work and start all over housewife again.

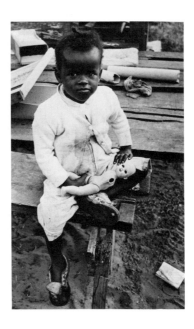

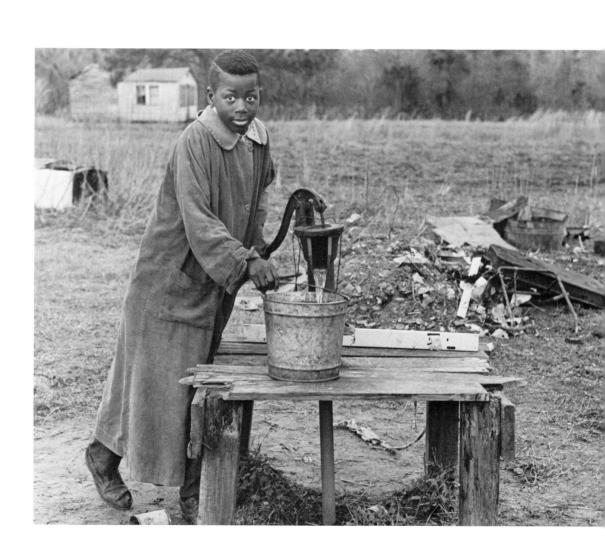

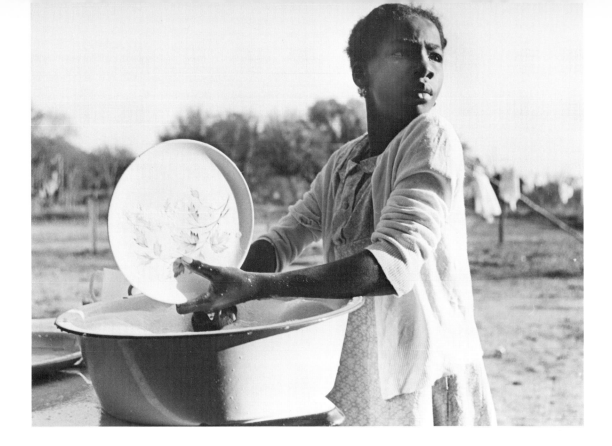

Miss Yvonne Hunter
ALL US WORKS

I am in third grade. I got left down one year because my mother was in New York one spring and I didn't have no shoes. I take arithmetic, language and reading. I like arithmetic best. When I grow up, if I don't be a secretary, I want to be a nurse.

For lunch at school we have popcorn, links, milk, roll, and have soup sometime. We have to pay for it. Sometime we take sandwich. At home we have grits, sometime rice for breakfast. Put milk and butter on rice. And have bread. Supper we have chicken and rice. Have greens, sometime cornbread and soup—vegetable soup. When Itchy and Joe go in the creek, we have oshters, crab, clams, fish.

Mother want us in bed at six o'clock. Sometime we go to bed seventhirty. Six sleep in a room. Tina and me sleep together, and Patricia and her two children sleep together, Mama and Papa sleep together, and Itchy sleep on the chair, and David and Johnny sleep on the couch.

We get up six o'clock. The bus come by at seven. School start at eightthirty. It takes five minute to get to school in the bus. I wash dishes before I go to school.

All us works. Sometime I wash dishes and I sweep the floor and I mop the floor. I cook. I cook grits, rice, cornbread. I cook meat, fry chicken, and I can make macaroni, and I can make salad.

I don't know if I want to get married. I don't like boys.

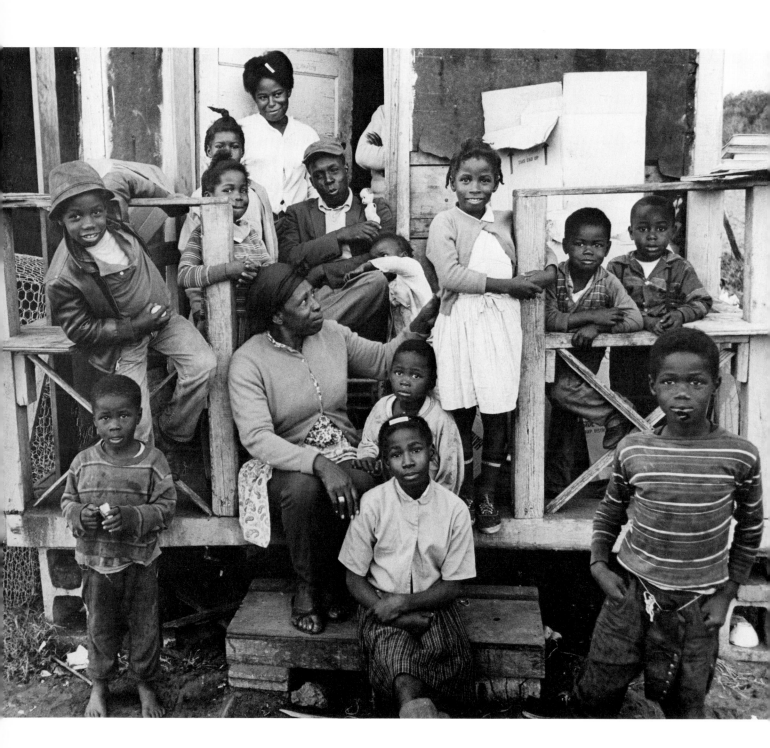

Mrs. Janie Hunter

IT'S A SMALL PLACE, BUT I RATHER
HAVE ALL MY FAMILY TOGETHER

I lost my house, a seven-room house, but I feel like it is the Lord's will. 'Cause I was burning oil stove from '41 up to now, and this have never happen to me before.

One day I went to work. I wash Tuesday night and leave a tubful of clothes for my daughter who always takes care of the house, and I told her to hang the clothes out. So she take my little battery radio in the yard under the tree, and she was hanging up the clothes, and when she look up, she saw smoke. She ran back to the house, but she couldn't even get in; the fire knock her back. She remember one of my little grand was sick in the house, and all she could do is run in the house and grab her. My son Johnny grab the rest of the children and take 'em over to my neighbor house and somebody call me.

One of my neighbor call me on my job, and my lady brought me home, must be about seventy mile an hour. I didn't feel so bad then, 'cause I thought fire engine would save at least some the furniture, but then I could see the housetop was falling in.

Then when everybody was together talking, I was sitting off by myself on Moving Star Hall, was thinking what would be best. I didn't feel like going anywhere far from the neighborhood. I have different friends offer me to come stay with them, and Mr. Jenkins, the place I raise on, he had a little empty house there, but I didn't want to go there either. I always want to be close to my meeting—Moving Star Hall.

So my neighbor, Nancy Field, she give me this little place she had built for the Florida people when they come. Those Florida people, they come 'round every year for season to pick tomatoes and thing, and she kept that little place for them. They just stays in it for a season—they'll stay any kind of where, you know.

It's a small place, but I rather have all my family together. If all of us have to sleep in one bed, I rather have all together. She kept manure and corn and all such of things in there, and all the rat been in there, but I was happy for it. I just get out and by my children, daughters, son, husband, they help me, and couple days we had it clean out, so now is clean enough to sleep in and eat in. We just work night and day. I sit up 'til two o'clock some nights. My son Johnny, he makes two window so it's light now. Then we go and buy a wood heater so it's very warm and comfortable.

We getting 'long all right. I realize God give and He takes. He take down and He can build back up. He took everything from Job—wife, children, Job have seven boys. His wife say Job ought to curse God and die. But Job say, "You speak as a foolish. When I curse my God and die, what will become of me? But I'll wait on my appointed time until my change will come." So I'll wait, 'cause I know soon or late there will be some change. If you only got faith in God, won't have nothing to worry about.

And everybody was so nice to me, and that one important thing make me feel good. All my friends from here and everywhere come and give; those who don't have to give, come with a word of encouragement. I appreciate everything they did. My brothers, my sisters, my daughters, friends, what they don't have to give, they come and sit and talk and sing together encouragement, and this make me understand that this is the Lord will.

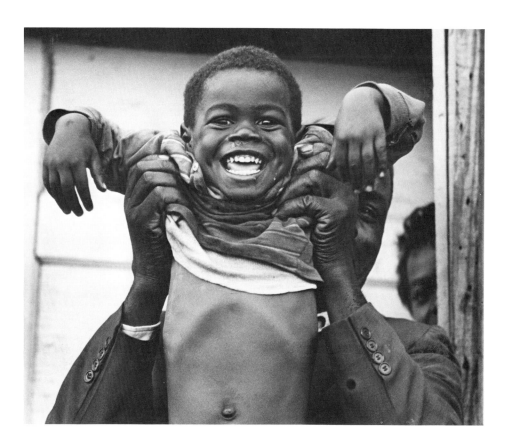

*Mrs. Bertha Smith and
the Moving Star Hall congregation*

THE STORM IS PASSING OVER

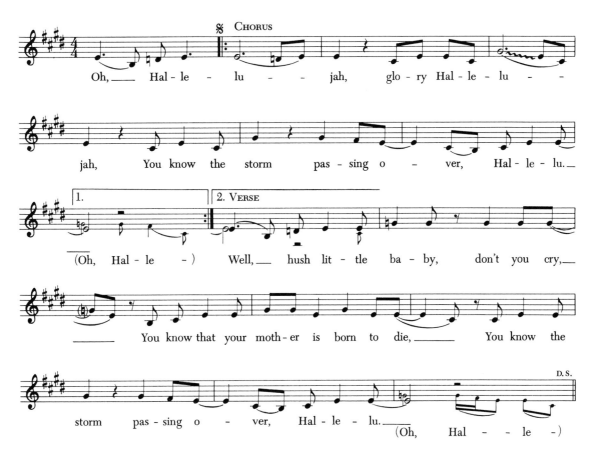

Oh,___ Hal - le - lu - - jah, glo - ry Hal - le - lu - - jah, You know the storm pas - sing o - ver, Hal - le - lu.___

(Oh, Hal - le -) Well,___ hush lit - tle ba - by, don't you cry,___

___ You know that your moth - er is born to die, ___ You know the

storm pas - sing o - ver, Hal - le - lu.___

(Oh, Hal - le -)

Sometimes I'm up, sometimes I'm down,
Sometimes I'm almost to the ground,
You know the storm is passing over,
Hallelu.

(CHORUS—2 TIMES)

Some say Peter, some say Paul,
Ain't but one God for we all,
You know the storm is passing over,
Hallelu.

The tallest tree in Paradise
Christians call the tree of life,
You know the storm is passing over,
Hallelu.

(CHORUS—2 TIMES)

3. ALL THINGS ARE

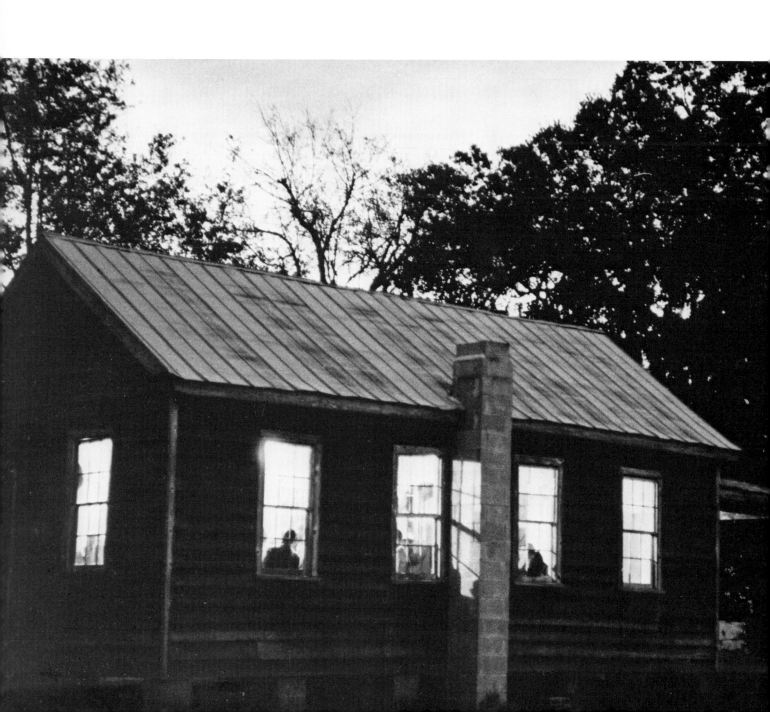

POSSIBLE IF YOU
ONLY BELIEVE

MEETING AT
MOVING STAR HALL

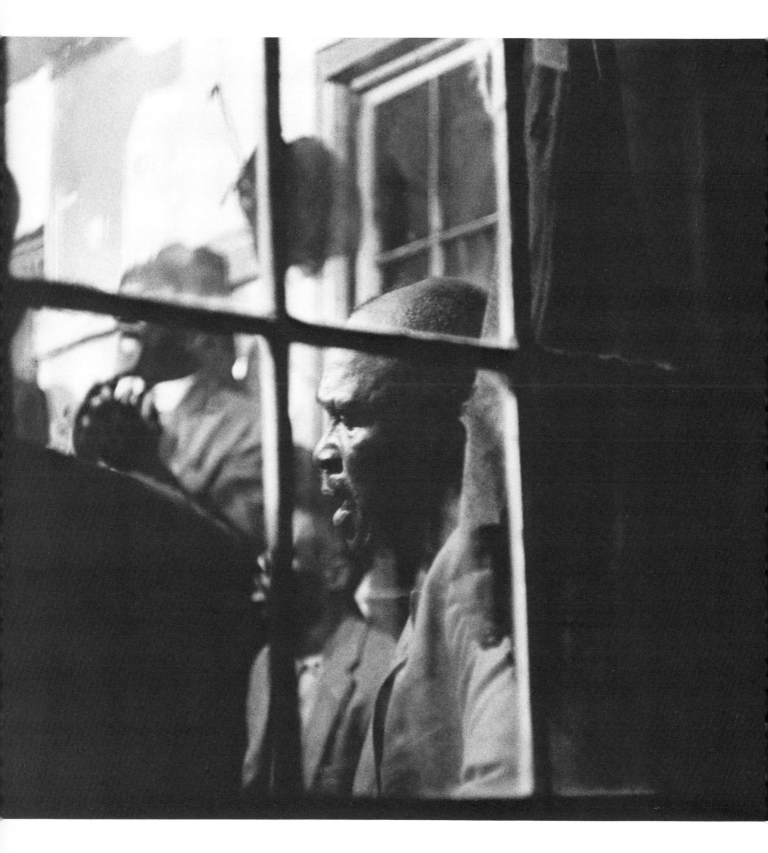

Mr. Esau Jenkins
SHOUTING FOR A BETTER DAY

Every Sunday night these people have meeting at Moving Star Hall. Every December 24th they have what we call a Christmas watch night meeting, and every December 31st, a New Year's watch. They sing from twelve o'clock until day clean.

They know the tune, they're ready to shout. They're giving praise to the great Supreme Being who have stood by them in the past days from slavery up to this present. Just to hear these songs remind us of our hardship. Those songs are the ones that made them happy, made them go through those hard days—the days when they didn't have a place to live of their own, didn't have a piece of land of their own, and were living on a plantation.

These people are hard-pressed people, and they are optimistic enough to believe that there are better days coming. When they get into these religious shouts, they feel so happy until that's all they can do but shout. The motions go into the hands and into the feet and they start clapping, and you can't keep them sitting—not when they start clapping, brother. They feel so happy 'til they got to shout. People sixty years and seventy years old clap and shout and jump all over the floor without falling down.

These people are trying to satisfy themselves, satisfy their soul. It's the only place they could be happy because life is so hard and sometimes there are any number of persons who do not know where the next meal is coming from. They can't talk back if they go on the farm regardless of how mean they were treated. Sometime their task they had was overburdening. Sometimes somebody watching them that they didn't have a chance even to stoop. They sometimes sad. But they're trying to get rid of it. If you could come and see them how they look when they singing and shouting, you can see they singing for a better day, shouting for a better day. And that's the thing that make them keep on shouting.

Mr. John Smalls
ANYTIME YOU COME, YOU IS IN

We don't charge nothing to come in Moving Star Hall. Moving Star Hall are free, and the door are open for each and every one. Whether you are white, whether you are dark like myself, or different color, come in. If you can preach, come on. We all preach. Don't say, no, you can't come up to this table. You can preach, pray, or testify. If you want speak, anything you want say, you got the opportunity—we give it to you.

'Cause we know we are in God hand. God made *all* of us. Don't make a few and somebody else made some; God made all. So I am happy to meet you all.

I hear the white madam say a while ago she glad we let 'em come in. "No, don't worry with that, Madam. Anytime you come, you is in. Bring friend, whatever; you's in." So sing, shout, get happy. But don't fall out!

Mrs. Janie Hunter

LEAD ME TO THE ROCK HIGHER AND HIGH*

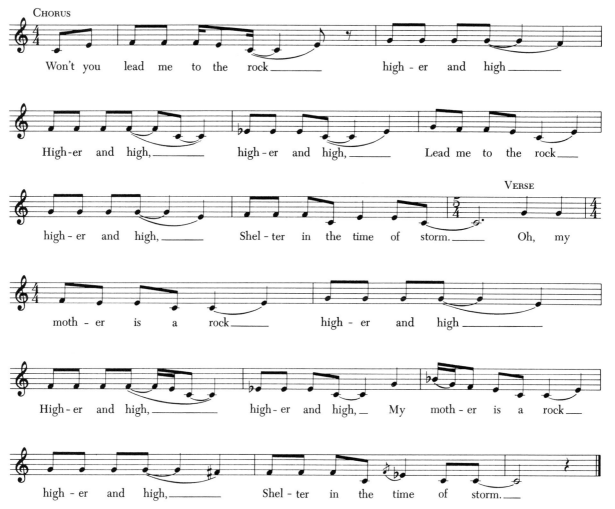

° *Also sung elsewhere in the South "Lead Me to the Rock Higher Than I."*

(CHORUS)

Won't you lead me to the rock higher and high,
Higher and high, higher and high,
Won't you lead me to the rock higher and high,
Shelter in the time of storm.

Oh King Jesus is a rock higher and high,
Higher and high, higher and high,
Oh King Jesus is a rock higher and high,
Shelter in the time of storm.

(CHORUS)

Oh my God is a rock higher and high,
Higher and high, higher and high,
Oh my God is a rock higher and high,
Shelter in the time of storm.

VARIANT OF VERSE:
Oh my God is a rock in a weary land,
Weary land, weary land,
God is a rock in a weary land,
Shelter in a time of storm.

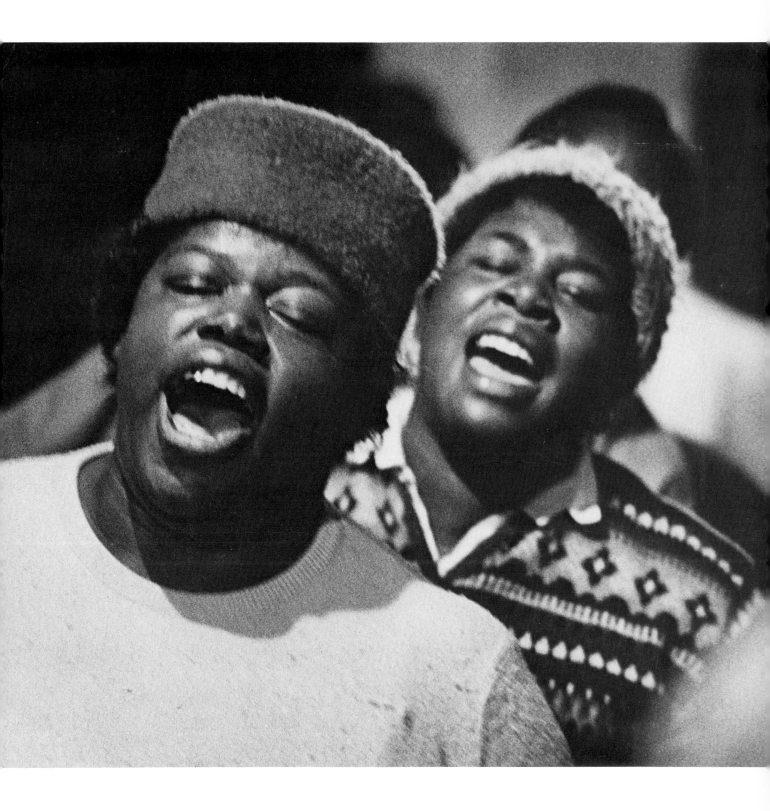

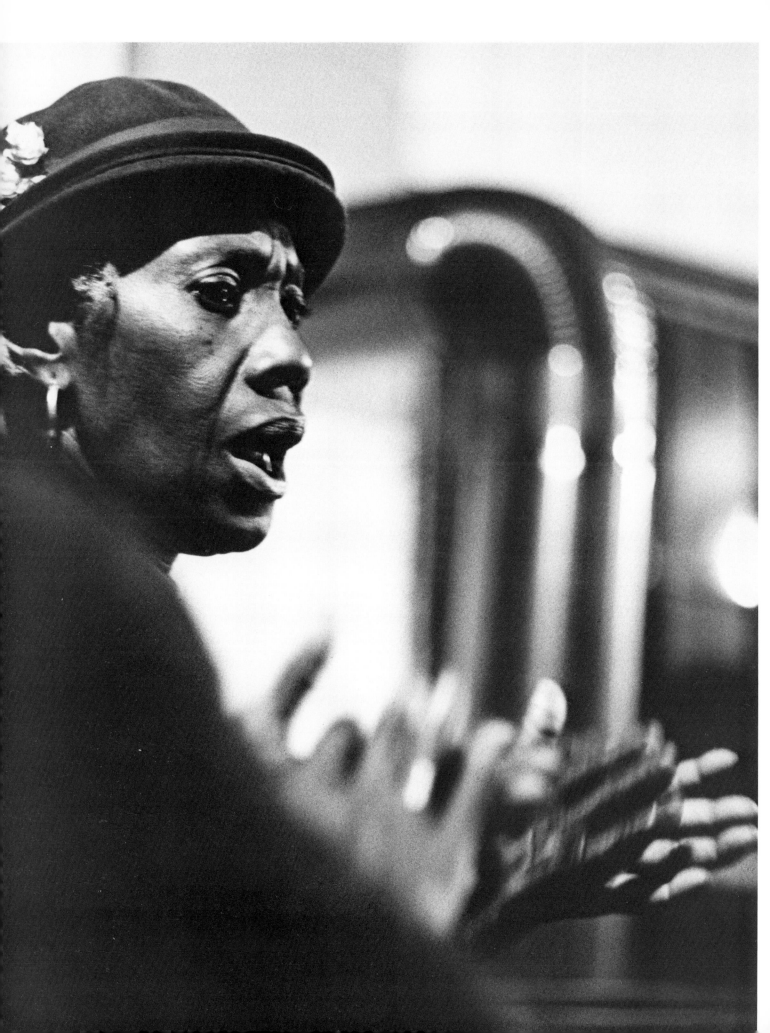

Mr. James Mackey
SHOUT

That's so much the most thing I could do—shout. I'll tell you, with the spirit of God, you don't care what pain you got. You forget about that when you shout. When I going out, I feel so painful I scarcely don't go. But I say to myself, just as well if I go now, 'cause will come a day when the limbs fail me.

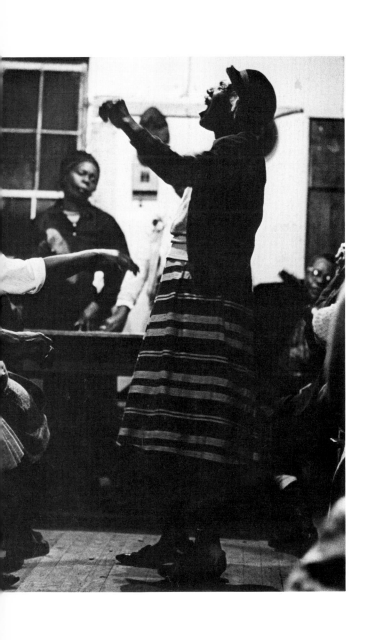

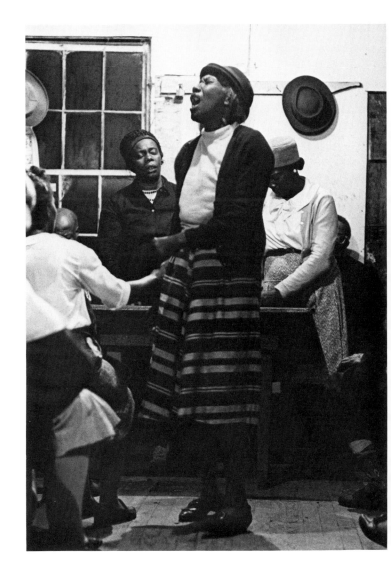

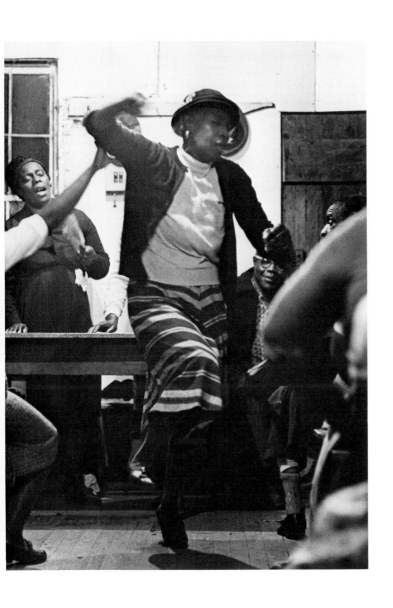
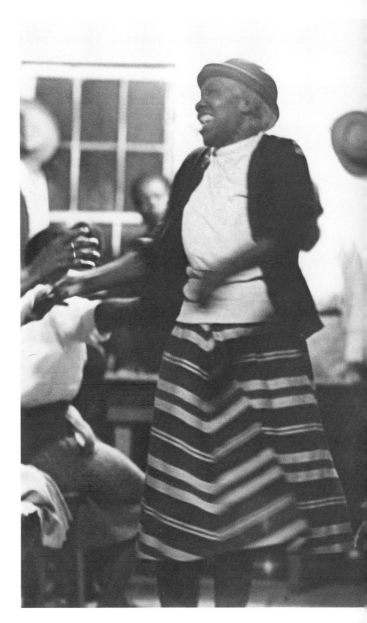

Mrs. Isabel Simmons

ALL JOIN AND MAKE THAT HALL

The only time they miss me at that hall, I either sick or off on some church duty. That hall mean a whole lot to me. It give me strength, spirit to carry on. I know everybody who comes. Some is friends, cousins, sisters; some neighbors.

I remember when Moving Star Hall was built, 'round about 1913, '14. Father help build the hall. Mother too. We all throw money until we gets enough to buy the land. All pay seven dollars for the lumber. All join and make that hall. They used to have prayer service in the house—only family then. Afterward, they began to have joint class from house to house. Then when we get the hall, we begin to have meeting there.

My daddy teach we how to sing, teach we how to shout, teach we how to go fast, teach we how to go slow. And then going to meeting, or later going to church, he'll teach we how to behave yourself when we get out to different place, before we leave home.

Used to be plenty people there—all them old people. They sing those old time spiritual, better than how we sing it now. Joe Bligen and Levy Green. Joe Deas was a good singer too, when he was much younger. Had plenty of singing womans, too.

That hall be full of people. Every Sunday. We have meeting in the neighborhood three time a week—Sunday and Tuesday and Thursday night. They keep a meeting going from eight until twelve. Then I get out, tomorrow morning I go on the farm make a day's work, too.

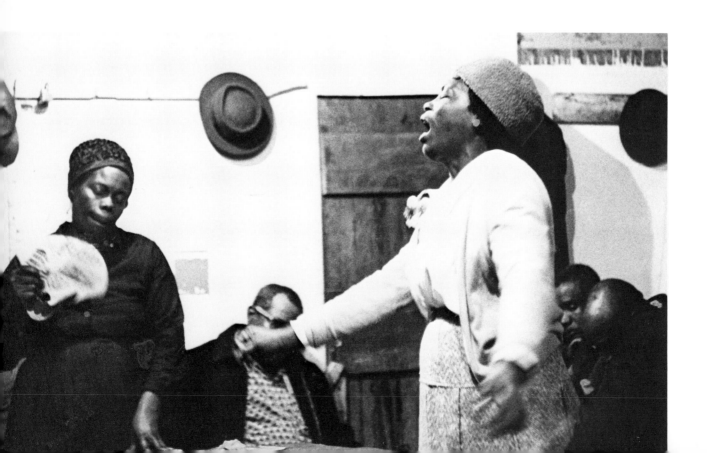

Mr. Joe Deas
THE SICK BENEFIT, AND DEATH BENEFIT

In the old days people couldn't afford insurance so we make up that Moving Star Society from ten cents each from Sunday School. We decided to bought a piece of ground to build that hall. And after we got 'em built we give 'em name: "Moving Star Hall." We got member from all different church. Generation after generation join and come out, join and come out. Some die and gone. The sick benefit. And death benefit. We still yet going on. By the help of the Lord we 'spect to go on 'til we are done.

Mrs. Alice Wine
THAT SOCIETY THERE, THEY TREAT YOU ALL RIGHT

Society is better than insurance to me. That society is supposed to tend the sick and bury the dead. Everybody who in there pay dues. They write from twenty-five cents up to one dollar a month. You is a twenty-five-cent member, you get twenty-five dollars when you die; you is a fifty-cent member, you get fifty dollars; you is a seventy-five-cent member, you get seventy-five dollars; you is a dollar member, you get a hundred dollars. Just as much as you pay, that's as much you get out. If you be sick, society service two person out to sit down with you all night, every night, until you get better or worse. If you don't go and sit, you be have to pay a dollar fine. If you sick and aren't able to pay your bills, they keep it up for you, live or dead; they elect money from the table and they keep you arrear. Insurance not going to do that.

And then the insurance man going to give you your money—put it on the table. Now, how you going to bury? That money can't move to dig grave. But that society there, they treat you all right. They don't give you your money and leave you there. They give you your money and give you attention. And we got pallbearers and everything in there. We got the pallbearers to take you from the undertaker and bring you to the church; take you from the church and carry you in the graveyard. They put you down there, and we got the member to cover you up. See, that's done.

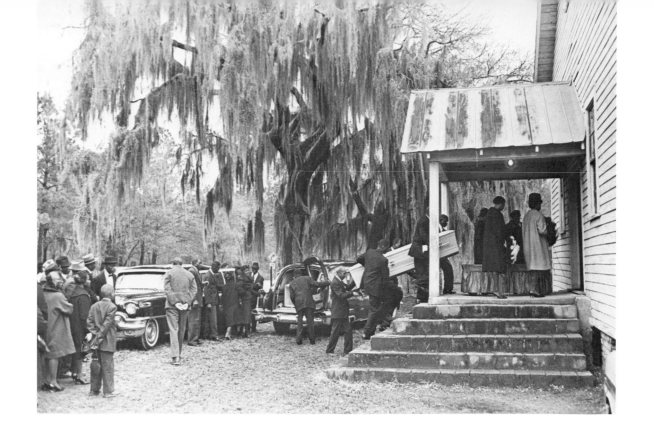

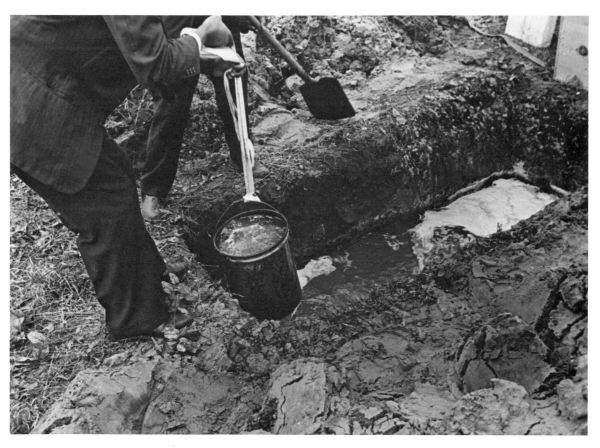

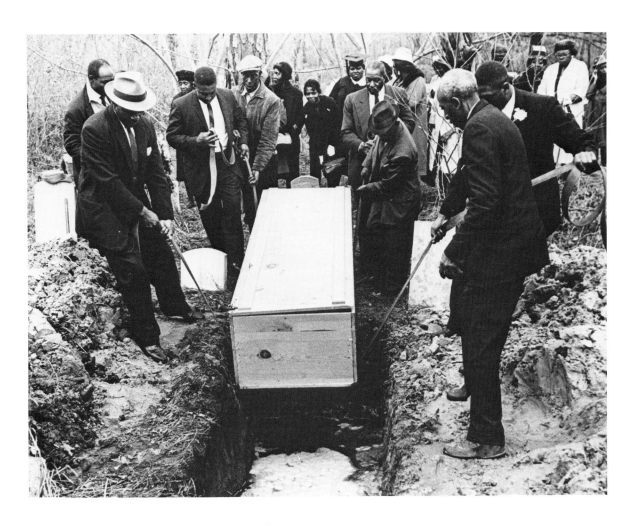

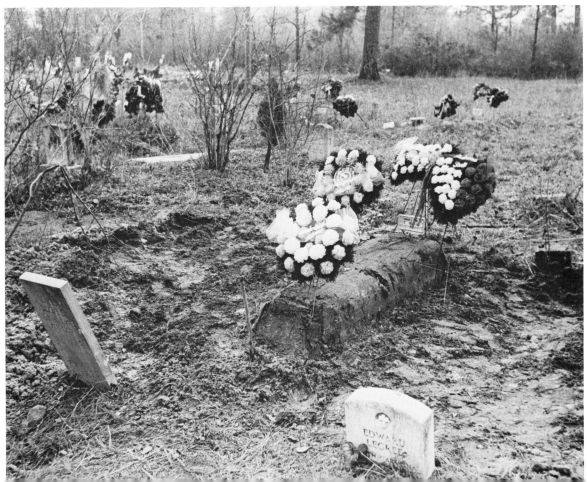

Mr. John Smalls
EVERYBODY HAS A TURN

In the meeting, Brother Joe Deas, he are the oldest person in there, we takes him for the leading man. We put him in the front to take the text. Then take myself, I follow. Then whosoever I wanted to assist—Eli Smith or any other leader. And we go on that way. Everybody has a turn.

We have prayer service the first Sunday night in the month; and the second Sunday night let the brothers preach; then the third Sunday night we let the sisters testify; then we go right back on the fourth Sunday night the brothers will preach again. We used to had it just how it come. We feel like prayer meeting tonight, we have that. But later days, we decided we would mark it out, that every person would know where he going.

That way we trying to do it now. Brother Deas takes the text, when is preaching night, and the boys supposed to preach from that text he give you. You can go preach anywhere you want to preach, but you come right back to that same text.

Any individual, soon as the man finish preach, if you wanted to raise a song, you raise it. And another way, anytime we call someone up to preach, if anybody want to sing for you, can sing you up there. Then one can sing you down. Anybody. They can't sing long as you're talking; wait 'til you finish talk.

Mr. John Smalls
TURN THESE BIG FISH LOOSE

Now friends, we still moving on.
I'm not going to linger with you
'Cause I want to turn these big fish loose.

Brother Deas will come and set the foundation,
The road we going to travel by,
That all of you could know the way to go.

Mr. Joe Deas
TONIGHT YOU GOT A BLESSED CHANCE

I thank you for this great privilege I have before you.
You know from last January '64, I didn't have to been here.
My face could have been under the clay.
But at this same particular hour I have a chance
To rub shoulder to shoulder with you,
I can speak language to language,
I can look face to face.
It is a great joy.

Now we started on a new task, started a new race.
From the twenty-fifth morning we been running,
We been wrastling to behold this very hour of the night.
How many haven't lived to been able to see the day?
Some gone by car,
Some pass away with fire,
Some gone by water.

All part of the world is stirred up now.
Tonight you got a blessed chance to go to the house of God.
Some want to come out tonight and can't come,
And some can come that wouldn't come.
But the day will come.
The day will come.

Mrs. Janie Hunter
YOU HAVE A CHANCE TO EXPLAIN YOURSELF

You can feel yourself in that hall. You have a chance to explain yourself
—anybody who want to. But in church on Sunday, we just have one preacher
talk. And you might get a chance to raise a song or pick out one person to
make a few remarks. But to that hall, everybody could have they way, tell
your own story. That's the difference it makes.

Mr. John Smalls
GOOD MORNING WARRIORS

Good morning Warriors!
How y'all feel?
I'm feeling special alive.

I just rise to tell you all my aim
And whole heart's desire.
My desire is to go the whole way.
I give thanks for being brought
Not from just last December
But from an infant birth.

I can say, "Are we yet alive
To see each other's face."
Thank God for His redeeming grace.

Since last January
Rocky was my road,
Tedious was my journey.
What troubles have I seen,
What conflicts have I passed.

If I had ten thousand tongues
It wouldn't be enough
To give thanks to Thee
Who took my feet out of the miry clay
And put them on a solid rock.

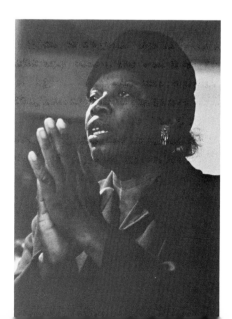

Mrs. Mary Pinckney and the Moving Star Hall congregation

FIX ME JESUS

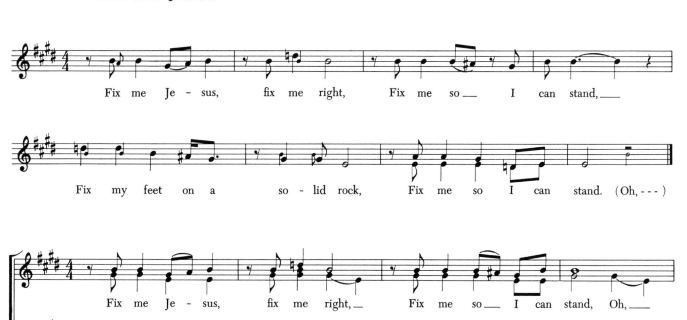

Fix me Je - sus, fix me right, Fix me so __ I can stand, __

Fix my feet on a so - lid rock, Fix me so I can stand. (Oh, - - -)

Fix me Je - sus, fix me right, __ Fix me so __ I can stand, Oh, __

Oh, fix me right, Fix me so I can stand.

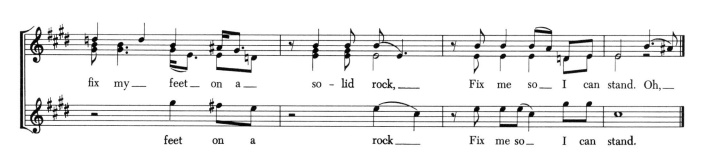

fix my __ feet __ on a __ so - lid rock, __ Fix me so __ I can stand. Oh, __

feet on a rock __ Fix me so __ I can stand.

My tongue tired and I can't speak plain,
Fix me so I can stand,
Fix my feet on a solid rock,
Fix me so I can stand.

Fix my home, Lord, fix it right . . . etc.

Fix my family, Lord, fix them right . . . etc.

Fix my neighbor, fix them right . . . etc.

Fix me warrior, fix me right . . . etc.

Fix me Jesus, fix me right,
Fix me so I can stand,
Fix my feet on a solid rock,
Fix me so I can stand.

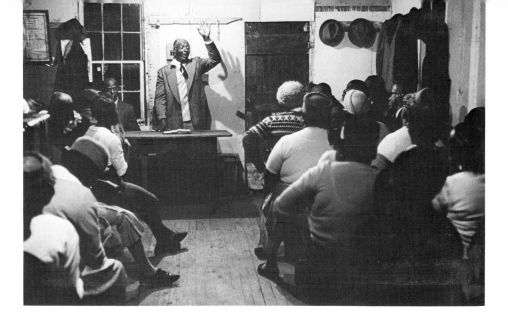

Mr. Benjamin Bligen

A SERMON: LET NOT THEM THAT EAT DESPISE

I'm not gonna tarry before you, Warriors. I'm glad to be here to mingle my voice among my sisters and brothers. I hope and trust that if this sermon don't do you any good, I hope it won't do you no harm.

You know you can go from one part of the Bible to the other. God say we should love one another. Let not them that eat despise them that eat not. Let us remember one another. Don't let us be like Dives now. Let us try to be just as Lazarus. Dives despised the poor. Lazarus went and ask just for a crumb that fall from the table, and before Dives had the passion on him to give, he call the dog on him. But the poor beast have compassion and lick Lazarus.

Time going pass and go on. Time come along when the poor man die. He went on home to God and been at rest. Rich man Dives die, and his home was in Hell. When he lift up his eye in Hell and saw Lazarus in Heaven, he began to memorize. He know he didn't do right, but he cries, "Oh Father, let Lazarus come and dip his finger in the water and cool my trials and trouble."

God says, "No. You had all the good times, plenty of money. You didn't need Lazarus at that time. You need him now, but it too late."

Dives say, "I got five brother. Just give me a chance that I may go back and tell them to get their heart right, that they may shun this torment place I'm in."

And He say, "No. I got Moses and I got the prophets; let them hear what they say. If they don't believe the prophets, they won't believe you, Dives."

Pray for me, Warriors. Let us sing like we singing for the last time. Let us pray like we are praying for the last time. Take no thought for tomorrow, for tomorrow the sun may shine on your grave. Jesus told us to dig deep and lay your foundation on a solid rock, that when the storm of life blow against you, you're gonna find your Father rock. If you dwell upon Him, everythin' will be all right. The world can't do you no harm.

Mrs. Bertha Smith
I DON'T KNOW HOW FAR I'M GOING

Good morning, Warriors,
I'm sitting down right now,
I feel like singing and shouting, Jesus,
But I got to be very careful.
I don't know how far in '65 I'm going,
For my heart pump me from one side to the other,
And then it hurt me from one side to the other.
I don't know when my awful day will surely come
And then my appointed hour.

I can say this new brand morning
In another January,
"Are we yet alive to see each other's face."
Oh glory, and praise Jesus,
Give us of His dying and redeeming grace.
I know from last January,
Many days have I looked up on the highway
Wondering which way I must go.
Lord, you know I thank you for this hour of
The morning,
For I know it's none of my goodness,
I know if justice had plumb the line
All my daily travels would have cut off
And then never no more return.

If I shall cut off from God
I don't want to have no gathering to do.
I want to live so that I shall pass from
Life unto death.
I don't know if I going to be in my bed,
And then I don't know if I going to be on the highway.
I know this hour of the morning
I got peace with everybody,
And then I got peace
With all my neighbors' children.
I can say this hour of the morning,
I am just what I am.

Thank you, Jesus,
I don't know how far I'm going,
Got a pain racking the body right now.
And then I got to be very careful, Jesus.
I ask you all to pray for me
So I may be able to run on.

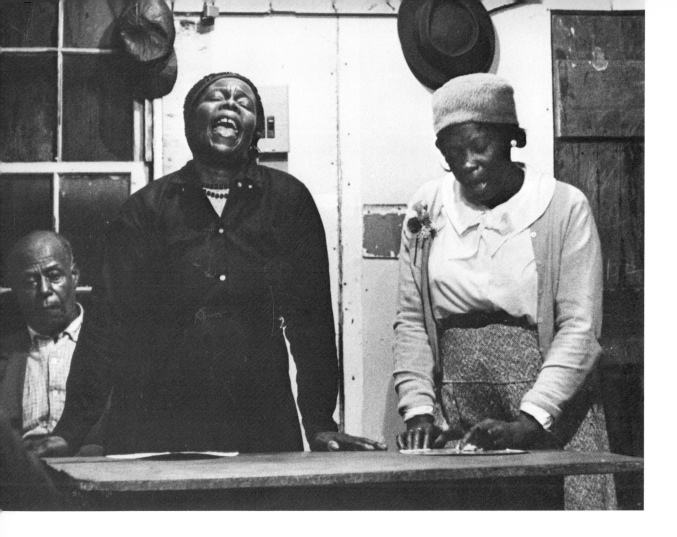

Mrs. Janie Hunter and the Moving Star Hall congregation
ASK THE WATCHMAN HOW LONG

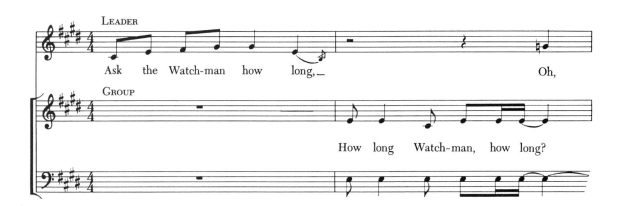

LEADER: Oh ask my brother how long,
GROUP: How long Watchman, how long?   Oh all my neighbors, how long? . . . etc.

In sixty-four how long? . . . etc.   Oh before the roll call . . . etc.
Well, ask my daughter how long . . . etc.   Oh just a few more risings . . . etc.
Well, ask my preacher how long . . . etc.   Oh ask my leader how long . . . etc.

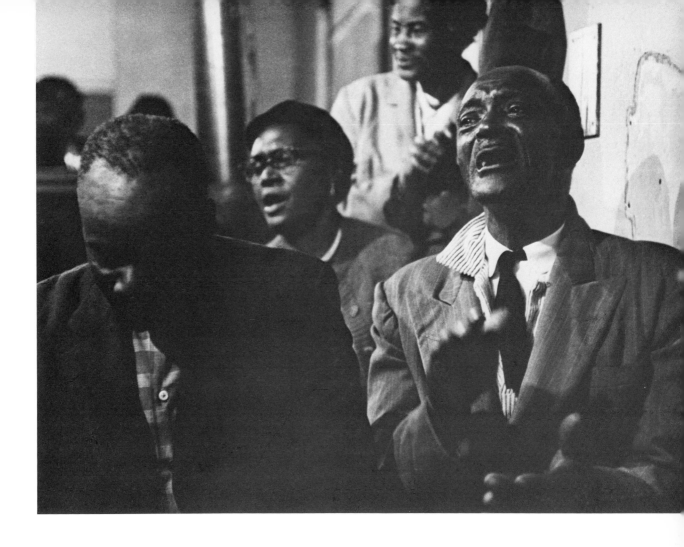

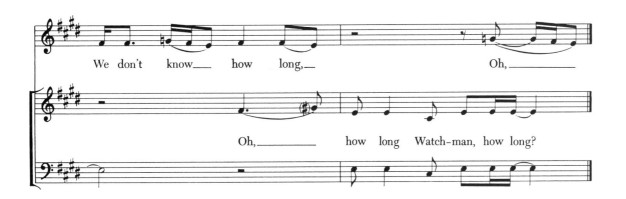

We don't know___ how long,___ Oh,_____

Oh,_____ how long Watch-man, how long?

Well, all my neighbors how long? . . . etc.

Oh soon it will be over . . . etc.
Watchman, how long? . . . etc.
You know how long, how long . . . etc.
Ask my friends how long . . . etc.

Brother Jenkins, how long? . . . etc.

Oh, how long, how long,
How long Watchman, how long?
How long, how long,
How long Watchman, how long?

REBORN AGAIN

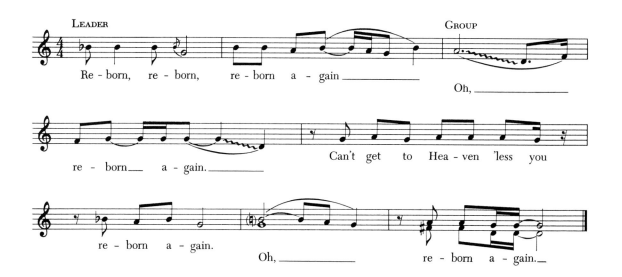

LEADER: Won't you reborn Member, won't you reborn again,
GROUP: Oh, reborn again.
LEADER: Well, you must keep a-rollin', got to reborn again,
GROUP: Oh, reborn again.

Oh, reborn warriors, won't you reborn again,
Oh, reborn again.
Yes you can't get to Heaven 'less you reborn again,
Oh, reborn again.

Oh, goin' to the river, gonna take my walk,
Oh, reborn again.
Meet Jesus mother, gonna stand and talk,
Oh, reborn again.

Just let me put on my travelin' shoes,
Oh, reborn again.
I'm goin' to Heaven, gonna carry the news,
Oh, reborn again.

Let me tell you the natural fact,
Oh, reborn again.
Can't get to Heaven, ain't comin' back,
Oh, reborn again.

When I get to Heaven, gonna sing and shout,
Oh, reborn again.
There ain't nobody there gonna turn me out,
Oh, reborn again.

When I get to Heaven, gonna sit right down,
Oh, reborn again.
Ask Jesus mother for my starry crown,
Oh, reborn again.

Oh Satan is mad and I'm so glad,
Oh, reborn again.
Lost the soul he thought he had,
Oh, reborn again.

Oh Satan he walking like a snake in the grass,
Oh, reborn again.
He always walk in a Christian path,
Oh, reborn again.

Wonder what Satan keep growlin' about,
Oh, reborn again.
He chained up in Hell and he can't get out,
Oh, reborn again.

Oh one of these mornings and it won't be long,
Oh, reborn again.
I'll see some grapes a-hanging down,
Oh, reborn again.

I pick a grape and I suck the juice,
Oh, reborn again.
Sweetest grape I ever taste,
Oh, reborn again.

Reborn, reborn, reborn again,
Oh, reborn again.
Can't get to Heaven 'less you reborn again,
Oh, reborn again.

Rev. James Grant

GET ON YOUR HOLY HORSE

Be careful, my friends, because sometimes the
Chairman of Hell begin to saddle up his pony.
He gonna override somebody.
You walk down the road
And somehow your feet begin to be tangled.
The road become rocky, hard to cross.

Hallelujah, my friends,
Put on your travelin' shoes.
Get on your holy horse
Because sin are now pressing hard,
Many dangers follow.

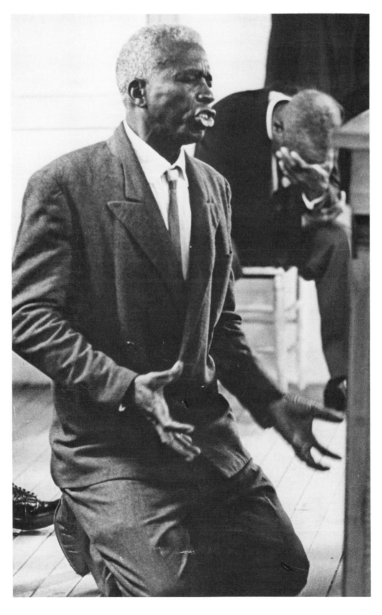

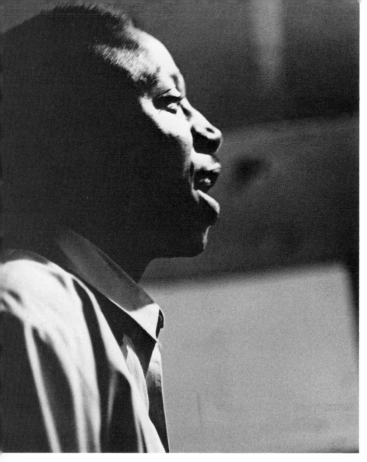

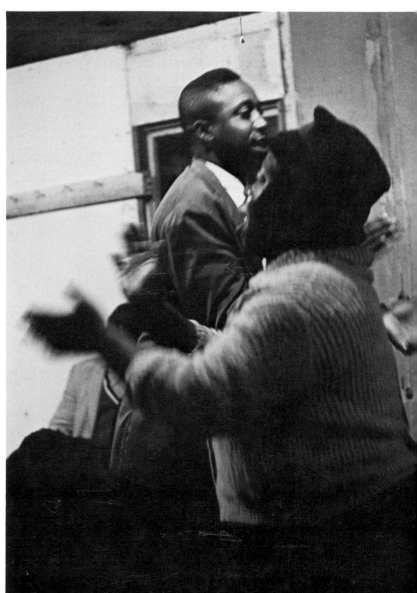

Mr. Benjamin Bligen
I REALIZE I'M HERE FOR SOME PURPOSE

I was about twenty-seven when I start to go to Moving Star Hall regular. Since I was a little boy, Mom used to take me there on her back—I was so small to walk in the dark, you know.

There was a time when blues was all that was on my mind. But the truth is the light, and after getting old in age I realize that I'm here for some purpose. Father always teach me the Bible, teach us how to sing and how to pray, and tell us what must not do and what must do to inherit life everlasting. So I stop and ask myself some question. Then I just had to change from singing blues and begin to go back to what my old parents said—singing spiritual songs.

And I found out that's better.

Mr. William Saunders
THIS IS GOOD, BUT IT DOESN'T HELP YOUR EATING

We all as kids went to Moving Star Hall. As far as I was concerned, I just had to be there. We used to enjoy the singing and the shouting. And at a certain period of the night, all the youngsters in there had to go up front and kneel down and everybody prayed. That place used to be full—three nights a week. You couldn't get in that place if you be late on Sunday nights. And it was so much young people. All of a sudden it just start dying off.

For one thing most of the young people started going away. Like me, I went in the Army. I was about fifteen. Once the kids start going to different places, and we start to be more enlightened, then we start getting away from this old type of thing. As we get more education, we come to find out that this wasn't the type of thing we needed to help us through the world. We needed more than this. This is good, but it doesn't help your eating. Why waste time with something that you aren't gonna get anything out of at all? You gonna be looking forward to when you die, and man, you hungry now.

That Moving Star Hall business just about died out completely. Then they started building it back up again. Now some of the people, the Moving Star Hall Singers, are enjoying some of the fruit of their labor.

Mr. James Mackey
MORNING

Here am I again once more, Heavenly Father,
The worm of the dust
Ready to bow this hour of the morning
On my bruised and bending knee.
Thank you, My Father, for your guardin' angel,
That guard me all night long
Until morning light appear.
And before he went from his watch,
He touch my eyes this morning with a finger of love,
And my eye become open
And behold a brand new Monday morning.
Oh, God, if you so please
Give us that holding out spirit,
That you may own us all
When we done trod across the many street of Charleston.
Oh God, what I say for our neighbors,
And the neighbors' children around in this vicinity,
Oh please, Our Father,
Make them more patient, more acknowledge,
May we love each and one another.
Help us to help each other.
And each other's cross to bear.
And Our Father, if you please,
Remember the President of this United States,
Oh, remember the officials.
And Our Father, once more I say
For the President of the N.A.A.C.P.,
Throw thy arms of protection around them,
May they achieve victory in whatever they may undertake to do.
Lead them, Our Father,
Through the unfriendly world where there's no friendly grace.
We know we must fight to increase our courage
That we may be able to endure the pain.
I ask you to please remember mankind far away,
Whatever his town may be.
Make him realize, that awful day will surely come.
And then have mercy, My Father,
When I done walk the last mile of the way,
Done all that you 'signed my hand to do,
When I shall come down off the stage of action,
Must surrender under the black banner of Death,
Ask you, Jesus, give me a resting place
Somewhere in your Kingdom
Which Job declare
The wicked cease from troubling.
Amen.

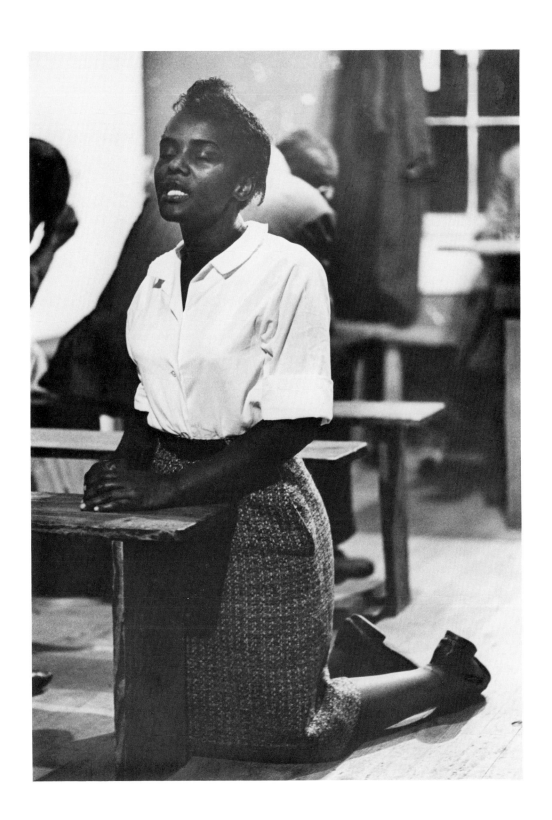

Mrs. Ruth Bligen

ALL THINGS ARE POSSIBLE IF YOU ONLY BELIEVE

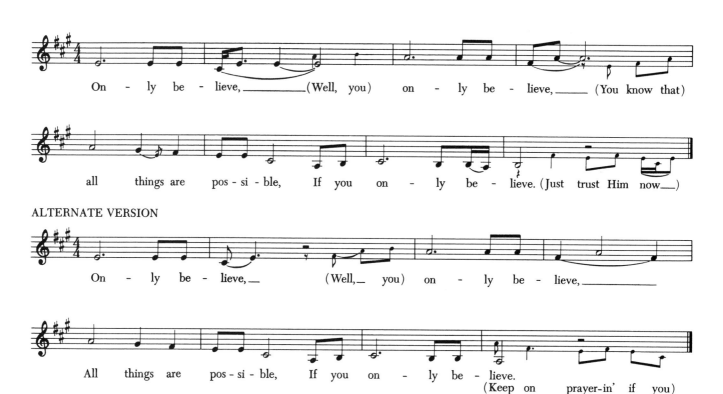

On - ly be - lieve,———(Well, you) on - ly be - lieve,——— (You know that)

all things are pos - si - ble, If you on - ly be - lieve. (Just trust Him now—)

ALTERNATE VERSION

On - ly be - lieve,— (Well,— you) on - ly be - lieve,———

All things are pos - si - ble, If you on - ly be - lieve.
(Keep on prayer-in' if you)

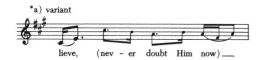

*a) variant

lieve, (nev - er doubt Him now)—

Only believe, (well, you) only believe,
(You know that) all things are possible,
If you only believe.

(Just trust Him now) only believe, (well, you) only believe,
All things are possible,
If you only believe.

(Keep on prayerin', if you) only believe, only believe,
All things are possible,
If you only believe.

(Tell the warriors, if you) only believe, only believe,
All things are possible,
If you only believe.

Only believe (never doubt Him now), only believe,
(You know that) all things are possible,
If you only believe.

(He'll be your {mother, if you) only believe, only believe,
{father,
All things are possible,
If you only believe.

92

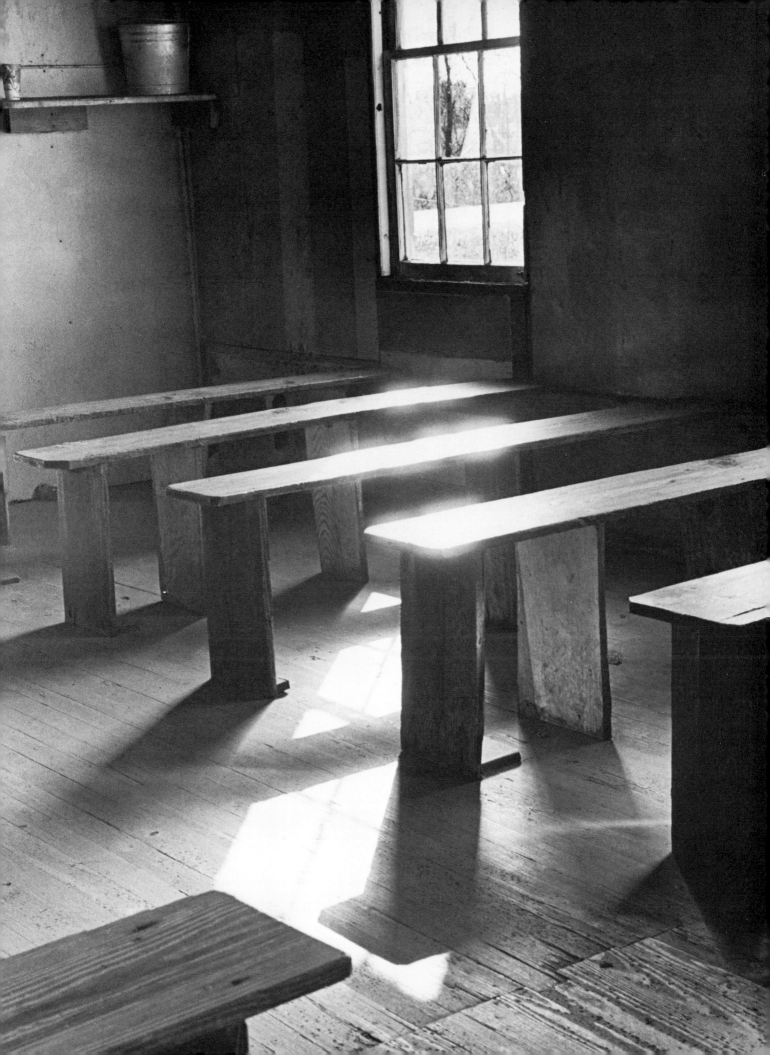

4. TALKIN' 'BOUT

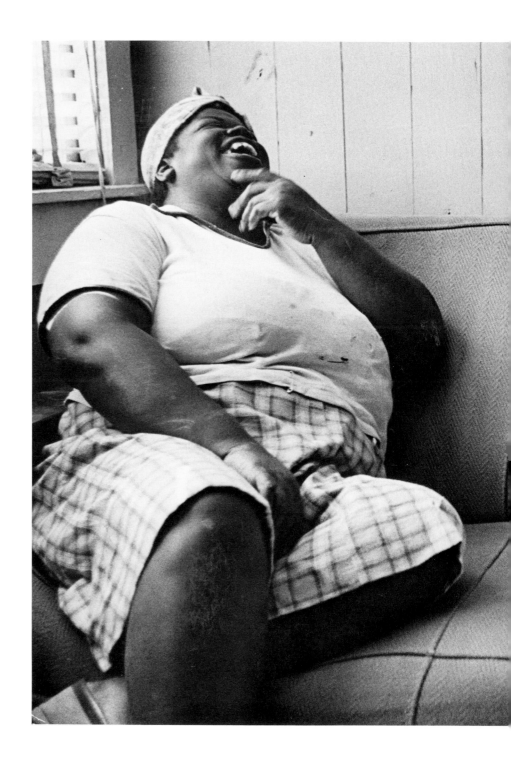

JOKEY

A GOOD TIME

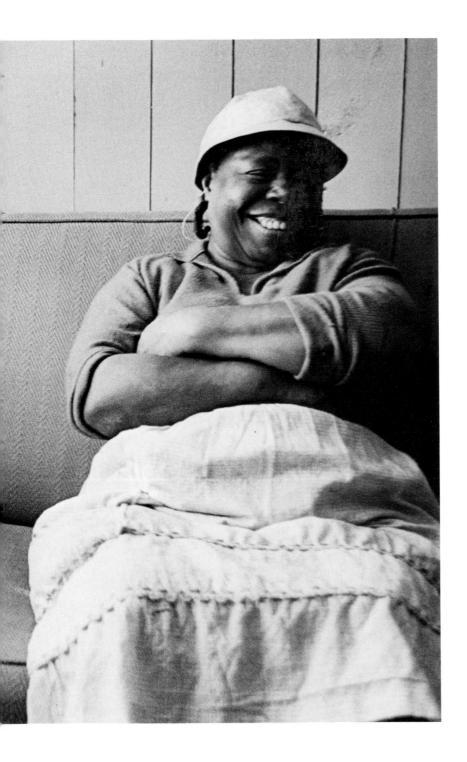

TIMES

Mrs. Janie Hunter
STORIES

When we was small, we didn't 'low to go no place, but we have all we fun at home. On weekend when we do all work what told to us and after we finish work at night, we sit down and we all sing different old song, and parents teach us different game and riddles. We go and cut the wood and wrap up the house with green oak and muckle wood, then we all stays by the fire chimbley and listen to stories.

96

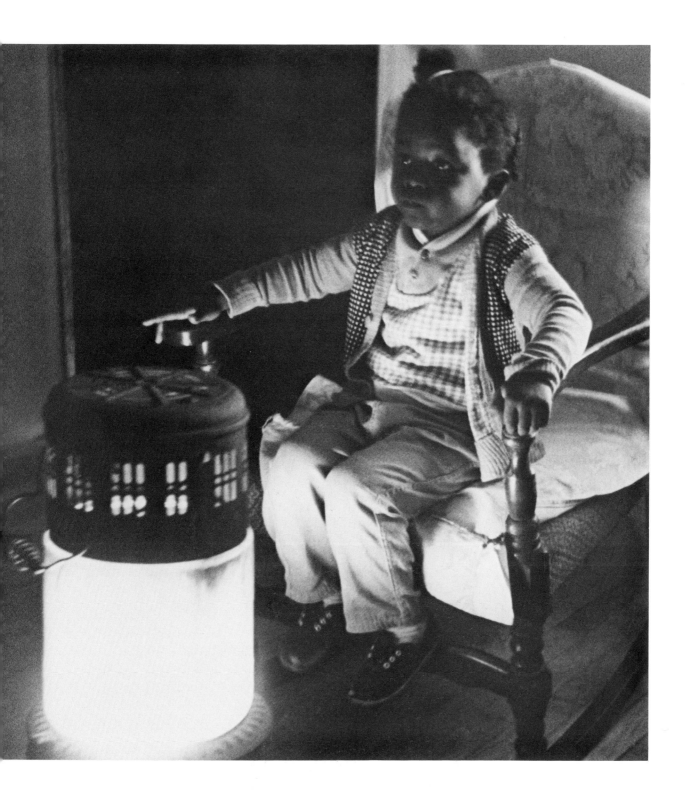

JACK AND MARY AND THE DEVIL

This is a old story. Very old. Way back in the time I heard my old parents talk about. Slavery time. Time when the Yankee beat the Rebel. They said it was a true-life story of Jack and Mary.

Jack and Mary was brother and sister. Mary was old enough to keep company, so a young man come to Mary mother house one day, and ask Mary mother could he keep Mary company. Mother ask Mary, "Do you love him?" And she said yes. So mother tell him, "Yes, I don't mind."

So after a while Mary mother tell this young man that he could take her out. But Mary didn't know who this young man was; this young man was the Devil. He had horse feet and he had horn on his head, but he had all of 'em cover.

Jack heard his mother tell Mary she could go, so he went and say, "Mama, could I go with my sister?"

She say, "I don't mind if Mary don't mind." But Mary tell Jack, "No, I don't want you to go with me; you is too young."

The old Devil had a high-top buggy and horse. And Jack had a horse. Well Jack was a very wise boy, so he study a plan, and full his pocket with corn. Then Jack went on ahead, and he get in a store and turn into a gold ring. All that time Mary and her boyfriend get in the cart and began traveling. When they get to the store Mary said, "Oh, I love that ring."

The old Devil—young boyfriend—say, "Jump out and price it."

The man say, "Nine thousand dollar."

Devil say, "Well that just my pocket change." So he got it. All that time Mary didn't know she brother turn to a ring in the store, and that's the very ring Mary have love. She put her brother on her finger and didn't know. And all that time they travel until they get to this young man home. And when they go in, oh he had a beautiful home.

Then when time come to eat she ask what they are going have for supper. He say, "Oh, pull out one of them drawer and cook one them dead man in there."

And then Mary began to get trouble in mind. She realize she was down in Hell. She said, "Lord, when my brother have want to come with me, I should of saw right and let him come."

And then, Jack disappear off Mary finger, say, "Oh Sister, when I ask to come with you, you run me back, but how now?" And then Mary was so happy. Then when time come for go to bed that old Devil put her to bed and fall on the floor and start for sleep. Mary knew that Jack was on her finger. As soon as the old boy got fast asleep, Mary and Jack began to travel.

Well the old Devil had a rooster; he was a teller. And as they began to travel, old Rooster get in the Devil face and spur 'em. Say:

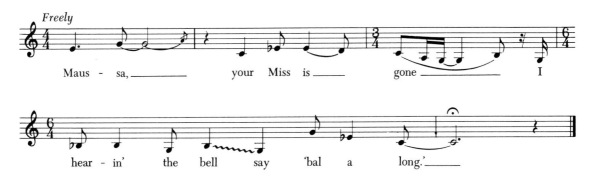

Devil say, "How long gone?"
Say, "Long time."
Then he tell the rooster, "Go down yonder and get my old bull that jump fifty mile away." And the Devil get on the old bull back, say:

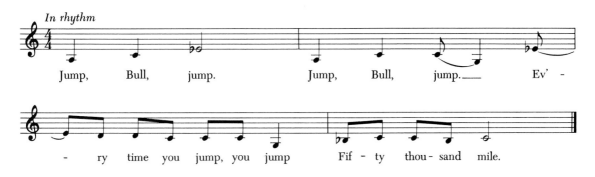

Well, he made one jump, he jump right by Jack and Mary, and Jack drop one grain corn, and it turn a ocean of water. And all that time it take for that water to dry up, Jack and sister was far away. Then the Devil made a loud cry, saying:

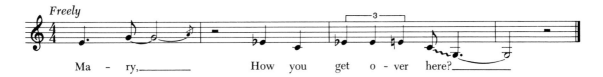

Mary say:

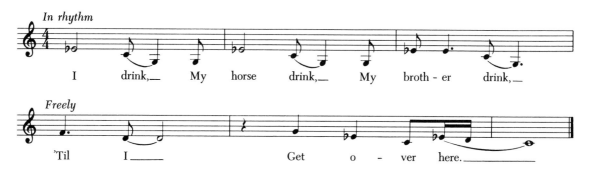

In rhythm

I drink,__ My horse drink,__ My broth - er drink,__

Freely

'Til I_____ Get o - ver here._____

Old Bull say:

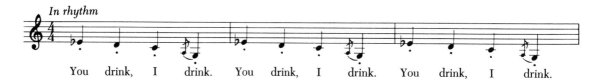

In rhythm

You drink, I drink. You drink, I drink. You drink, I drink.

He drink, and bust the bull belly loose, and when he think the bull was going fifty thousand mile an hour, the bull couldn't make but five mile an hour. And old Devil take some string and tie the old bull belly up. And all that time Jack and Mary was far away. Then he get on the old bull back and say:

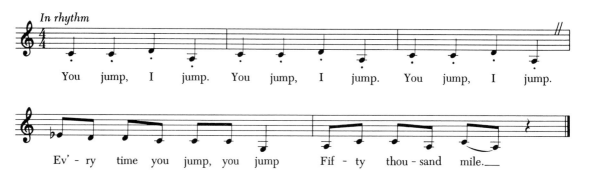

In rhythm

You jump, I jump. You jump, I jump. You jump, I jump.

Ev' - ry time you jump, you jump Fif - ty thou - sand mile.__

And jump right by Mary and Jack. Then Jack drop another grain of corn, and it turn a whole mountain, 'cross and 'cross the world. Old Devil say:

"Mary,
How you get
Over here?"

100

Mary say:

> "I climb,
> My brother climb,
> My horse climb,
> 'Till I get
> Over here."

Bull say:

> "You climb, I climb,
> You climb, I climb,
> Every time you climb,
> You slide back down."

Now he couldn't climb. Every time the bull climb to catch Mary and Jack, he slide back down. And when he did climb the old mountain down, then Jack and Mary was across a bridge another three miles away, and he was about getting given up in mind. He say:

> "Mary, tell me how you
> Get over here?"

Mary say:

> "I root, my brother root,
> My horse root,
> 'Till I get over here."

Bull say:

> "You root, I root,
> You root, I root,
> You root, I root."

Then old Devil and old Bull root beneath the pine tree, and that pine tree fall 'cross the bridge, the bridge bend, and that's the way that story end.

Mr. Benjamin Bligen
THE RABBIT AND THE WOLF AT THE DANCE

The Rabbit and the Wolf been going to a dance one night, and the Rabbit tricky, you know. The Rabbit was in love with the Wolf girlfriend, and the Rabbit want to get close to she. So after they went to a joint, and the music start to play, Rabbit ask Wolf girlfriend to dance. It was a fast dancing record, but Rabbit walk up and tell Wolf, "Wolf, this music call for close dance." He tell Wolf that music call for close dance that he would get a chance to talk with the Wolf girlfriend. Well, the Wolf see him dancing close with the girlfriend, Wolf wouldn't take it for no harm. That was cut and dry, see. Cut and dry.

Mrs. Janie Hunter
THE RABBIT AND THE PARTRIDGE

Everybody think that a rabbit have the most sense, but one day the Partridge outsensed the Rabbit. This day the Partridge went out on a walk, come back home with his head under his wing. On the way back he stopped at Bunny Rabbit's house and say, "Oh Rabbit, how you like my head?" And all the time he had he head under he wing.

Rabbit say, "I like it fine; where *is* your head?"

Partridge say, "You old fool Rabbit, you ain't got no sense. I leave my head home for my wife shave."

The Rabbit take off and went home to his wife, say, "Old Gal, I got a job for you. Come on and chop my head off. I want you to give me a haircut."

She say, "Oh Rabbit, no! I not supposed to cut your head off. If I cut your head off you'll die."

Rabbit say, "No I won't die either, 'cause the Partridge cut he head off, leave 'em home for he wife to shave. I don't see why I can't cut mine off."

So he argue and argue until he make his wife get the knife, and the wife chop the old Bunny head off. And then the Bunny die. The old lady cry. Then she skin the rabbit and eat him.

The old lady went to the Partridge and say, "Partridge, why you did that?" Say, "Why you take your head under your wing and fool the Bunny that you leave your head home for your wife to shave, when you know it wasn't true?"

Partridge say, "Well, you ain't no fool, and if you'll only keep that up, we sure will get along." After that the Partridge have two wives—have his wife and then the Bunny's wife.

BARNEY McCABE

We learn some these stories from my uncle, Harry Williams. He was kind of rough, but he really could tell some stories.

Once upon a time it was a twin sister and brother. The sister name was Mary and the brother name was Jack. One day they decided to go on a long traveling. But Jack was a wise child and he told Mary to go in the house and ask Mother could we go. Her mother say, "Yes, you could go, but take care." So Jack say, "Wait a minute, Sister," and went to the barn and get four grain of corn. And Mary said to Jack, "What you gonna do with that corn?" Jack said, "In a long while, you will see." So he put the corn in his pocket.

Then before he leave home Jack told his mother, say, "Mama, I got three dogs—Barney McCabe, Doodle-le-doo and Soo-Boy. I going to leave a glass of milk on the table. If you see that glass of milk turn to blood, I want you to turn my dogs loose."

So they went on traveling and all the time wondering what was the end going be. Pretty soon it come dark and they begin to get weary. They knocked at an old lady house. The old lady run to the door, say, "Who is it?"

Jack say, "Me, Mama. Could we spend the night here? 'Cause we far from home and we very tired." Old lady say, "Oh yes, come on in."

All that time she was a witch-craft and the children didn't know it. She fed them and put them to bed. She had a knife she call "Tommy Hawk." After she put the children to bed she began to sharpen it up:

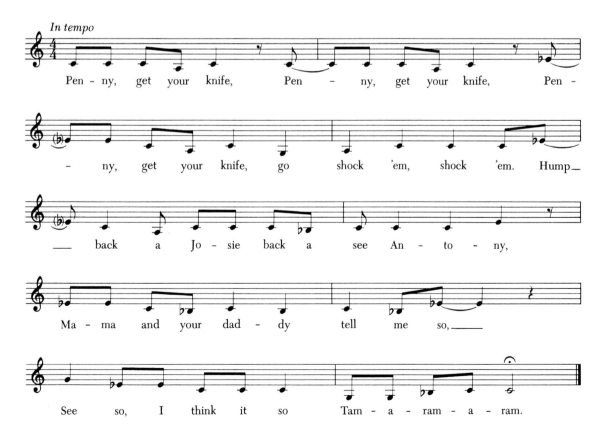

In tempo

Pen - ny, get your knife, Pen - ny, get your knife, Pen - - ny, get your knife, go shock 'em, shock 'em. Hump— —back a Jo - sie back a see An - to - ny, Ma - ma and your dad - dy tell me so,— See so, I think it so Tam - a - ram - a - ram.

Children say, "Grandma, what's all that noise? We can't sleep."

She say, "That ain't nothing but your grandma frock-tail switchin' to get your supper hot. You all go back to sleep."

So Jack begin to wonder how they can get out of there. Then he remember the old lady have a room full of pumpkin. Jack takes two pumpkin and put 'em in the bed and cover 'em over, pretend it was he and his sister. Then Jack throw one grain of corn to the window, and it turn into a ladder. Jack and Mary climbed the ladder down and they start traveling for home.

The old lady sharpen her knife faster:

"Penny, get your knife,
Penny, get your knife,
Penny, get your knife, go shock 'em, shock 'em.

Hump back a Josie back a see Antony,
Mama and your daddy tell me so,
See so, I think it so
Tam-a-ram-a-ram."

She didn't hear no noise, so she sneak in the room and chop up the pumpkins in the bed. Then she ran in the kitchen and got a dishpan, and pull back the cover. And when she think she putting the meat in the pan for cook for breakfast, she drop the pumpkin in the pan. And Jack and Mary was long gone.

She get mad, grab Tommy Hawk and flew down on those children. The children drop another grain of corn and it turn a tall pine tree. And Jack and Mary flew up in that tree. The old lady start cut on the tree, say:

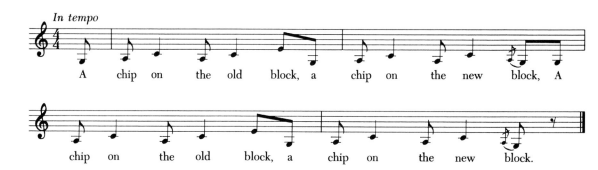

Then Jack drop a grain of corn down from the pine tree, and back home that glass of milk turn to blood. Them dogs begin to holler. Jack's mother ran in the yard and turned the dogs loose. Jack say:

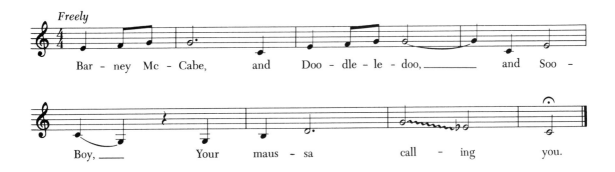

Bar - ney Mc - Cabe, and Doo - dle - le - doo, _____ and Soo -

Boy, _____ Your maus - sa call - ing you.

Dogs say:

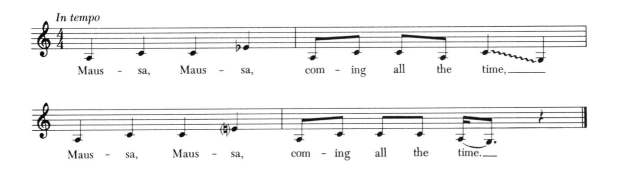

Maus - sa, Maus - sa, com - ing all the time, _____

Maus - sa, Maus - sa, com - ing all the time. ___

Old witch say:

> "A chip on the old block, a chip on the new block,
> A chip on the old block, a chip on the new block."

Every time she chip, the tree lean and lean. Jack call:

> "Barney McCabe, and Doodle-le-doo, and Soo-Boy,
> Your maussa almost gone."

Dogs say:

> "Maussa, Maussa, coming all the time,
> Maussa, Maussa, coming all the time."

Jack drop another corn, the last corn, and it turn a bridge. And then
when the old witch pull the ax up for take the last chop and chop Jack and
Mary in the head, the dogs ran up. Barney McCabe cut her throat, Doodle-
le-doo suck her blood and Soo-Boy drag her on the bridge, the bridge bend
and that's the way that story end.

Mrs. Mary Pinckney
I TOO SCARED THEN

People say if you look over your left shoulder you'll see ghosts. Tell about hag and all kind of thing like that. I look back over my left shoulder all the time, I don't see no ghost. I never see none, but I believe in ghost. Some call 'em ghost, some call 'em spooks, boodyman. That's the way we is call 'em when we was little—boodyman.

That old man, Michael Brown, he's always be to our house. I guess he's 'round about seventy-five. He is come over every Sunday and he sit down and talk about all these old-time thing. Talk about old-time ghost. He say when he go home nighttime he have to carry a stick and feel his way, 'specially if it dark, 'cause ghost is crowded in the path. He take stick go "whicha-whoocha-whoocha," clear his way. I be glad when he go home 'cause he talk about those thing and make me scared. Mama like to listen. Not me. I say, "Take your hat and go home." I too scared then. Ghost!

Mr. James Mackey
THEY'LL KNOCK YOU OFF YOUR FOOT

Some people died, their spirit walk around. If a person died happy, they don't bother you. But people died bad, well, they'll knock you off your foot.

One most knock me off my foot one night. I was coming out just about dusk-dark and something come around me like a long black snake—tie around me. It shoot up and I ain't feel like I was onto the ground at all. Only way I came back in this world, a dog smell my scent and that dog bark. Didn't for that, I'd been *gone*.

When my foot touch ground, feel like I been off the ground. I go and curse 'em. They say if I pray I might of get off much better. The more I curse, the more I guess he try to knock me.

When the feeling get back to me, then I start to walk—taking my time just like when a person sick—and I could imagine he up behind me. My hair on my head just tauten up. I got back home, gone to bed that night with *all* my clothes on.

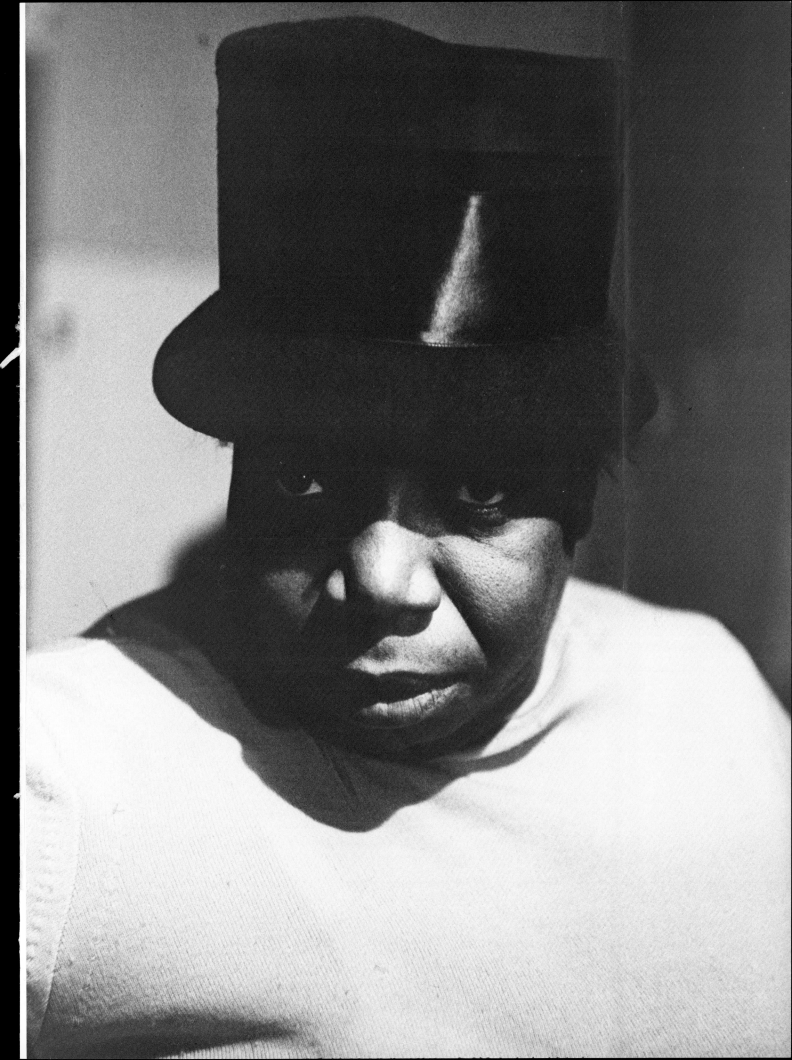

Mrs. Janie Hunter
WHEN YOU GET TO OLD AGE YOU TURN A HAG

I say see it to believe it. Ghosts shows up to some people, and some people they don't. But I'm not scared of 'em. I'm more scared of live.

But hags, that's real. When you get to old age, you turn a hag. Hags come to your house and hag your children. Children can't sleep, or a hag take somebody child and put 'em under the bed. Sometime a hag sit on you and keep you from getting up, try to smother you.

But you could tell a hag. I heard my old people say, if you want to tell a hag, put a broom 'cross your door. If that's a hag, he going take up that broom, ain't going step across it.

If hag bother you, use salt and pepper. Sprinkle either by your bed or 'cross your door and they won't come in. The salt burn their skin.

Mrs. Mary Pinckney
I GOT A BLUESY FEELING

I like blues. My uncles Benji and Willis—oh, they could sing! Willis is come home 'round twelve and one o'clock in the night and wake up everybody on the hill. Go one side by the pump and he sing that blues from then 'til four in the morning. Wake up everybody. Mama is come outside, say, "Willis, why don't you come on in the house?"

"Can't come in the house right now, Doll, I got a bluesy feeling." He sing.

And Benji, Benji could sing! He have one them cowhorn and he get up and put it to his mouth and blow 'em. Just like a trumpet. And Willis be singing the song and he be blowing the horn and they going down the road blowing and singing. And I be right there listening to 'em. I follow them too. They is like for I follow them 'cause I sing right along with them.

My brothers sing blues too. Joe, he like all different kind of song—spiritual and blues. Sometime he be home by heself and go on the road or stay on that porch or go under a tree, sit down and just play his guitar and sing his song. And I'll go and help him.

Mr. Joe Hunter

WHAT YOU GONNA DO?

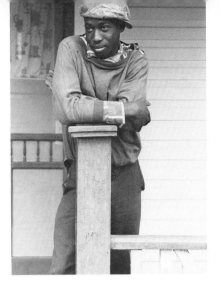

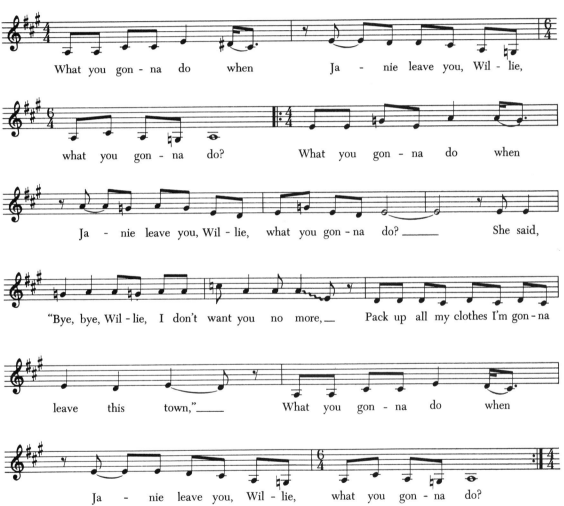

What you gonna do when Janie leave you, Willie, what you gonna do?
She said, "Bye bye, baby, I don't want you no more",
Sitting here crying, Janie, please don't go,
What you gonna do when Janie leave you, Willie, what you gonna do?

What you gonna do when Janie leave you, Willie, what you gonna do?
She said, "Bye bye, Willie, I'm putting you down,
Pack up my clothes I'm gonna leave this town",
What you gonna do when Janie leave you, Willie, what you gonna do?

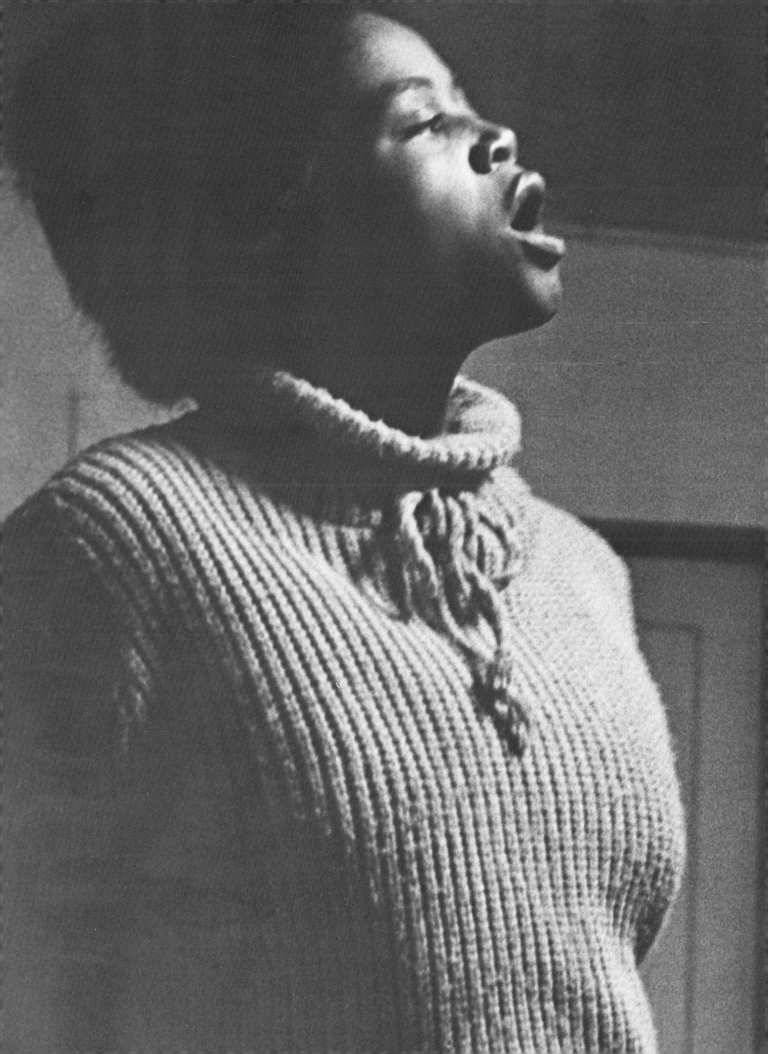

Mrs. Janie Hunter

WATER MY FLOWERS

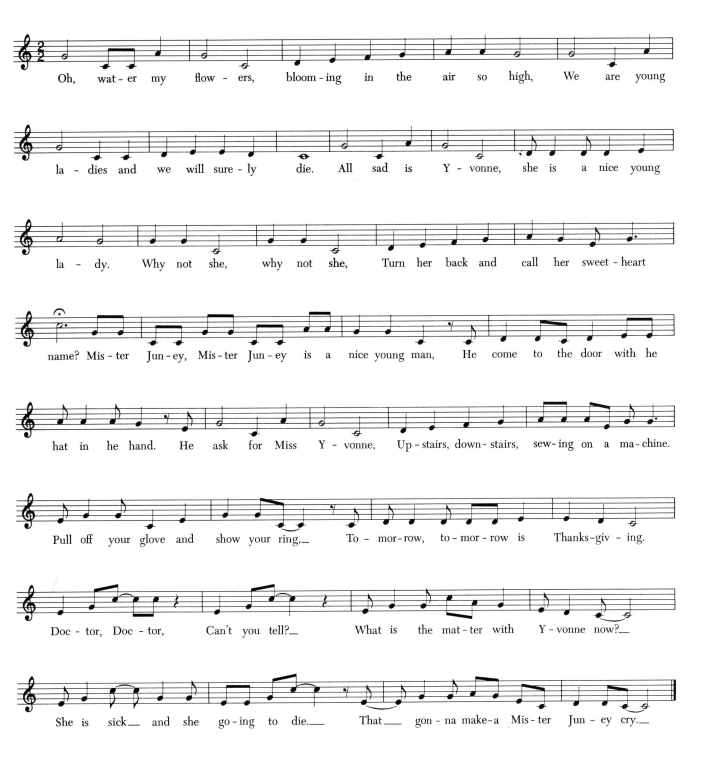

Oh, wat - er my flow - ers, bloom - ing in the air so high, We are young

la - dies and we will sure - ly die. All sad is Y - vonne, she is a nice young

la - dy. Why not she, why not she, Turn her back and call her sweet - heart

name? Mis - ter Jun - ey, Mis - ter Jun - ey is a nice young man, He come to the door with he

hat in he hand. He ask for Miss Y - vonne, Up - stairs, down - stairs, sew - ing on a ma - chine.

Pull off your glove and show your ring,— To - mor - row, to - mor - row is Thanks - giv - ing.

Doc - tor, Doc - tor, Can't you tell?— What is the mat - ter with Y - vonne now?—

She is sick— and she go - ing to die.— That— gon - na make-a Mis - ter Jun - ey cry.—

111

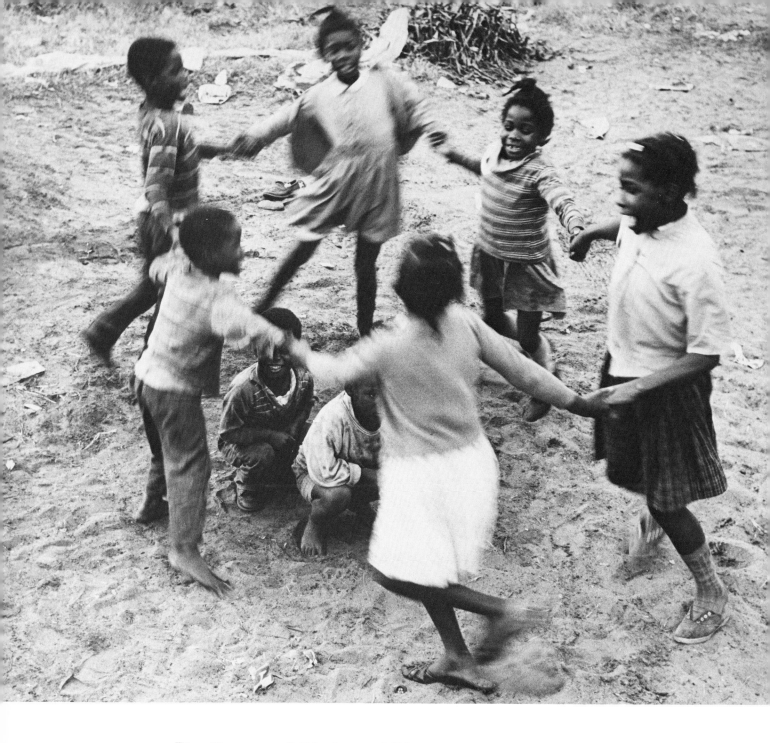

The Hunter and Pinckney children
SALLY ROUND THE SUNSHINE

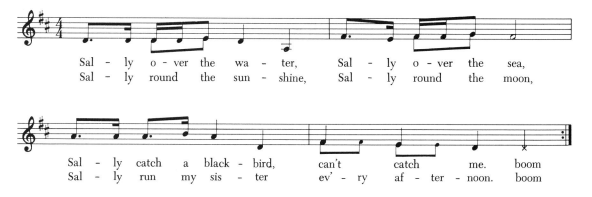

Sal - ly o - ver the wa - ter, Sal - ly o - ver the sea,
Sal - ly round the sun - shine, Sal - ly round the moon,

Sal - ly catch a black - bird, can't catch me. boom
Sal - ly run my sis - ter ev' - ry af - ter - noon. boom

112

Mrs. Janie Hunter, Mrs. Mary Pinckney, and their children
OLD LADY COME FROM BOOSTER

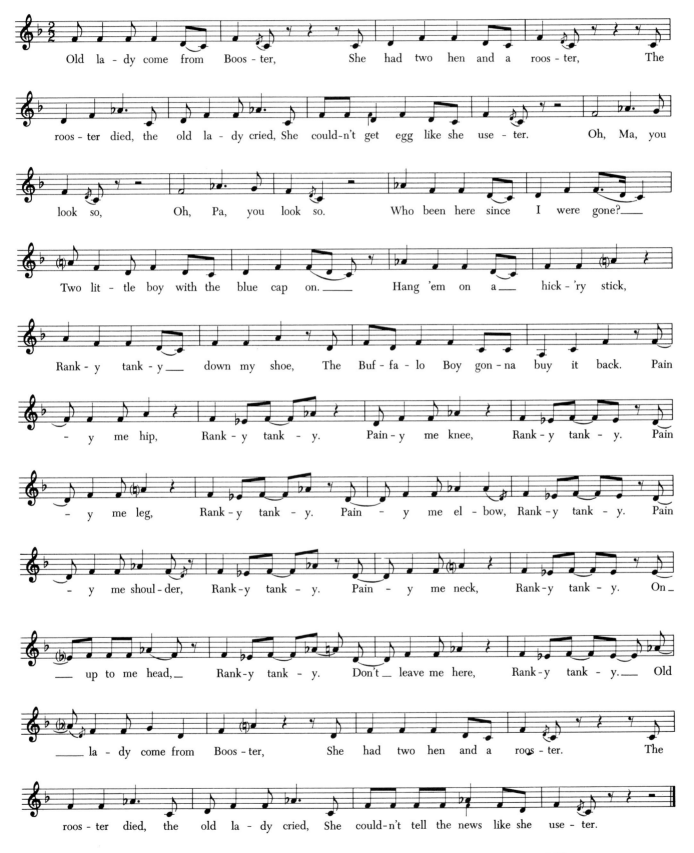

Old la - dy come from Boos - ter, She had two hen and a roos - ter, The

roos - ter died, the old la - dy cried, She could-n't get egg like she use - ter. Oh, Ma, you

look so, Oh, Pa, you look so. Who been here since I were gone?

Two lit - tle boy with the blue cap on. Hang 'em on a hick - 'ry stick,

Rank - y tank - y down my shoe, The Buf - fa - lo Boy gon - na buy it back. Pain

- y me hip, Rank - y tank - y. Pain - y me knee, Rank - y tank - y. Pain

- y me leg, Rank - y tank - y. Pain - y me el - bow, Rank - y tank - y. Pain

- y me shoul - der, Rank - y tank - y. Pain - y me neck, Rank - y tank - y. On

up to me head, Rank - y tank - y. Don't leave me here, Rank - y tank - y. Old

la - dy come from Boos - ter, She had two hen and a roos - ter. The

roos - ter died, the old la - dy cried, She could-n't tell the news like she use - ter.

113

Mrs. Janie Hunter, Mrs. Mary Pinckney,
and their children

SHOO TURKEY SHOO

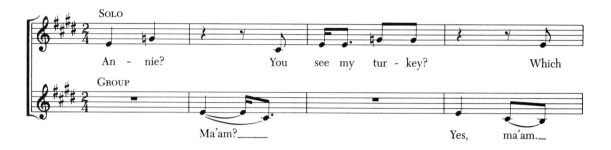

An - nie?　　　You see my tur - key?　　Which

Ma'am?　　　　　　　　　　Yes, ma'am.

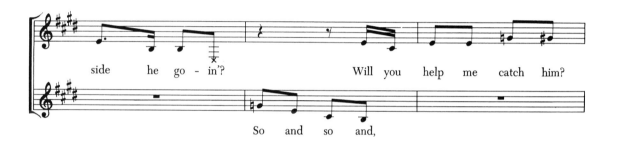

side he go - in'?　　　Will you help me catch him?

So　and　so and,

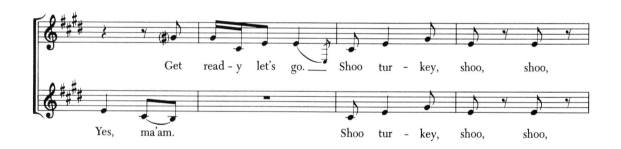

Get read - y let's go. ── Shoo tur - key, shoo, shoo,

Yes, ma'am.　　　Shoo tur - key, shoo, shoo,

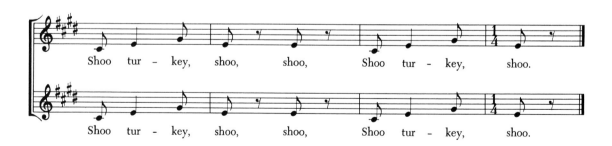

Shoo tur - key, shoo, shoo, Shoo tur - key, shoo.

Shoo tur - key, shoo, shoo, Shoo tur - key, shoo.

Clapping pattern often used

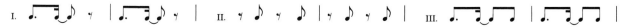

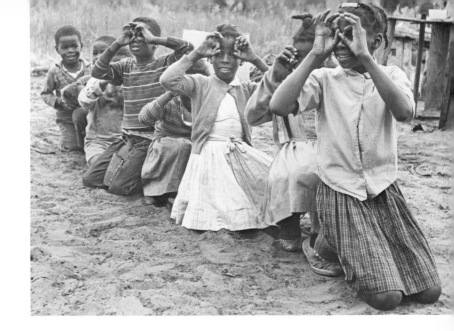

SOLO: Annie?
    GROUP: Ma'am?
SOLO: You been to the wedding?
    GROUP: Yes, ma'am.
SOLO: Did you get any cake?
    GROUP: Yes, ma'am.
SOLO: How nice that taste?
    GROUP: Nice, nice.

Annie?
    Ma'am?
Did you been to the wedding?
    Yes, ma'am.
Did you get any wine?
    Yes, ma'am.
How nice that taste?
    Nice, nice.

Annie?
    Ma'am?
You see my turkey?
    Yes, ma'am.
Which side he gone?
    So, so.
Will you help me catch him?
    Yes, ma'am.
Get ready, let's go.
ALL: Shoo turkey, shoo, shoo,
    Shoo turkey, shoo, shoo,
    Shoo turkey, shoo, shoo,
    Shoo turkey, shoo.

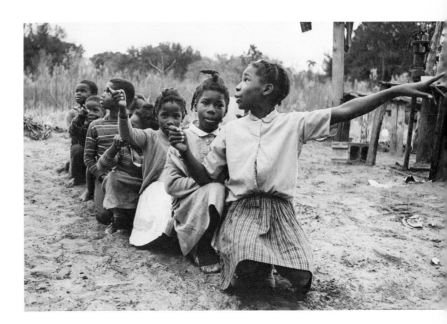

Miss Yvonne Hunter

A LOT OF KIDS PLAY THOSE GAMES

I learn some songs and games from my mother, some from my brother, and then I learn some in school. A lot of kids play those games. Mostly girls. Kids that are seven, eight, nine, ten, eleven, twelve play. There are some that don't like to play the games.

It's no music teacher at school. Our teacher have times for teaching songs. They have piano. When Mama teach us songs, she teach us until we learn it good.

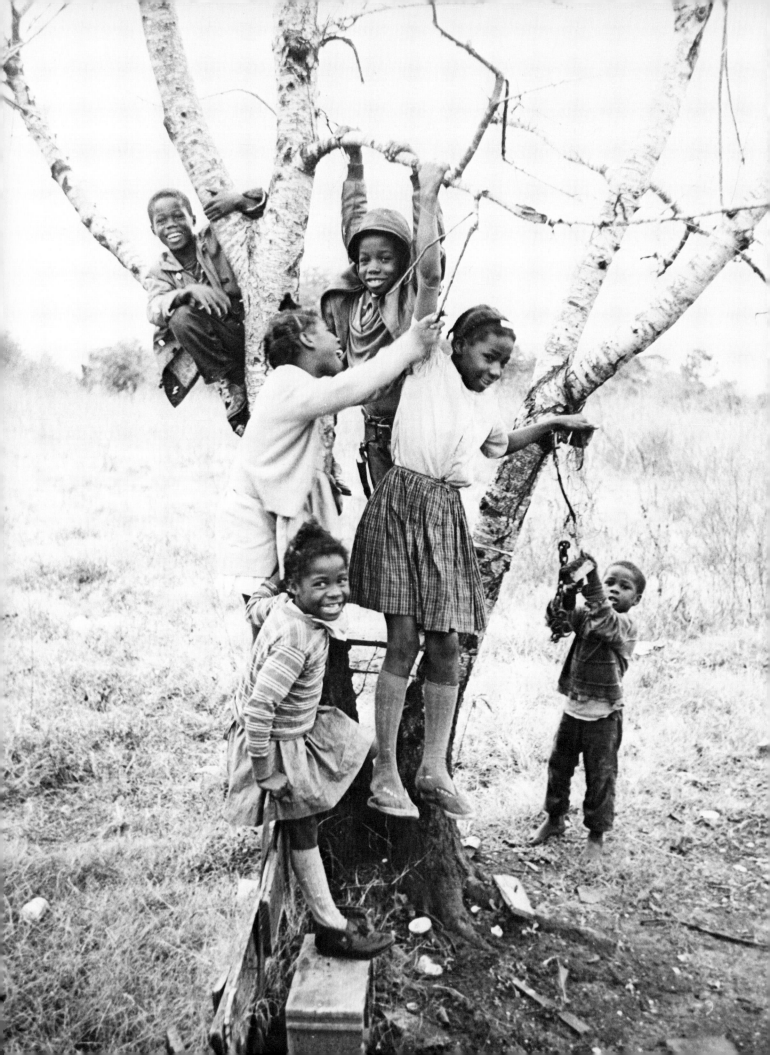

Mr. Benjamin Bligen and the Moving Star Hall congregation

TALKIN' 'BOUT A GOOD TIME

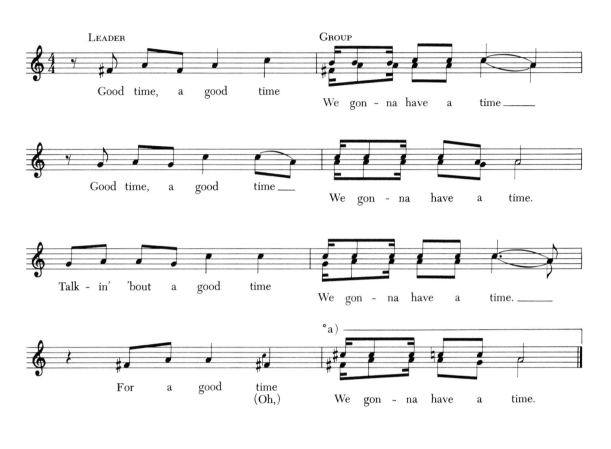

LEADER GROUP

Good time, a good time

We gon - na have a time_____

Good time, a good time ___

We gon - na have a time.

Talk - in' 'bout a good time

We gon - na have a time. _____

For a good time
(Oh,)

°a)

We gon - na have a time.

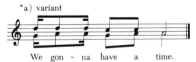

°a) variant

We gon - na have a time.

LEADER: Singing for a good time,
GROUP: We gonna have a time,
LEADER: For a good time,
GROUP: We gonna have a time.

Praying for a good time . . . etc.

Let's have a good time . . . etc.

Talkin' 'bout a good time,
We gonna have a time,
For a good time,
We gonna have a time.

117

5. DOWN ON ME

RACE RELATIONS

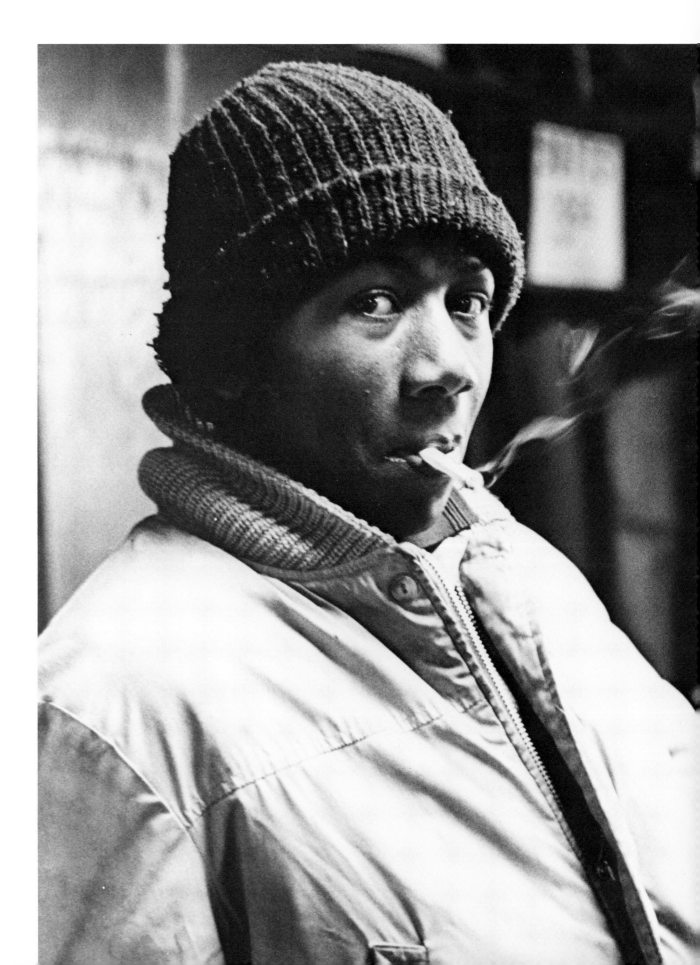

Mr. Joe Deas

YOU IS ABEL CHILDREN AND I'M A CAIN

There ain't but two race. Two brother children. If you don't work with me I ain't work with you. You can't do without me and I can't do without you. You may don't want me to your table, but you can't do without me. Cain and Abel—you is Abel children and I'm a Cain. So I got to work with you and you got to work with me. Ain't but two race, and there ain't but two place to go—that's Hell and Heaven. If you miss that, you just forever done. That's all.

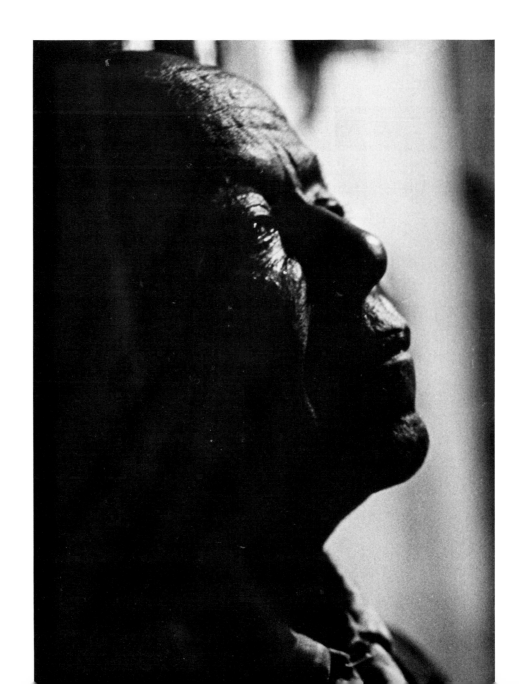

Miss Laura Rivers
THAT'S ALL RIGHT

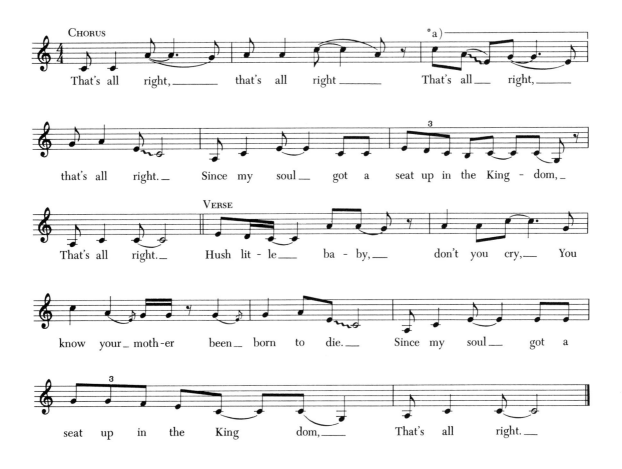

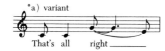

You go brute me, you go scorn me,
You go scandalize my name.
Since my soul go a seat up in the Kingdom,
That's all right.

(CHORUS)

One of these mornings, it won't be long,
You ask for me and I'll be gone.
Since my soul . . . etc.

Two white horses side by side,
One of those horses Jesus ride.
Since my soul . . . etc.

(CHORUS)

Mrs. Betsy Pinckney

YOU CAN BE BLACK OR SCARLET

Now some people after slavery times think to themselves, "If I see a white and he needs help, but they didn't tell me to do it, I wouldn't do it anymore." But me, I go there and they ain't call me neither. He need help and his family need it, and that's the reason God help some people to get along so good.

I treat everybody right; my heart open for all. And that's why people treat me well for it. That's right! Sometime I pick the bean and I say, "I ought to give 'em a quart of bean." Well, when I send that bean, how they glad.

I don't care what kind of people, I going there and help 'em. I do it, sir. I got proof! You can be black or scarlet but it don't make no difference. The pure in heart shall see God.

Mrs. Alice Wine

NOW THE WORLD IS NOTHING BUT WHITE PEOPLE

When I were growing up, I must have seen one white man in my life. And I was so scared of that white man I never see his face. You might see but two white man in the whole Johns Island then. But now the island is full of white people. There so many white people it seem like there always one now. Before then you wouldn't see no white people there in six or seven months. But now, the world is nothing but white people. White people!

The Bible says you must love your fellow mans, 'gardless of what color you are, you must love 'em. Ain't no need for I love my color, hate you. 'Cause God don't please with it. 'Cause we all is God's children. We must love one another.

The church doesn't do a thing for you no more than preach a sermon. That's all the preacher do for you. But you got to live a life living right here. The way you walk and the way you talk, the way your action—there's your sermon right there. You preaching your sermon before you die.

The way you treat people, that's your heaven right there. Now if you born dumb, you just dumb. If you're a mean person all your life, you're just a mean person; people can't say good for you. If you're a good person all your life, that's all people will say is he's a good person. Got to first have heaven here before you have Heaven. If you have speck in your heart, you cannot get in God's kingdom. I never been up there yet, but I feel about it.

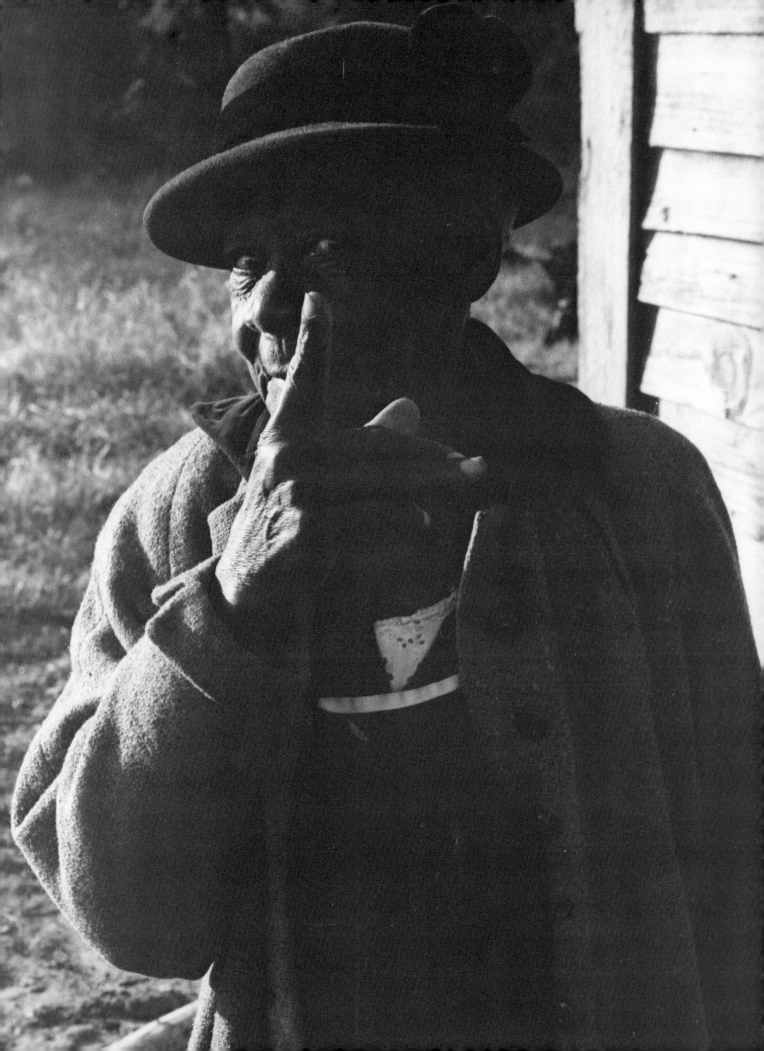

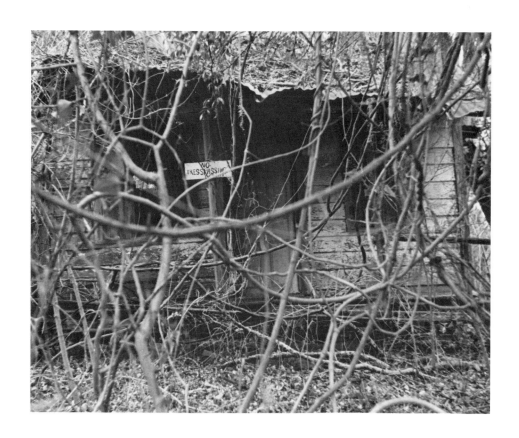

Mr. William Saunders
I COULD HAVE BEEN SOMEBODY

I apply for a job and you apply for a job, and I'm the better man, then I should get the job, not you because you're white. I believe to myself that the biggest mistake that I've made was not being born white. To me I could have been somebody if I was born white. I felt before that I had the intelligence to be somebody . . . now I'm nothing.

Mrs. Belle Green
WE'RE THEIR ONES HERE IN THE WORLD 'TIL GOD COME

We're their ones here in the world 'til God come, but they don't like we colored people. All these here want out you is work. And they can get 'em—give us our three dollar a week. You not going to feed yourself with that. Outside of that, you can go.

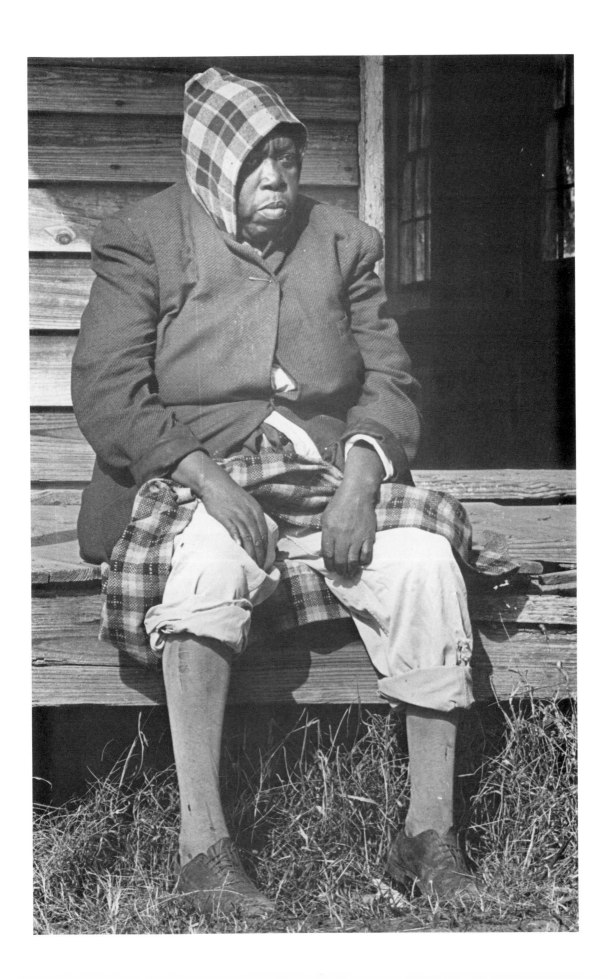

Mrs. Janie Hunter
I CAN'T FIGURE IT OUT

You find people 'ssociate with Negro 'round here, Charleston is not their home. That is one thing I can't understand, because we have to do everything for them. I was working for my lady for three years. I raise her baby. Mostly all these people have a maid or baby-sitter. You can't 'ssociate with 'em and then people want you to cook their food and take care their children. I can't figure it out.

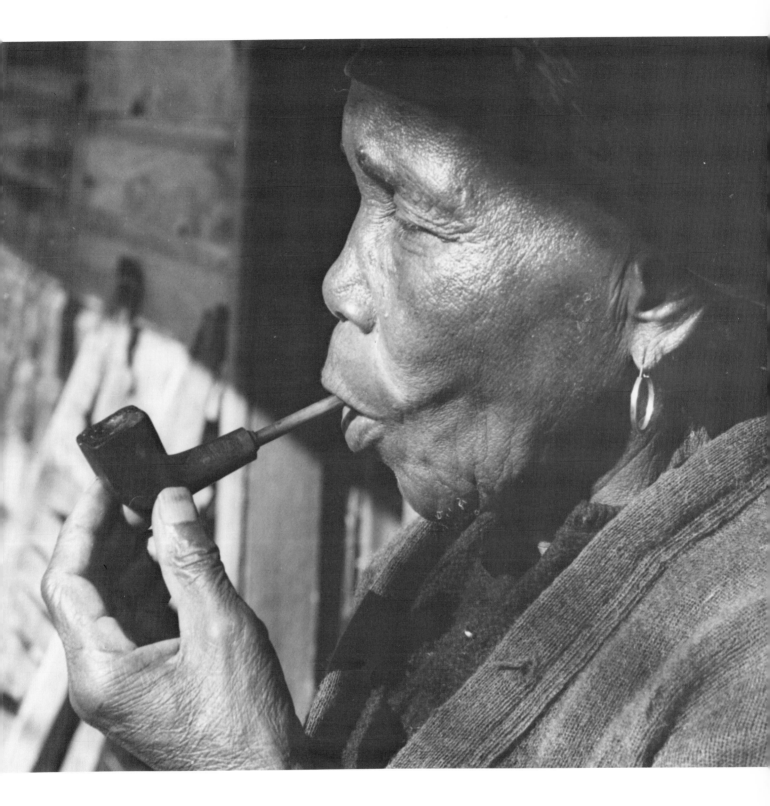

Mr. William Saunders

THEY DON'T WANT TO GET OUT ON A LIMB

I believe, in my honest opinion, that there's a whole lot of white people on this island that's not bad at all. And I think they would like to see everybody happy, but they don't want to get out on a limb from their own people, be called "nigger-lovers" or any other stories that the people can dream up for them.

I knew a white guy and we sat around and was drinking beer and talking and he was saying that he was with the Negroes in most of the things that they wanted and he believed that most of the things they wanted was right. He said he has never done nothing to hurt the Negroes. I told him that I felt like he hadn't done anything to help the Negroes either because he just sat back and was sort of looking out for his personal self, instead of saying to his friends, when they have gatherings and the question comes up, "I don't believe that we are right in what we are doing. I believe that everybody should have a chance."

I think seriously that we got a whole lot of Negroes that are hurting us more than the whites, by acting content—like the maids in the house. Any time the madam would say something to them, they would smile even though within themselves they were unhappy. But this is what was expected of them and so this is what they're doing. They have been conditioned to this. They are not frank and not honest with themselves or the people they deal with. I believe this is one of the things that's hurting us because then the white man feel that he could always push you back, because you're just that way; you're not going to stand up to nothing.

Mr. William Saunders

ALL WOULD BE GETTING EQUAL EDUCATION

As far as Johns Island is concerned, we got a long way to go. I believe sincerely that there will have to be something that happens real bad to change the situation here. We've coexisted all these years. We have accepted this, and the white man have accepted it. Very seldom do we have to come together on any major thing. So in this respect we could make it if we could keep on going like that, but we can't. Because we have gotten to the place now that my kids are not wanting what I wanted, or *thought* I wanted.

Nobody has applied yet to go to the white high school. But I think when it come right down to it, it's gonna be accepted. Actually Johns Island is real poor and I don't think nobody could afford for money to be cut off from the schools. The superintendent of the schools told me that if the schools were closed, the Negroes would suffer more than the whites. I don't believe this, and I don't believe that he believes it, because actually to me then we all would be getting equal education—nobody gets none.

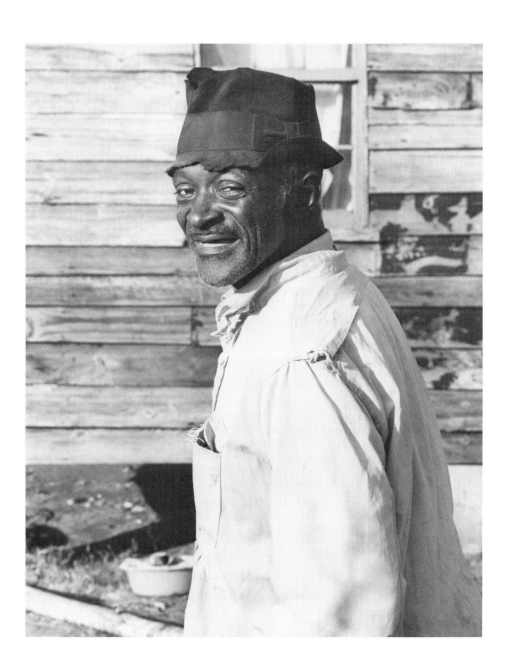

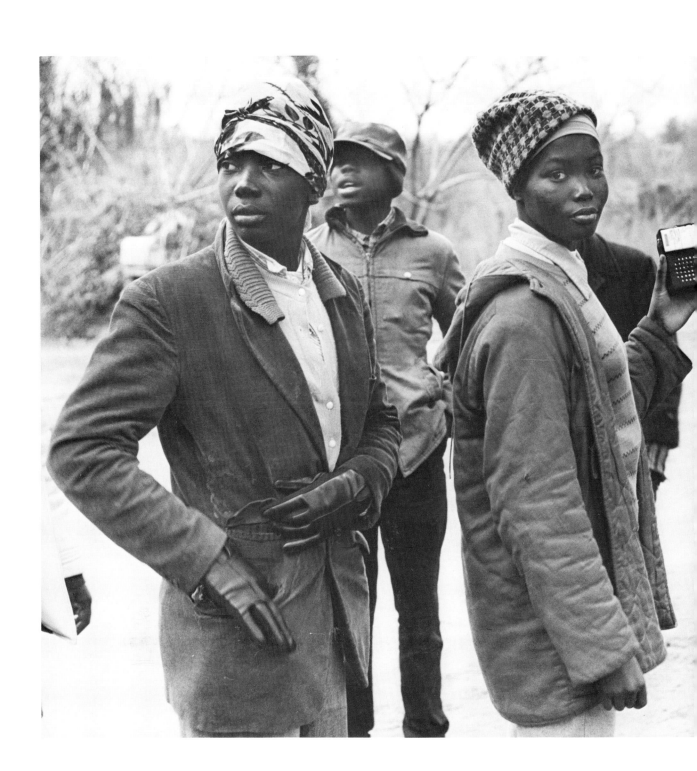

Miss Carol Bligen
I KNOW BE TROUBLE

If they integrated Haut Gap School, be trouble. I know be trouble, 'cause I don't like nobody to tease me. If one of them come and tease me, first thing I do, I going fight.

Mr. William Saunders
INTIMIDATION HAS BEEN BAD

The whites and the Negroes on this island haven't gotten involved in violence. But the intimidation, I think, has been bad as far as the white is concerned. Like making a person feel like he might not have a job tomorrow. This is something that bothers the Negroes a whole lot. Although it never bothered me because I feel like anybody that works me, he's working me because he's making some money off me, he's not working me because he likes me. He's working me because I'm a good worker and he needs me. And I believe that we all need each other—without the whites the Negro couldn't make it; and I believe without the Negroes the whites couldn't make it.

They've used the migrant workers in this intimidation. When I first knew about the migrant workers, they were really, really treated bad. They had no place to stay when they came here, and they were always treated bad. But since the integration movement has started here on the island, I think the white farmers have really gone for the migrant workers because they know that the migrant laborers really don't stand for nothing. They're just somebody to work.

Most of them, I've found out, have been in trouble before. They had trouble somewhere, or they couldn't make it at home, or something like that, and that's how come they become migrant laborers. So the white farmers figure, "Here's a chance for us to use the Negroes without the Negroes really being able to do anything about it. We don't have to worry about them getting an education. All they want to do is get our crops out, and then we can sort of hurt the Negroes here on the island by doing it this way."

The biggest farmer here, during the last season, he was working the migrant laborers three days and the regular Negroes on the island two days a week. So this is something where the Negroes used to look forward to making during the summertime eighty or ninety dollars a week, it be cut down to thirty-five or forty dollars a week.

This is to try to keep the Negroes from participating in things. It doesn't matter whether he or she has been participating or not, he's automatically placed in this category. Two farmers came by the Progressive Club last year during the workshops there and acted like they were taking down license numbers. Nobody knows if they were actually taking down the numbers or not; they never published them, but this really scared a lot of Negroes and they wouldn't even want to bring their cars around.

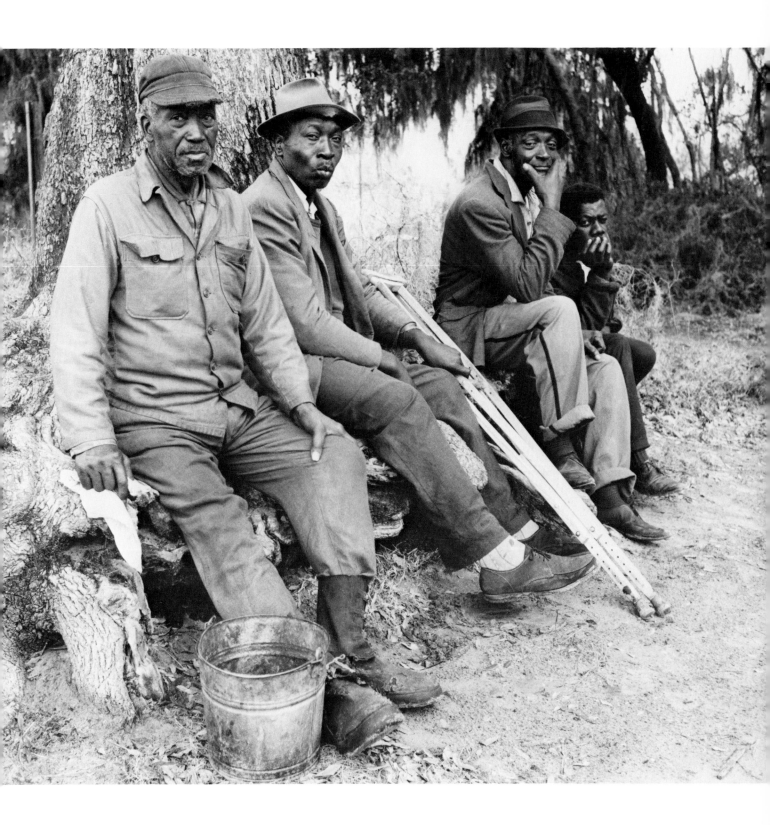

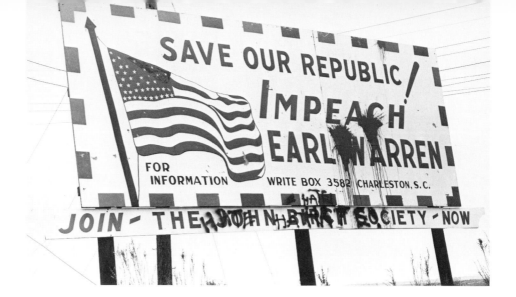

Rev. G. C. Brown
WE GOT ALONG

The Negroes have been afraid to trust the white. They feel he isn't wanting them to begin with, and the white men feel that they are superior. That's what we have on this island.

There has never been any race problem since I've been here. By race problem I mean there hasn't been any violence. We got along. The Negroes just used to take things as accepted course. They been resigned to their fate, most of them, and satisfied with that.

You can tell the difference in the whites' attitude since 1954. They weren't quite as friendly, some of 'em, as they had been, because they thought there was going to be a rushing into the white schools, and they didn't want that. But I don't think they have to fear about that. Nobody's ever tried to go there.

It's just a matter of time until they are going to accept integration. Well, I don't know about Johns Island. I won't say that here because, you see, people accept according to their education, I believe. The more a man knows, the more intelligent he becomes of worldly affairs. But now this island here is going to be a long time, I think.

The newspaper see a relation between the two races, they make that white man a Communist. Infiltration! Any time relationship between Negroes and whites, always be somebody tag 'em as a Communist. That's one of the policies of this Southland you'll find. They don't have anything else to say, they just say that. Just like Martin Luther King. They say he's a Communist and that's not true. Just a man trying to get what belongs to him.

Mr. Esau Jenkins
WE NEED TO MAKE FRIENDS

I have a white friend and we usually be frank with each other. He ask me, "Don't you think that the Negro want integration because they want to marry white women?"

I laughed. I said, "Are you kidding? You ever know any garden that's pretty without having a variety of flowers?" I said, "If you have all black flowers or all white flowers you don't have much of a garden, but if you have all kinds of flowers it looks pretty. Now Negroes can choose from almost white to the very black and different shades between, and then he's just wanting to have integration to marry a white woman?"

Years ago the Negroes on this island were skeptical of a white person if he show as if he want a friendship with them or help them, because only thing they know about the white folks is go out and work for them and they treat them as animal, and that's all. That's the kind of relationship they call good—to go out and do what they want done and then go home. Years ago, Negroes have never seen a white person come around, no more than if they come out to the house to ask them to work. They wouldn't even much come in, and the Negroes couldn't even go in the white folks house regardless of how much they work. But now things are changing a little bit.

Some time ago I went to a white home here, and I rung the bell, and to my surprise, the man invited me into the kitchen. We began to talk together, and the white girl came and peeped through the door to see who the daddy was talking to. And she went back to the mother and I heard the mother say, "Who is that?" and the girl say, "Mr. Jenkins." I was surprised she had said that. I just want to know what the mother thought when a white girl calling a Negro *Mister* Jenkins. That was a surprise to me. But we talk in a friendly manner 'til I ready to leave.

And I think it is because of these white persons who have come here, who have stayed with me lots of times, we have gone around together, we have sung together, we have prayed together, we have eaten together. And I think some of the white folks here are being ashamed of themselves just now. They can see the handwriting on the wall. We need to make friends.

You can see a change in the most of them. Not too many have come out openly and invited me in their home and sit with them as these one or two. The white magistrate has invited me in his home. We sat to the table together and discussed things on the island and the betterment of Negroes, and some white farmers have call me and we begin to talk. Not in the masses, but you can see the feeling, and they respect you much better. It's not the kind of relationship they were calling good relations some years ago, that you go out and do what I tell you to do and then go home.

Mr. William Saunders
FREEDOM IS WORSE

Really to me, freedom is worse in New York than it is on Johns Island. Because on Johns Island the white people are honest in letting you know that they don't want you to associate with them. In New York, if we go to a hotel and want a room, there's no segregation, they just ain't got no rooms.

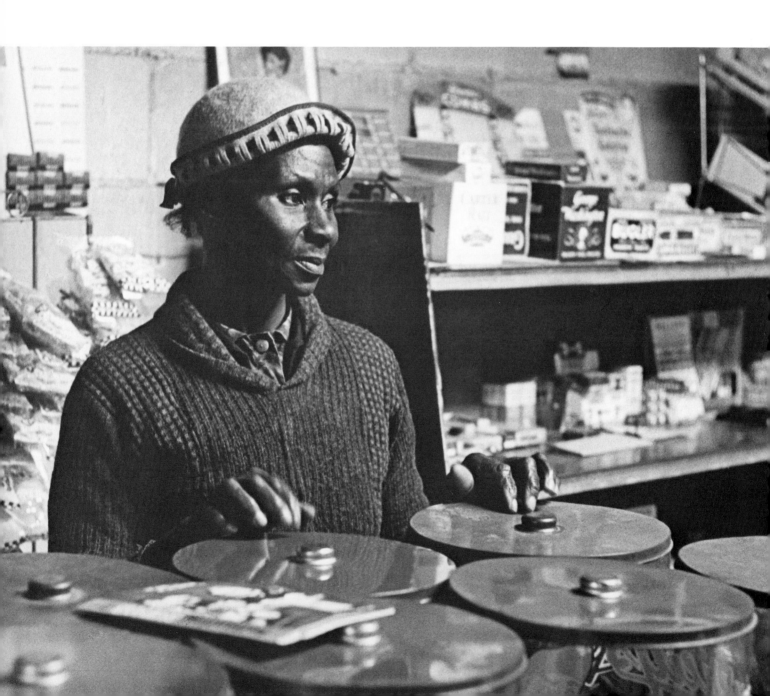

Mrs. Mary Pinckney

DOWN ON ME

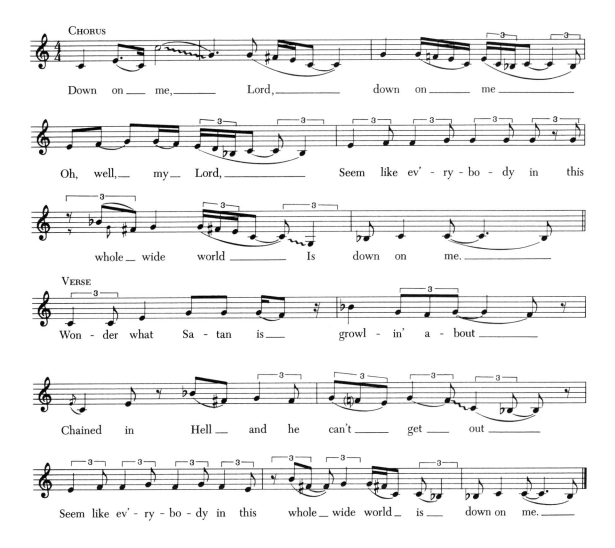

Chorus

Down on me, Lord, down on me

Oh, well, my Lord, Seem like ev'-ry-bo-dy in this

whole wide world Is down on me.

Verse

Won - der what Sa - tan is growl - in' a - bout

Chained in Hell and he can't get out

Seem like ev'-ry-bo-dy in this whole wide world is down on me.

I been buked and I been scorned,
I been talked about sure as you're born.
Seem like everybody in this whole wide world
    Is down on me.

When I get to Heaven going to sing and shout,
Nobody there going to put me out.
Seem like everybody in this whole wide world
    Is down on me.

You can talk about me just as you please;
The more you talk the more I'll bend my knees.
Seem like everybody in this whole wide world
    Is down on me.

One of these days and it won't be long,
You go look for me and I'll be gone.
Seem like everybody in this whole wide world
    Is down on me.

(Chorus)
Down on me, Lord, down on me.
Oh, well, my Lord, seem like everybody in this whole wide world
    Is down on me.

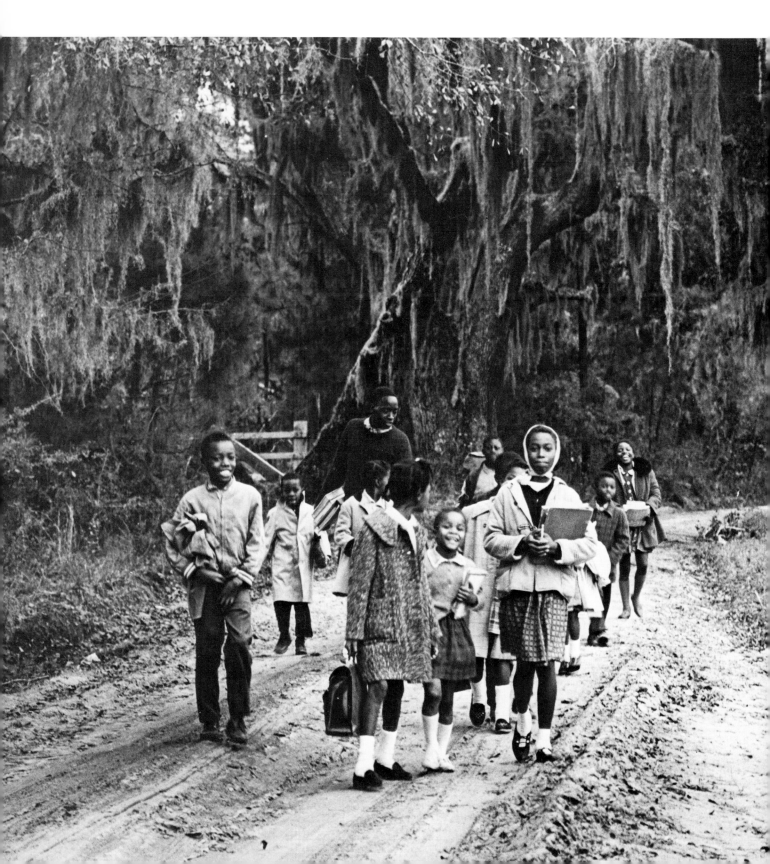

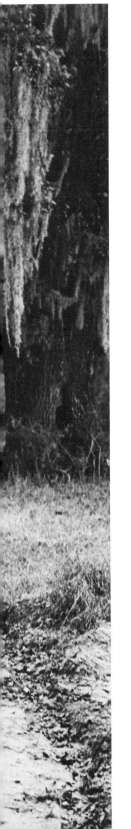

RIGHT TO THE TREE OF LIFE?

OF LIFE?

PROGRESS ON JOHNS ISLAND

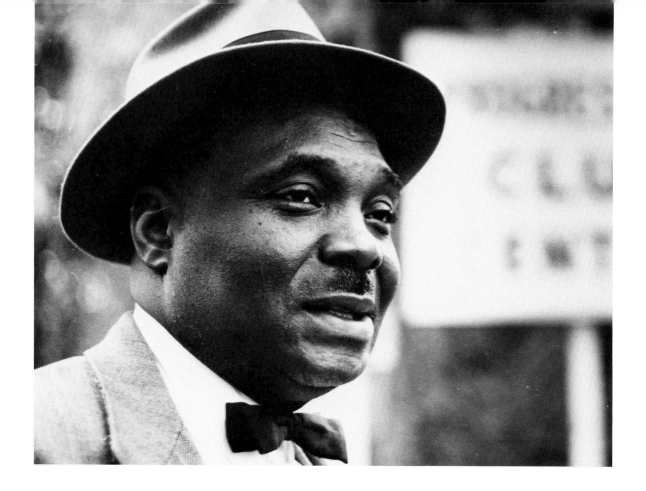

Rev. G. C. Brown

THE STRUGGLE HAS COME WITH ESAU

He's a self-made man—what you call pulling up by your own boot-straps. Everybody here live practically on the same level, but Esau is in a class all by himself.

When we first came to Johns Island in '36 I saw there was a future for Esau. He used to come to me for night teaching. I taught him, right here in my house, to continue his English and grammar and reading. Then, when he stopped coming here, he went to night school at Burke in the city and developed and increased his knowledge.

There's not another one here like him. I knew his father. He belonged to this church, but his father was not that type of person. He was the kind of "you doing too much, Esau . . . ." You know.

We have a civic organization here on Johns Island and Esau is the president. He's tried to let other people take over, but we elect somebody, he serve maybe three months and give it up, and Esau just have to take it back over again. That's why he's stayed in office so long. Others become discouraged and quit. But he hasn't ever become discouraged. He just work on through.

There's always two groups when somebody like Esau builds himself up—one that appreciates and another that doesn't think too well of it. I think now most everybody sees what he's done and I don't think he has much opposition. But he had opposition to begin with—opposition from his own people. They went to the white people, and they gave him hard knocks, but he kept right on persisting; didn't never stop. But now they see he's going to make it anyway, so they just decided to let him off.

One reason people criticized Esau so much, they afraid he going too fast. They been resigned to their fate most of them, and satisfied with that. The struggle has come with Esau. Esau has advocated justice, and don't be satisfied until you get justice.

There's been a great awakening through television and through the news media. They all begin to know now that we've been treated wrong for a long time. They are more conscious of that every day now. And you'll find a greater desire on the part of the individual to get some of the good things of life. But now, people still don't help Esau as much as they should. The prophet is without honor in his own country.

Mr. Esau Jenkins
AM I MY BROTHER'S KEEPER?

Long years ago I ask myself a question, Am I my brother's keeper? And the answer that I got was, You are. So then I decided to myself, since I'm no better than anybody, I don't feel I'm any worse than anybody. I decided to do anything I can to help people in order to help myself.

I have two question asked to me by other people. The first question was, how was I able to educate five children and live, born and raised on Johns Island—have never taught a school in my life, have never work for the government—and they all have made good grades in school, and they have been very mannerable to everybody. The way you raise your children, you can make 'em be lovable in this world, or you make 'em be hated by people, so it's your responsibility. Since God is kind enough to give you a child, then you ought to raise 'em the way he should go.

Then a man came to me and ask me, said, "Look, I notice them buses you have look so nice, and I understand you have sent all your children to school and you have gotten some property you own and doing some business. Where do you buy your hoodo root from?"

Now you know that's silly. Hoodoo business. That's the thing that make people poor, because they believe in root. So I said to him (I didn't have the answer right away because I might have said something bad to him), but I said, "Look friend, where I got my root from, it only takes obedience and a simple mind to go home and go into your closet and get on your knees and ask God for what you want."

And I tell you one thing: every progress that I have made in life, it came to me while I was doing some good for somebody.

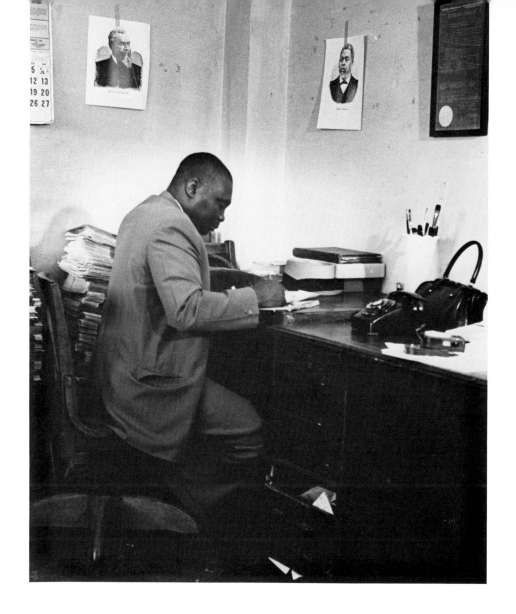

Mr. Esau Jenkins
THEY PAINTED IT BLACK

I haven't gotten any further than the fourth grade in grammar school here. I had to work, and because of that I had to leave school. And then too, the school we had here wasn't encouraging to go to. We had around fifty children and one teacher with a one-door school.

And beside that, they painted it black, that we could be identified as to who go to the school. It discouraged me when I got some pride. I left school and went to Charleston and started working on a boat. But I still was serious about getting my education. I know I couldn't have done anything out of a fourth-grade education.

Then I got married some years later and find out that I have a great responsibility, and I know that my education was limited. So I decided that I would work and go to school at the same time. I went four years more, which help me to transact my own business, and now I'm happy to say that

I was able to have my children educated. One son is a captain in the Army, one a navigator in the Air Force, two daughters are teaching, one son is a professor of music.

And now there are other folks on this island being encouraged to send their children to get a higher education. We know that some day in the near future Johns Island will be a better place to live.

Rev. G. C. Brown
ESAU STARTED THE MOVEMENT, WITH HIS OWN CHILDREN IN A LITTLE TRUCK

When I came here thirty years ago, there was no chance for any schooling beyond the fifth and sixth grade. Esau started the movement by going into Charleston, with his own children in a little truck, taking them to Burke High School.

Then the County eventually consented to pay the tuition at Burke for all who graduated the eighth grade here. And the load kept increasing as the nine little schools on the island educated a group every spring. So they decided it would be better to go ahead and build a school over here with the people, and consolidate rather than to pay this tremendous tuition cost and transportation to Charleston. And that's how Haut Gap High School came to be here.

Esau started it. He's the originator of it. They might not give him credit for getting that school built, but I know 'cause I was here.

Mr. Esau Jenkins
IT'S GOOD TO DO YOUR OWN FIGURING

I shall never forget those days when I have worked long on the farm— for fifty cents a day—plowed, lined out straight rows to spread fertilizer in, and come back and put the potatoes in the trench and cover it up.

At that time I was about eighteen or twenty years old. I married when I was seventeen, and because I felt like that wasn't any kind of money to support a family with, I left and went to work somewhat for myself.

My father was a farmer and a carpenter. He was doing carpenter work when he was much younger, and he tried to teach me how to do it. I worked with him for a while, but I didn't like carpenter work too well. I imagine I was a little bit lazy, that kind of thing. But my father was very smart in carpentry. He built a house in a few days if you just give him the material. But then as he got older he turned more to farming.

My father was a man believe in whatever the white folks said. He didn't want to hurt them a bit. I know after I start farming with him, one day we went to carry some cotton to sell. The white man who figured what the cotton come to, he gave us a certain price. I started to figure mine.

Daddy told me, "Don't do that. The white folks never like that, Son."

I say, "Well, I'm not figuring for the white folks at this point, I'm figuring for my own benefit."

Well, he never figured, but I figured mine. Unfortunately, mine was wrong when the white man figured, but I wouldn't take it. I waited until everybody got the money, including my daddy, and I went to him. "According to what you paid me, my money didn't come to what it should come to for the amount of cotton I had."

So he said, "Well, let me see." Sure enough, he found out that he made a mistake.

But now if I said that before everybody, there might have been everybody who was there think that his own was wrong too. And everything might have been, but I *know* mine was wrong. And I certainly glad I was able to figure.

I told my daddy, say "Now Daddy, you see I don't know how long this man doing it, but this figuring was wrong, and I don't know how many other person was wrong, but I didn't say it because I was afraid that everybody would say the same thing, and then he would blame me for it. But can't you see it's good to do your own figuring?"

Of course, I convince him at that time, but he never would do it.

Mr. Esau Jenkins
THEN I NOTICE THE GREEKS

I planted cotton for about four, five years—my father. and I together. It takes one whole year to harvest cotton. Then my mind tell me to start with vegetables. Then most of the people start on vegetable farming—truck crop farming, where you can plant three vegetables a year, no doubt four. That's what prompt me to buy a truck.

Then I notice as I go into the city to sell my vegetables, most of the stores are operated by Greeks. They buy all kind of vegetables. So I thought the best thing for me to do then is to try to learn the Greeks' language. I could sell more stuff and help me to do more business and help my family better. So I went and took Greek. I took Greek for about a year and a half or two, and I was able to understand the Greek language in everyday speaking in business, and that helped me to go on. That is the thing that helped me to educate most of my children.

Mr. Esau Jenkins
HERE'S A MAN BEING SHOT FOR A DOG

Two evil things that happened motivated me to get involved in my work on Johns Island. In September of 1938 two Negroes were riding in a truck. A dog ran out of a gate. The man driving tried to avoid it, but he couldn't, he hit the dog and killed it. The dog's owner, a white man (he wasn't a native of Johns Island, but had come here to live), jumped in his own car, and he carried a shotgun and ran this man down.

The fellow who wasn't driving tried to plead with him, ask him not to shoot him because he didn't mean to run over this dog, but he shot this fellow dead.

The family got a white lawyer from Charleston to try to bring that case in the court, and from 1938 until this present time, nobody heard any more of that case.

Well, that's something that I felt like people who have good will and think about decency and human dignity should do something about.

Then in the early '40s a white man, Mr. Malone, move from Mississippi onto Johns Island. He was sixty years old, his wife was twenty. They had a female dog and as a rule at certain times of the year, several dogs will go around these homes with female dogs. For some reason her dog was across the street one morning at a Negro man's home. She heard her dog's voice hollering as if somebody was beating the dog, and she went over and asked this Negro man by the name of Sammy Grant if he put his dog on her dog.

He said, "No, I didn't."

She said, "Yes, you did."

And he said, "Whoever said I put my dog on your dog tell a damn lie."

So she went back home, and we don't know what she told her husband.

Every morning Mr. Malone caught a truck about seven o'clock to go to work. The next morning, when the truck came by, he stopped it and called to Sammy Grant. By the time Sammy came around by the tail of the truck, Mr. Malone shot him right there. He was so close, and with a 12-gauge gun, this boy bled a lot.

The man who owned the truck stop a car and rush him to the hospital. By the time he got there, he had bled out the blood that would keep him alive, and the doctor asked this man to rush out and get some blood right away, 'less he was going to die.

The man came down to the city market where people sell the vegetables to find the guardian of this boy or the mother to try to get some blood, or try to get some money to buy blood for him. She said she didn't have any money. Everybody was standing around saying it was wrong, he should not have been shot. But I said, "Are you trying to help this boy? You can't listen to people say it's wrong. If they feel sorry for the boy they'll go down and give him blood."

I said, "Wait a minute, I'll get two of my brother-in-laws and I will go down and give him blood." So we went down. I gave the first pint and my two brother-in-laws gave the other two pints and save his life.

I ask him to tell me the truth what happened. I said to him, "Sammy, just as I gave you my blood to save your life, I will spend every dime and make sacrifice for you to help bring this thing to justice through the court." And he told me just what I've said.

So I went on Broad Street and hired a lawyer. He ask me to find a hundred dollars because he said he have to hire a stenographer to carry to Johns Island. The magistrate might not stick to the word he said in the court, so he need somebody to keep a record.

For a long time we heard nothing about the case. Finally I called up this lawyer and ask him what's wrong. I fussed at him a long time. Then we heard from the other man's lawyer that he wanted to make some kind of deal with Sammy. And we went and met with this lawyer.

I told him, "Mr. Malone shot Sammy with malice of forethought. Now I realize that it's a bad thing to call a woman a liar, but I don't think a man should be shot down for calling somebody a liar."

I said, "You know we have had one man shot dead over a dog and nothing came of it. The family paid a white lawyer to look out for the family and bring this thing to trial and nobody heard anything from it yet. Here's another man being shot for a dog. Now this is bad for race relations."

I told him if he were to come to Johns Island, with one man shot outright and another shot and left for dead, he might not be safe—and he could be ever so right, but because of the things that happened, Negroes began to get malice in their heart for white folks. We can't afford to let things like that go on. We, as people who know better, should make it better and make race relations better.

So he decided to pay us what Sammy had lost. He said that he hadn't felt like he was going to lose the case, but if he had won the case in court and then heard what I had just told him afterward, he never would have felt himself justified.

These are the things, then, that motivated me to organize in 1949 a progressive movement, that we could help the people to be better citizens, give them a chance to get a better education, and know how to reason and look out for themselves, and take more part in political action.

Mrs. Janie Hunter and
the Moving Star Hall congregation

YOU GOT TO MOVE

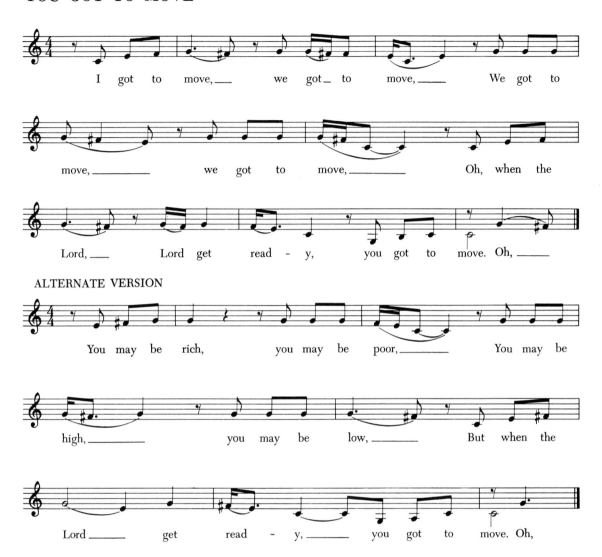

I got to move, ___ we got_ to move, _____ We got to

move, _____ we got to move, _____ Oh, when the

Lord, ___ Lord get read - y, you got to move. Oh, _____

ALTERNATE VERSION

You may be rich, you may be poor, _____ You may be

high, _____ you may be low, _____ But when the

Lord _____ get read - y, _____ you got to move. Oh,

My brother move, my brother move,
My brother move, my brother move.
Oh, when the Lord get ready, you got to move.

O sometime I'm up, sometime I'm down,
Sometime I'm almost to the ground.
Oh, when the Lord get ready, you got to move.

Oh we got to move, we got to move,
We got to move, we got to move.
When the Lord, Lord get ready, you got to move.

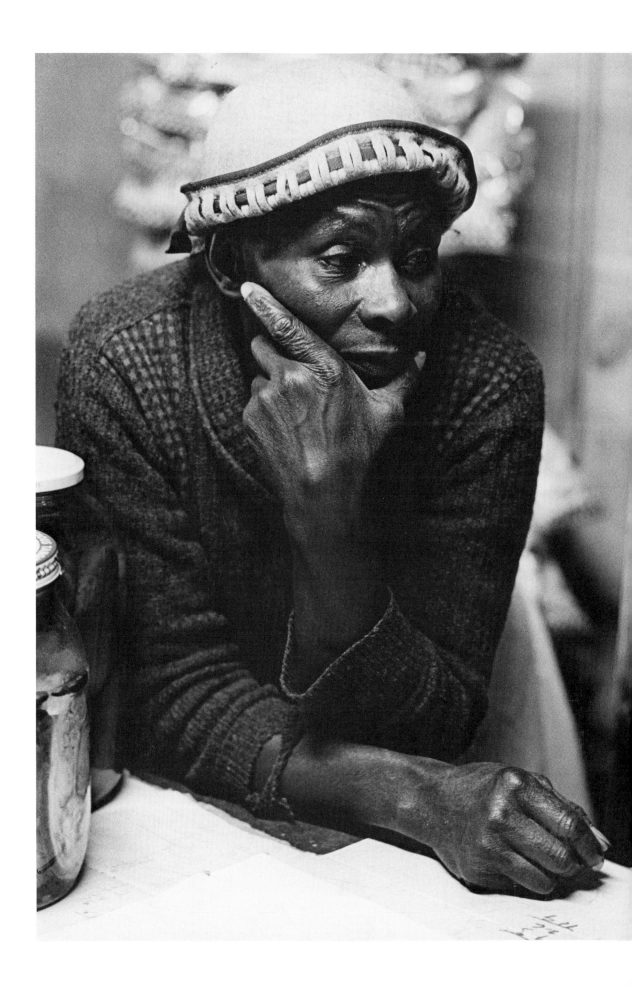

Mr. Esau Jenkins

"MR. JENKINS, I WOULD LIKE VERY MUCH TO BECOME A REGISTERED CITIZEN."

On Johns Island, in the year of 1948, I saw the condition of the people who had been working on the plantations for many years. And I knew that we were not able to do the things that would need to be done unless we could get people registered citizens.

I operated a bus from Johns Island to Charleston carrying people to their jobs. So I decided to get a group in the bus in the mornings and teach them how to read the part of the Constitution that we have to read before we are able to become registered citizens.

One of these mornings I was teaching the group to read the Constitution, a woman by the name of Alice Wine said to me, "Mr. Jenkins, I would like very much to become a registered citizen, but I cannot read this Constitution because I did not get but just so far in school, and I cannot pronounce these words. But if you are willing to help me, I will show you that I would be one that would be willing to vote in every election."

So I decided to pay more attention to her, and I helped her at more times than I do the regular times when we have school in the bus, to get her prepared to register.

Mrs. Alice Wine

EVERYBODY READ AND GET A PAPER

I come around to registering through Mr. Esau Jenkins. I used to ride his bus, and he said, "I want to carry you down to register." I said, "I can't read those hard thing yet," and he get the book and he start to learn me.

He start to help me read and when I get to them hard words I feel like jump it. My tongue so heavy until I couldn't pronounce the words, you know. But he said to me, "No, the hard word is the things for you to learn." And so me and them girls (and some of the girls could read 'em—dum-de-dum-dum-dum—right on through, right on through, but I couldn't do it), we tried 'em.

Then he take we up to a registration board on Society Street, and we get in line. Everybody read and get a paper, read and get a paper. And I be in line next to this girl, and she read and she stammer. And then the man put me for read, and I read those things just like I been know 'em. And I didn't know them things, I swear!

Mr. Jenkins figure I going fail. He been right outside there on the corner for listen. And when I come out he said, "Miss Wine, you get it?" I say, "Yes, sir." Say, "Well, sir!" I say, "I thought I couldn't read them hard thing." Them thing was *too* hard!

Mr. Esau Jenkins
EVERYBODY IS JUBILANT FOR THE HIGHLANDER FOLK SCHOOL

The Negroes outnumber the white here 'round about two and a third to one. The potential voting strength for Negroes is about two thousand against around one thousand white, if we could get them all registered. They have been doing it much faster now, because I know the last ten years before the new registration started, it took us ten years to get seventy-five or a hundred person registered, and then starting back in 1957–1958 it got better. Since then we put nearly four hundred people on the books. They are civic-minded now, and they want to take part in it. I think so much progress has been made in the last few years due to the citizenship school that was started here by the Highlander Folk School.

I first attended Highlander in 1954. They asked each individual to give the immediate problem in his locality. My immediate problem was adult education, because so many person were here who couldn't read and write and I know this condition, because I would have been almost in the same condition if I didn't go back to school. So I asked the Highlander Folk School officials if it were possible to help us set up night schools for these people to help them become better citizens.

They said if I could find a place, could find a teacher, they could help take care of the expenses. So they did. And that was very, very important to helping us to get as many persons registered on this island.

And then people on Wadmalaw and Edisto Islands found out later the reason Johns Island was so successful in registering Negroes. They ask me if it's possible to help them to get an adult school. So the next year when I went to Highlander, when it comes time for immediate problem again, I brought in Wadmalaw and Edisto, and they again say they will help if I could find a place and the teachers. I found the place, and today Wadmalaw registered more Negroes than ever registered in the history of Wadmalaw. In the 1964 election Wadmalaw had about two hundred Negro votes for Johnson. Most of the white folks were voting for Goldwater, but Negroes voted enough to hold it in the Democratic column. That's the only area in Charleston County that went for Johnson.

The same thing is happening on Edisto and all over the county. In 1954 in the county there were 'round about five or six thousand Negroes registered. In 1964 almost fourteen thousand. So everybody is jubilant for the Highlander Folk School, who have helped them to see the light.

150

Mr. Esau Jenkins
KNOWING HOW TO PLAY THE GAME

We had gotten quite a few people registered through that adult citizenship school, but they did not have the political education or understanding of voting. So we decided to teach them what the ballot means. I started what we called the "second step" political education school, because the people who registered to vote would vote because we told them to vote.

There were many persons who did not know how many men in the House of Representatives; why Charleston County has eleven in the House; how many men in the Senate; how many congressional districts we have in South Carolina; who are the men elected and sent to Washington to represent these two districts. We feel that if these people know about these things, they will be more interested in voting, and they will help others.

As you know as well as I do, that if a person doesn't know a football game, a basketball game, neither a baseball game, he hears other people laugh and sees how other persons play, but he doesn't know *who* plays well, because he doesn't know the game.

The same thing goes with some of the people who don't know anything about political action, so we felt like it was our responsibility to teach those people and have them well-informed.

Along with political education, we have taught a good many persons how to sign checks, fill out money orders, how to crochet, how to sew, how to fill out blanks for their drivers' licenses. I think it was a great success.

Then after I was elected President of the Citizens' Committee of Charleston and Charleston County, I set up what we call a voter registration and information center, to which place people will come in for information. Whatever information they need, they come to this center.

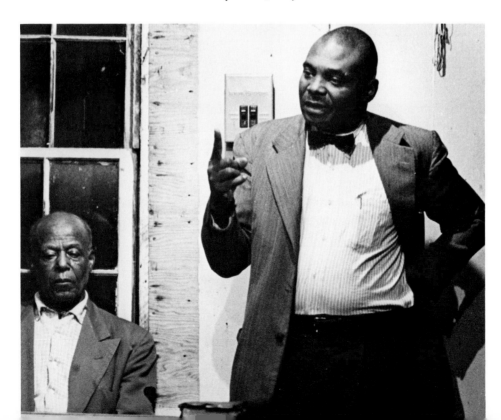

Mr. Esau Jenkins

"MAN, ESAU JENKINS' NAME ON THE VOTING MACHINE!"

Then I ran for the school trusteeship on this island. I ran knowing that I wouldn't have won unless a miracle had been done. They had three white persons to run. I made four. And I came out third, so I got more votes than one of the white candidates. That scared some of the white folks here, and the man who is on the county council decided that they would change voting for trustees on the school board. They would have it be appointed because Johns Island strength was growing too much.

The reason why I ran is because I wanted the Negroes to know that it is their privilege to go into any office they're qualified to handle. They are taxpayers and they have just as much right to run for public office as the white persons. I ran because some Negroes thought that if a Negro name ever was placed on a voting machine, that person would be killed. Or they thought that a Negro's name couldn't be placed on a voting machine.

And so I ran and my name was placed in alphabetical order and they saw it. And when one of the guys went in and saw my name, he went and told the rest, say, "Man, Esau Jenkins' name on that voting machine," says, "You better go on down there and vote." And that year we had about ninety-nine percent of the Negroes who registered vote. Encourage them ever since to vote.

Mr. Esau Jenkins

WE'RE NOT FOR SALE

After we got started and the Negroes started registering, then a bribe was made to me. They sent someone to offer me whatever I want if I would stop teaching Negroes to register and vote and go along with the white folks. Well, I didn't accept it.

My argument at that time was that we need a high school on Johns Island and we need to get our children off their feet who are walking ten miles per day to try to get an education. They walk in the rain, in the cold, and the sleet and we believe it cause a health hazard. So I told this man who offered me the money, "We're not for sale, and we're only going to support people who are willing to see to it that our children will get a high school, plus transportation to take them to and from school."

The white kids were riding in school buses, and the buses were warm when they got into it. When they got to the school, the schools were warm. Yet our children had to walk between eight and ten miles per day, go to a cold school with no heat. The teachers that teach the school, they live in Charleston—fifteen or eighteen miles away—and the children have to stand outside until the teachers come. Then when the teachers come, if they didn't have any wood, they got to go out in back of the school and get wood to make up the fire. Whether it raining, whether it cold, whether it snowing, those children have to walk there, and after they got the fire started, it being so cold, I don't think they could concentrate so well. And beside that they

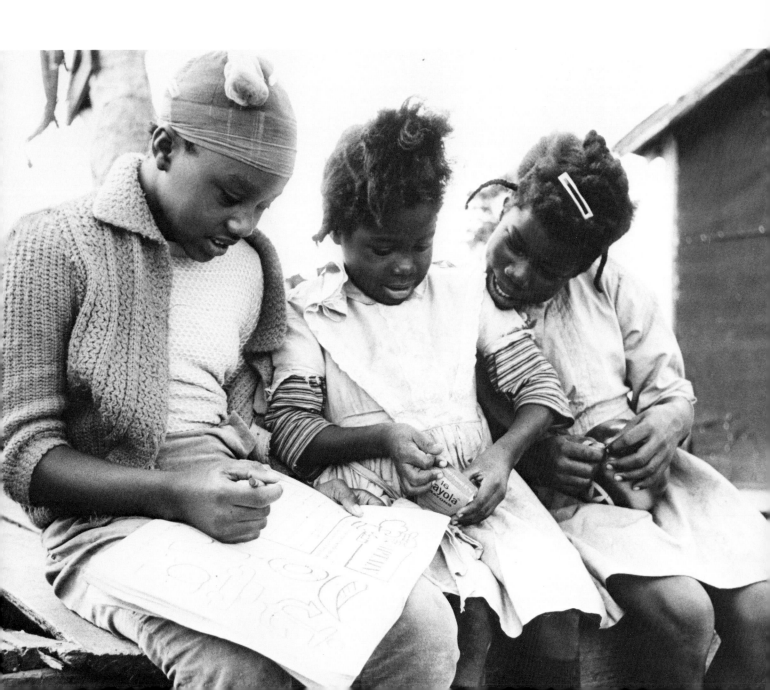

have forty to fifty children to one teacher, and have to carry 'em from scratch to seventh grade.

So we know that was a terrible condition, and that's the condition that I want to try to eliminate. And that's my reason for not taking this bribe. I know that we wouldn't have gotten anywhere, not as long as I was willing to take bribe and go along with the white folks. I had made some enemy by not taking the bribe. I had made some of my people afraid of me because I kept on fighting for the Negroes' right. But I didn't stop.

The white folks cut off this one big plantation that I used to haul to, as I had three buses and two trucks. Sometimes I make sixty dollars, sixty to eighty dollars a day, with three or four vehicle—twenty dollars for each one —to carry the people there. They cut that off, but I wouldn't stop. I keep on driving and keep on fighting.

Since we have gotten the high school, now we have had quite a few children graduated from the high school here on the island. Since then we have been able to get this consolidated grammar school, and we have buses.

Mr. Esau Jenkins
WE DIDN'T HAVE A CHANCE WHEN WE GO INTO COURT

I'll tell you another way voting was able to help us. I could remember not too long ago, we didn't have a chance when we go into court. I remember a day I was riding with a man coming to Johns Island from Charleston, and a white person ran into the back of his truck. When we stop to find out what happen to the person, the law took side with the person who ran into the back of his truck, and he had to go to court.

We all thought that the judge would say, "Well, somebody ran into the back of the truck, certainly seem like that person is wrong." Unfortunately, he said that the colored man was wrong. He didn't have a chance in the court. But we decided to change that thing by getting people to see the importance of citizenship, registration and voting.

We got them to be interested in organizing what we call the Progressive Club. I emphasize the word "progressive" which mean look upward, do something better. And in this club we told them that if you're not registered to start with, you're going to have to *become* a registered citizen if you join. And we ask every individual to pay twenty-five cent per month. For what? Just in case when you go into these unjust courts, your money pools and somebody'll stand the bonds, or pay the fine. Now things are changed. The time would come when this same magistrate who have never listened to Negroes would need their vote.

One year when he ran for the third time, the white folks decided to vote against him—not all the white folks, just about fifty percent of them. And he was thinking about dropping out of the election. He came to me and ask, "What can you all do? I understand that the white folks is against me because in the court sometime ago I was little bit lenience with Negro."

So I told him if he would promise that he would treat Negroes better, make them realize that they are human being when they come into the court, not charge them for everything or just assume that they are wrong, but just give them what belongs to them—if they are right, let them know they are right—I said, "We will vote for you. We got a few Negroes voting. If you got fifty percent of your people, the rest of the Negroes certainly would turn the tide."

And when that night came, he won by the many Negroes had registration certificate. That change the situation. That magistrate now, whenever our people go into the court, he is very frank and fair with us. And so for that reason, we felt like the more we could get people registered, the better it would be.

Mrs. Alice Wine
HE IS A WONDERFUL CONQUEROR

We start the Progressive Club with about two or three hundred head of people in '48 or '49. We used to meet in Moving Star Hall every third Sunday and pay twenty-five cents a head. And after we done pay out for that piece of property we got now, we stop paying monthly dues.

There was a schoolhouse there, but we turn 'em into a store after we buy 'em. We put all our money together and open 'em up. And we call 'em Progressive Club. We been growing and growing. We is still in debt, but we are going on. And Mr. Jenkins, he is so good, he is so kind, so soft-hearted, he don't care what the people said, but he going on. He is a wonderful conqueror, I tell you that.

And John Smalls, he just stick and stand right there as a sale-man. Sell in the store. He is the head of buying for the store. Bill Saunders is the Manager of the store. And I am the Treasurer. Mr. Jenkins is the President. So we stick and stand, thick and thin, right there.

I think this the best place on Johns Island. I say to myself, "is a Christian place" because the good Lord help us so far in all these years. We ain't had no bad quarrels yet. 'Cause they always divide a row. I not say no row don't be there. They be there. But if they know, Esau or John, they will divide the row. They will ask them nicely to quit. Or they put them out. We never had nobody hurt one another yet.

Mr. Esau Jenkins
NOW WE CALL IT SEA ISLAND CENTER

The Progressive Club grew a little bit. We finished paying for the old building. Then after we have taken out what it takes to run the store for the year, each member (thirteen people) gets a dividend. The first year it was twenty-five dollars. Next year each person got thirty dollars. I felt like it was some motivation for all of them to find out that we are now getting something back.

And then I said to them that since this building was bought old and is about to outlive its usefulness, that we need to build something that will be serviceable to not only this community, but for the whole sea islands. I thought that a place large enough for basketball and other games and workshops would be something that could bring in other people to give ideas what could be done for the community and other communities. I suggested to them that this ought to be done. I felt like if we got together and work heartily together, cooperatively together, that it could be done.

We have one or two person oppose my idea about a huge building like that, for fear that we wouldn't be able to pay for the thing, or that we wouldn't even be able to get it built to start with. One of the members stated that he hoped he could live long enough to see one side of the wall go up. When I was told that, I said maybe he didn't feel he have long to live. I guess he was surprised to see it go up.

One member couldn't believe that Negroes could get together and pool their money and buy something and get along all right. It took me ten years to convince him. He told somebody that when I first started the Progressive Club he thought I was looking out for Esau Jenkins and the family. This person told me, "But I found out when you went and bought that place. The money was loaned to you, and you put all as many names as possible on

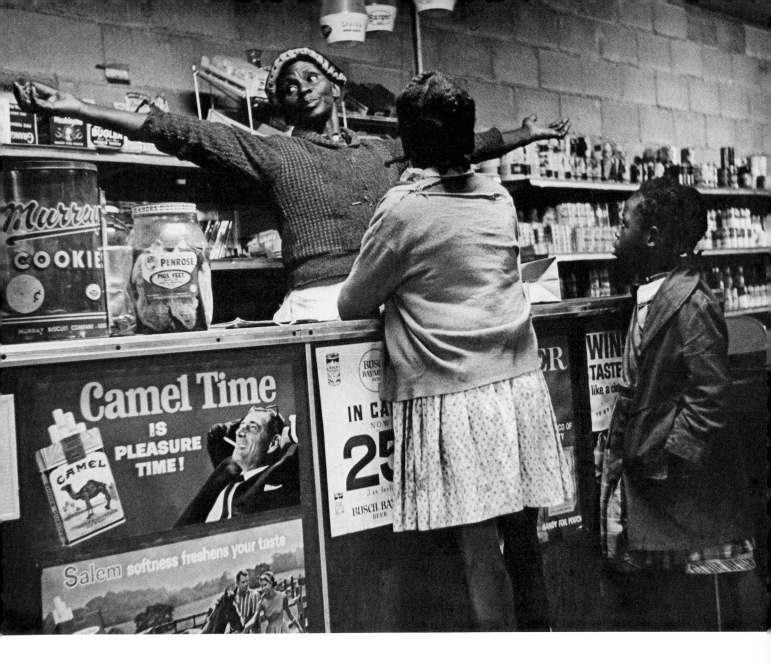

the deed, and let them run it, and just check with them once a month, so they believe you meant good for them. And now I have all the confidence in you." Evidently that's the reason why it took me ten years to make him realize we can get along together.

The whole entire group work faithfully with me now. I think we are doing very well because of the fact that we are working together. And more people are using the place now. They see the need for it.

They didn't have any place to go on this island for recreation. That's one reason we built this, and then call it "sea island" center instead of community center, because we serve James Island, Johns Island and Wadmalaw. Unless they play in somebody's yard, there's not a place where they can have a proper game on any one of these islands.

Our school doesn't have a gym, probably won't ever have one. In October of this year the basketball teachers came down to the Progressive

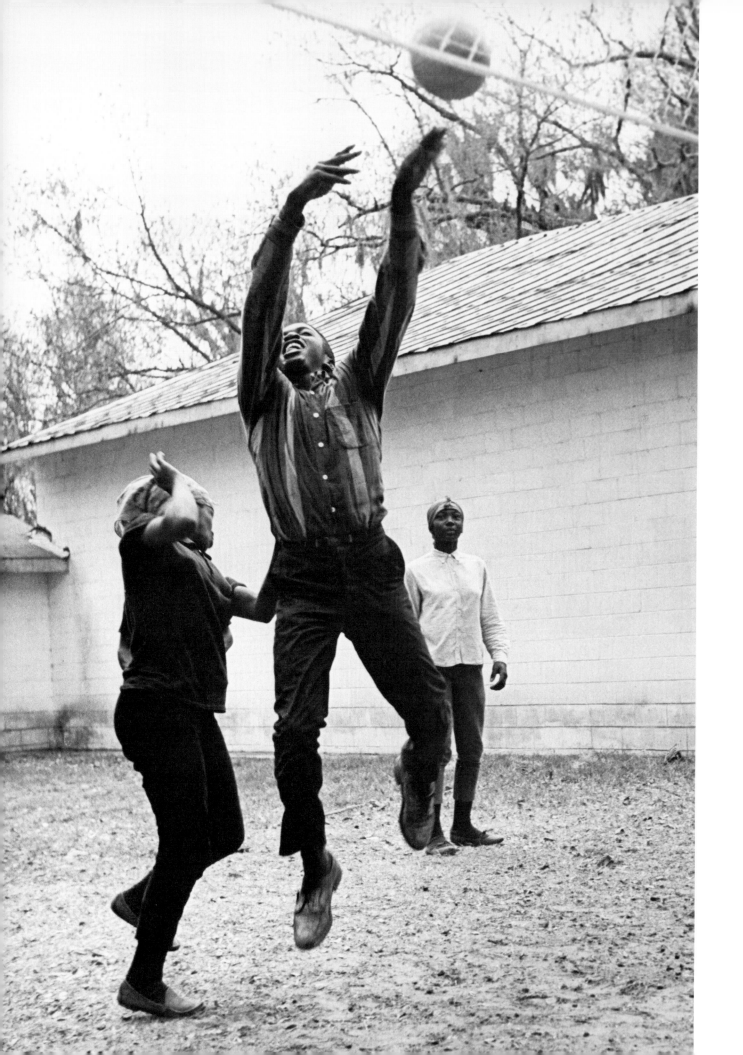

Club and asked us to let them play basketball there. They'd been playing outside during this basketball season, and they'd been getting beat eighty-something to twenty.

Last night we had the school come in and they had a talent show, and had a record hop behind it, and I understand about two hundred head or more were there. Then we started a Boy Scout here. We are interested in getting the boys because we feel like it would be a good thing for young boys to be a better citizen. They are planning to have their programs at the Club.

Then we have a young citizenship group that we organized. It concerns itself with race relations and voter registration or everything that goes to make the human being happy. They got a volume of encyclopedia to study a variety of words that they might have a vocabulary large enough to answer questions. And they feel happy about it, because that's one of the things kept them from running up and down the street and have nothing else to do.

I stated before that we emphasize the word "progressive." If we are going to be progressive on this island, we still have a lot to do.

Mr. Esau Jenkins
THOSE TYPEWRITER CAME FALLING DOWN IN THE SCHOOL, OVERNIGHT

We need better equipment and better instruction in our schools to make our children better able to compete with other children. I felt there are so many Negroes whose children wouldn't be college material, and so many Negroes' income wouldn't allow them to send their children to college. If a child goes to school and just take up home economics and some agriculture, they wouldn't able to use it when they come out, and they be just as bad or worse off than a child who hasn't gone to high school who will go on the farm and work and never think about it.

The child who had been through high school feel bad scrubbing somebody's floor or working on the farm—much worse than the child who never had any training. So my suggestion was that the school give shorthand and typing.

I told Robert Johnson, a man who is very energetic in doing things, to go to the Haut Gap School and ask the principal if it be possible to get in some typewriters and give shorthand and typing, that our girls who would want to be secretary and can't go to college would come out and know how to do something. They could take dictation and maybe could be hired in some of these lawyers' offices.

The principal told him that the boys and girls there don't have the aptitude for that kind of thing. In fact he said that on the national average the boys and girls who finish Haut Gap School are no more than about tenth grade scholars. So Mr. Johnson say, "I surprise to hear you say that, because it seem you ought to try to correct that kind of thing, if it be true."

The principal sent Mr. Johnson to the man who is the supervisor over the schools here on Johns Island. The supervisor told him that the typewriters would cost a lot of money. If he insist that his daughter or some other girls take typing and shorthand, they could go to the Negro high school on James Island. Mr. Johnson contention was that that would be too far away.

Then I found out one day that the white high school on Johns Island had typing and shorthand. A white man came to my restaurant to fix the cigarette machine and said to me, "Esau, I congratulate you for sending your children to college." He said, "I couldn't send my daughter, but she has a good job. She works for one of the lawyers downtown."

I ask him, "Where did your daughter get her training?"

He said, "St. John's High."

I said, "St. John's High doesn't teach shorthand and typing."

He said, "Oh, yes it does. That's where my daughter learned and she's making good now."

Well that burn me a little bit when he told me that, so I brought it up that Sunday in the PTA, and I talk a long time about it. I told the principal and the teachers, "This is our children being hurt. I went all out for a high school here on Johns Island—I guess a lot of people were afraid to walk with me, some of my own race—because I was fighting white folks. Yet I was fighting that our tax money would be beneficial to our children. Now we need typewriters here. If we don't get it, certainly I'll try to find anybody who I know, as many as I know, to send to St. John's High School."

Well, I know they didn't want the Negroes to come there at that time, because you know this thing hadn't gotten full under way yet about integration. But we could make some trouble.

So I was told that Monday morning somebody rush to the superintendent's office and said, "You know, Esau talk a lot down there yesterday, and that crazy Negro say he'll send somebody to St. John's High School." He say, "The best thing you better do, you better try to get them typewriters."

So those typewriter came falling down in the school, overnight just

160

about. I don't think they got the person to teach shorthand yet. Some of the teachers said it seemed like I was against them. I tell them, "I wasn't against any of you, but I asked you not to get in the way. You're not going to stand in the way of our children's education. You got yours."

Mr. Esau Jenkins
I AM TRYING TO GET HELP THROUGH THE WAR ON POVERTY

Because I feel there needs to be work here for our young people, and care for our children so their parents can also make a good wage, I am trying to get help through the War on Poverty.

I told the poverty committee that I am a native of Johns Island. I said that I have been working over the years trying to obliterate ignorance, to promote health, social, educational and civic welfare, and to combat juvenile delinquency and to secure a more rich and abundant life to ourselves and to our posterity. I told them that we have obligated ourselves and denied ourselves and begged and borrowed money to help build a center that our boys and girls and adults could have a place on the island where they can have games and workshops and where we have had some folk song festivals which have brought together people of both races.

Now our people are asking us to assist them in many areas in which we cannot give help unless we get some kind of grant. They are asking for day care for preschool children so that they do not have to keep older children home from school while the parents are out working. They are asking for classes which will help them to earn some kind of living here—sewing, crafts, adult remedial reading, music, some kinds of mechanical skills. They are asking for the creation of some jobs for children who have left school, and after-school jobs for school children.

These requests have come from parents who make from $600 to $2,000 a year and have from two to eight children in their homes.

If we receive the grant we have asked for, we can employ twelve or fourteen persons for the Progressive Club Sea Island Center's program—a director, assistant director, dietician, secretaries, teachers, assistants, and a janitor.

We promised the committee if they would give us this badly needed grant, which would help alleviate the cycle of poverty in this area, we are willing to do our part in seeing it become a reality.

Mr. William Saunders
WHEN YOU FINISH THIS HIGH SCHOOL, YOU AREN'T PREPARED FOR ANY JOB

Most of the kids that leave the island, I would say ninety percent of 'em go to New York. And to me, New York is about the worst place that any good youngster could go. They'll come back and tell you that they're living nice, everything is really nice. The young girls go away angels, have never had anything to do with a man, and they go away for about two years and come back with three babies. And a lot of the kids get to be addicts. Some of them do all right, come back driving big cars and really influencing the kids that are here to go away.

The kids that get college education, it might help them individually but it sure doesn't help this island. It seems like they forget from where they came, or what they've suffered through, and the help that the rest of the people need. And our schools don't offer what the kids need to go to college anyhow. Yet our kids will get out of school and won't come back home to try to help the kids to get what they really need to even go to college. You can be an A-student here on the island, which don't take very much, and go to college and be a C-student or even flunk out.

When you graduate from this high school you aren't prepared for any job, except farming. You can't borrow no money from the bank to start a farm of your own, so they just prepare you to work on a farm here. They now offer typing, but like my first cousin was an honor student at Haut Gap and her teacher told her that she was too smart to take typing and short-hand. She tried to get into this new Technical Educational Center here and she couldn't get in. So now she's in New York. I know she's an angel, but what's going to be her fate? We don't know. She wrote back home and told her daddy, "Please make sure my brothers and sisters (she got about six or seven) get shorthand and typing." So her daddy bought a typewriter and got everybody in the house typing now.

Rev. G. C. Brown
IF WE COULD ONLY KEEP OUR YOUNG PEOPLE HERE

If we could only keep our young people here, but now when they finish high school, most of 'em go. They don't stay here to help you develop things. They're looking for better wages—fact, they have to do that. There's nothing much for them to do here but cut cabbages or run a tractor, maybe drive a truck or do something in the field. And there's not much money in it for them.

They mostly go to New York and find jobs somehow or other—working as domestics or doing small factory work. Very few ever come back to live. They come back to visit about once a year. But they don't ever come back to live.

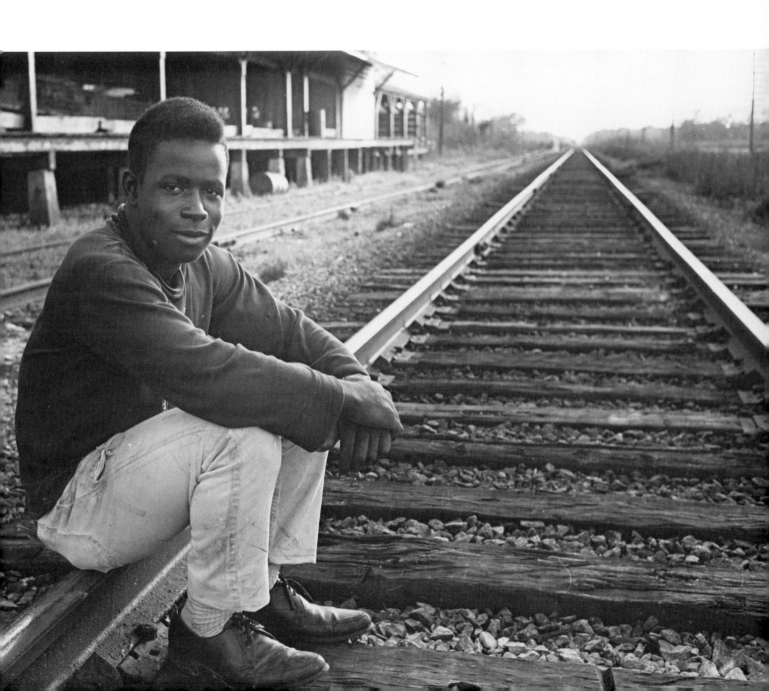

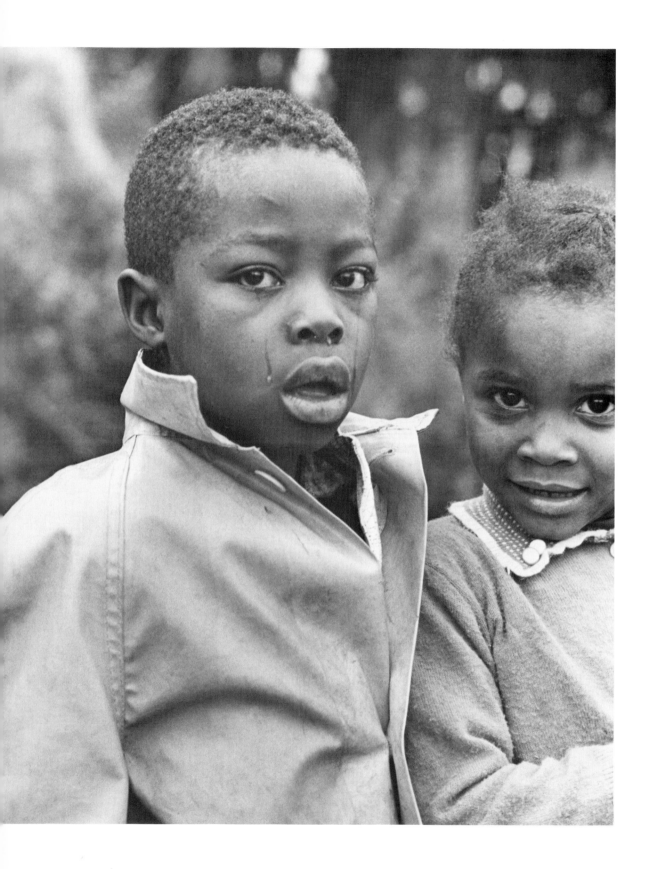

Mr. William Saunders
GOING TO NEW YORK IS AN ADVANTAGE
AND A DISADVANTAGE

Most people think about their kids. It's so hard raising kids in New York. And it's so easy for kids to go bad there. So most of the kids are left here with the grandparents while the parents are in New York working, and when they get a certain age they think about it. And they rebel. They find something bad to do. They try to get back somehow at their parents.

Most of the people that go away from here leave their kids. If the wife and the husband are going to be working, they have nobody to care for the kids, so they leave them home. And the grandparents have gotten to a certain age, they raised their kids, and they're so much more lenient on their grandkids than they were on their own kids. So this is one of the real big problems, I think. The kids suffer.

I was born in New York. I was one of these babies that was shipped here—not even somebody bringing me, they used to put tags on you and just put you on the train and say where you're supposed to get off at. I was raised by my grandparents and actually when a grandparent raise a kid, there are two generations between, and there's so much less understanding there. Things that the parents would probably understand, the grandparents cannot understand. And this was my problem.

This is something that is still going on, and I think it's gonna be going on and on. And this is one of the things that the Negroes have really been suffering from—this grandparents raising the children and the children not getting actually what they need. I believe if a kid really wants something, like he wants music lessons or he wants to study farming, or anything, if they say that they *want* to do it, I think that somebody should be there to help them with it. So even if they fail, they can't say, "I didn't have the opportunity." I think he should have the right to try, and if he fails, he can't blame nobody but himself because he just couldn't make it.

But like me now, I can sit back and blame my grandparents and my parents for not being successful. I don't know, I just feel to me that I could have been somebody. And I got somebody to blame for not being somebody.

Kids here need an opportunity.

Going to New York is a disadvantage and an advantage. To live I think it's a disadvantage. Some things are lacking here, but the children have a home. So we don't have everything that we want for them. But they have their home, so all they need is to get along like everybody else—daily living.

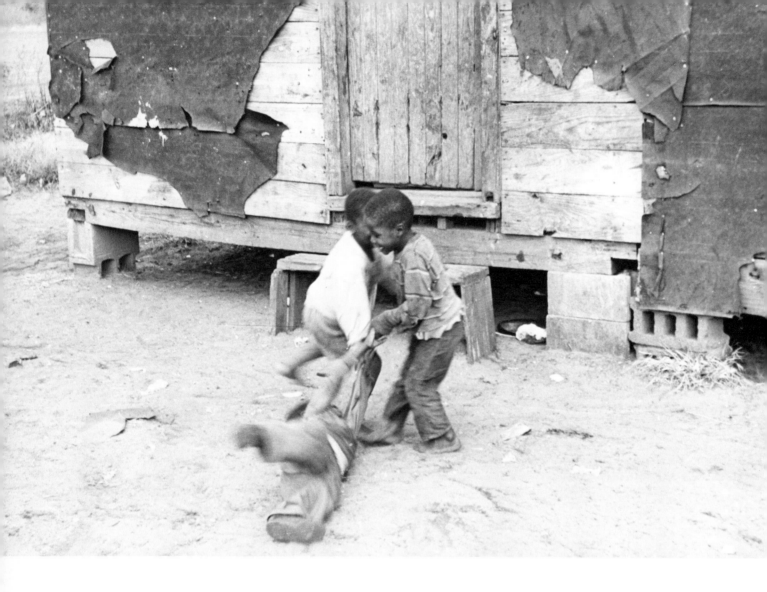

And it really shouldn't be that hard. The pay here is less, but you don't have
to pay rent, and the food is cheaper. They go to New York and then they
come back here on their vacation and tell you how silly you are to be here.
And what they bring here is a new car, but then you have a car and you
have a house, so what is it they're bringing? They're making more but
they're spending more. But yet you're here with your kids, and they aren't.

And really they miss everything about home up there. That's why you
find Christmas times or holiday times they don't want to be in New York,
they want to be home. They miss the atmosphere, the friendliness of the
people. You can go to anybody's house, the people don't have no money in
the bank, they don't have no money under their mattress, but they got a
whole lot of food. I don't believe there's a house around here where they
ain't got a whole lot of food, got a little moonshine to drink on the holidays.

A lot of my friends say if they could make even thirty dollars a week
less than they make in New York they would come back home.

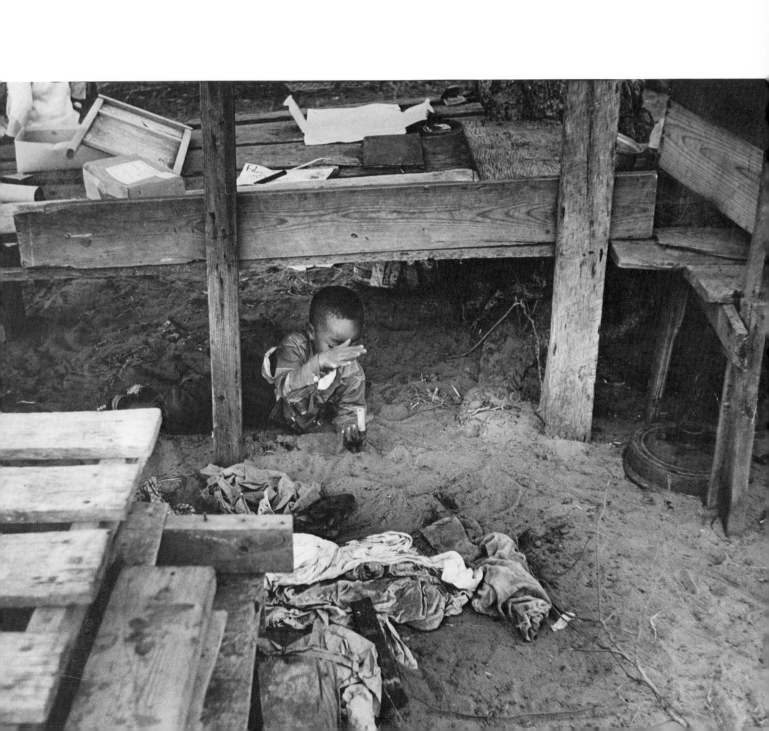

Mr. Esau Jenkins
OUT OF EGYPT I AM GOING TO CALL MY SONS

Now if anybody is happy, it ought to be Esau Jenkins, the person who is talking here to you. Why? Twelve years and some months ago in this community, I organized a club—what we call the Progressive Club.

You folks have helped me start as a man and form a group. You are selling groceries, you are selling gasoline. Besides that, some time the early part of this month you have paid out all your debt and yet left $175 to add to your store.

When I organized this Progressive Club, I could count the number of voters on my one hand, and I don't have but five fingers.

In twelve years you have caused this whole island to change. Today you got school buses running by your door and picking up your children, carrying them to a high school on Johns Island. Today you can say that my children will be educated—at least get a high school education on Johns Island.

Today you could say in the last election we built up our voting strength so high until the white men in Charleston have to ask us to be in the polls on Johns Island and Edisto and Wadmalaw. Negroes have helped work for the Democratic party.

Now you could not have said that twelve years ago because you didn't vote. You didn't have a school. But today you have children getting ready to compete with anybody's children, because of your cooperation.

My friends, I want you to help me that I may go on, come what may. There are any number of times that I have walked alone. There are a lot of people who are afraid, because if they be seen walking along with me, the white folks might say, "Well, he is one of these persons who are fighting me."

But share it with Esau Jenkins, and thank God that God has helped us. We made an achievement that we are not ashamed of. You don't know how much you have done, friends—how many people are talking about what you have done; how many people are reading about what you have done.

Together let us go—sisters, brothers, blacks, whites, yellows, whatnot. We are all God's people, so we got to go together. And friends, I think all over the world today, people who love freedom are saying this morning, "Out of Egypt I'm going to call my sons."

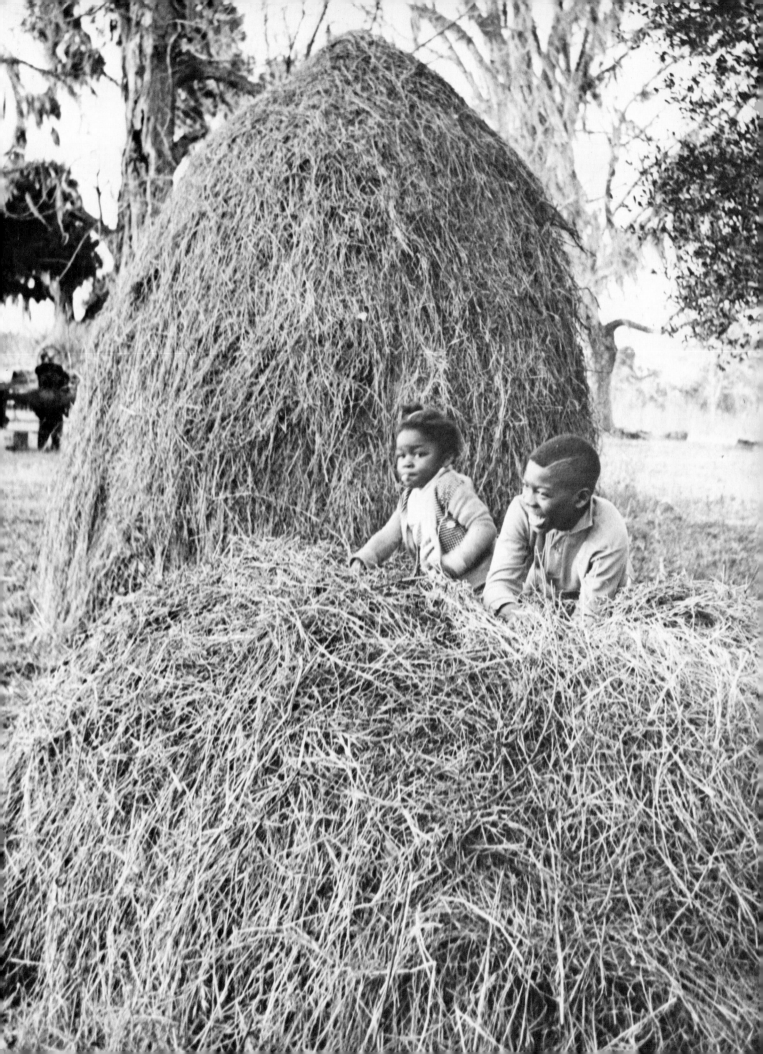

The Moving Star Hall congregation

AIN'T YOU GOT A RIGHT TO THE TREE OF LIFE?

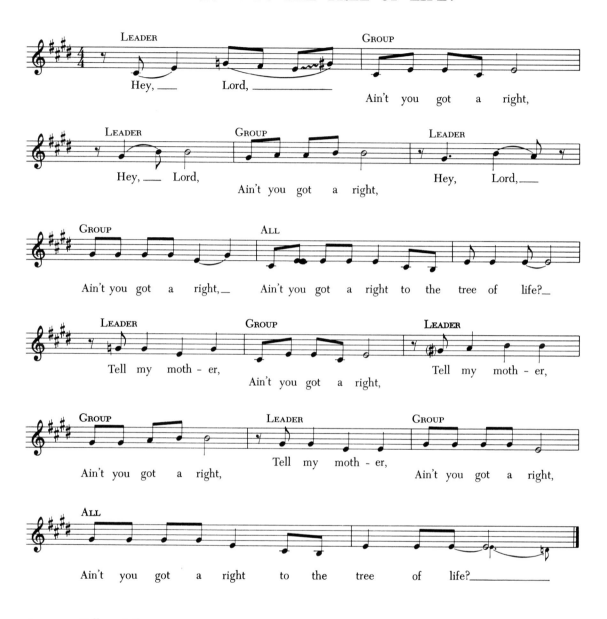

LEADER: Tell my father,
   GROUP: Ain't you got a right,
LEADER: Tell my father,
   GROUP: Ain't you got a right,
LEADER: Tell my father,
   GROUP: Ain't you got a right,
ALL: Ain't you got a right to the tree of life?

Tell my children . . . etc.

Tell the world . . . etc.

Hey, Lord,
   Ain't you got a right,
Hey, Lord,
   Ain't you got a right;
Hey, Lord,
   Ain't you got a right,
Ain't you got a right to the tree of life?

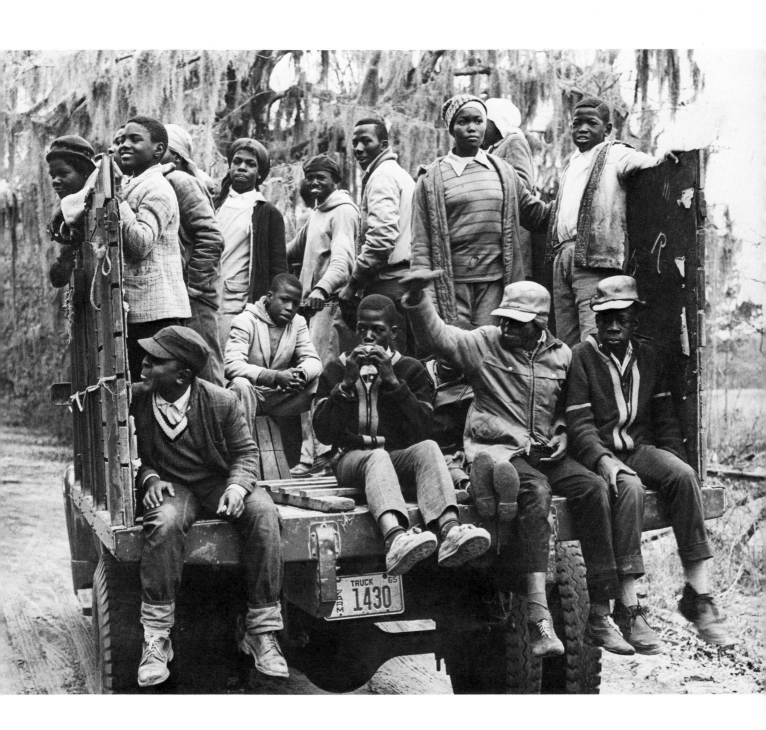

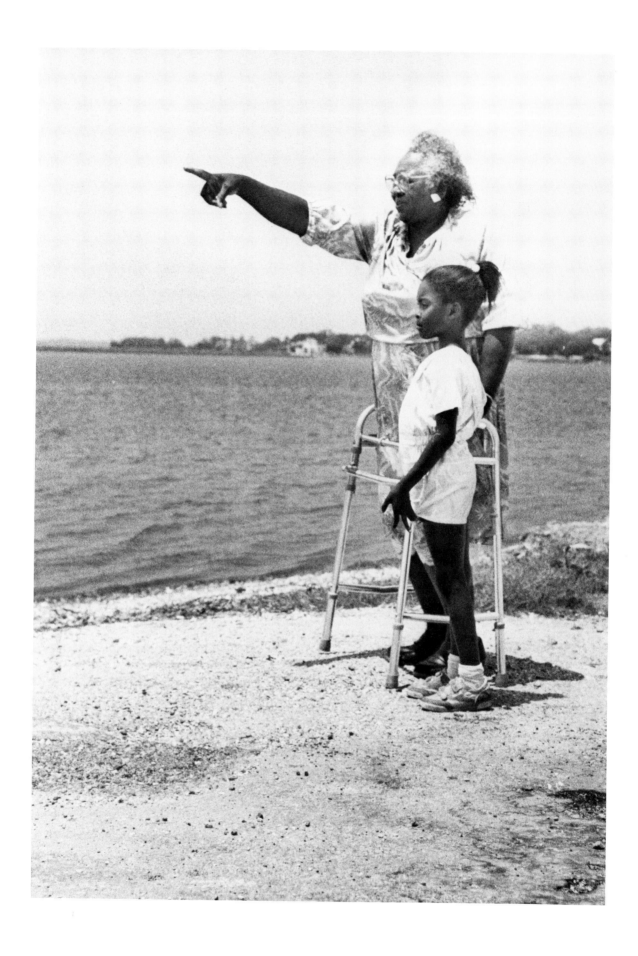

7. KEEP YOUR EYES ON THE PRIZE

THE SEA ISLANDS IN 1988

Mrs. Maggie Russell
ANYBODY WANTS TO GO BACK TO
THEIR OLD HOMEPLACE

You see that house through the bushes? That's Jenkins Point, where I used to live. They had houses built on the plantation for black people to live in because that was the people that worked for them. Now there are no black people living over there on Seabrook.

I married Dan Russell in 1944 and moved out to Wadmalaw. My husband was a crabber. We worked in the creek thirteen years together. I loved it.

You're not going to get onto Seabrook now. We tried to go in a boat one time and a man was standing up on the bank and shoots. He shoot up in the air. I say, "Dan, it sounds like somebody shooting." He say, "Cut the motor off." We cut the motor off and he was shooting up in the air telling us not to come over there. Then we see the sign says "no trespassing at any time." You can't even go in the little creek we used to go in to catch fish. He closed that out.

It's too bad because anybody wants to go back to their old homeplace.

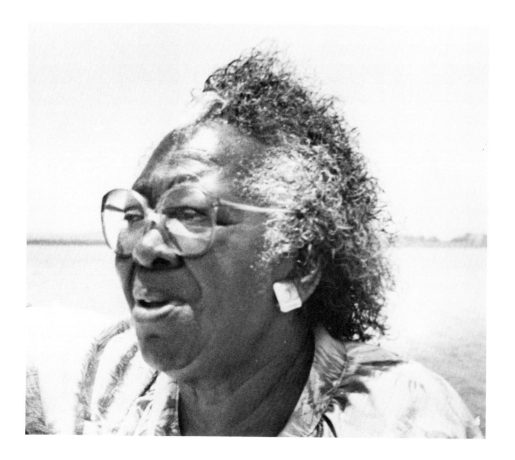

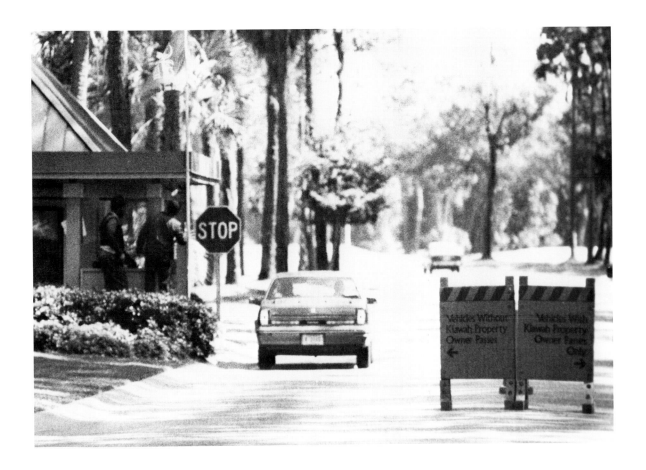

Mr. Abraham Jenkins
GOD AIN'T MAKING NO MORE LAND

Land on these islands got to be so valuable because of the development projects on Kiawah and Seabrook. At one time you could get an acre of land for less than fifty dollars. Now land costs a lot more. It's almost impossible to buy land now. We got people out here now that come to buy with cash money. This is a way of enticing and influencing people because people have spent all their lives trying to make some money and here this guy walks up to you with rolls of thousand dollar bills circled by hundreds and five hundreds and starts talking. Many of these people just want to take the money and I can understand it. But you have to let them know that God ain't making no more land, and if you got any, you better hold onto it and try to work some other type of arrangement like long-term leasing. Sometimes you can be land-rich, but you can lose it all.

Black land is a threat to further development. It's slowing things down. I'll give you an example of how these developers operate. There is a black family that used to own about seventy-nine acres of land on Johns Island. The land developers were out there like buzzards trying to find an heir to that property that would not have any interest in the property. In this particular case the heir was somebody in New York and the developer said, "I will give you X amount of dollars for what you own on Johns Island." He said, "Man, what are you talking about? I have never been to Johns Island." The developer said, "Yes, but you own something down there." The developer looked like Santa Claus to him and he just went on and took the money.

The developer took the signed agreement into probate court and started suing for partition. They couldn't agree on how to divide the seventy-nine acres. The court said since the relatives could not agree who was going to get the swamp, who was going to get the waterfront, who was going to get whatever, then the whole property should be sold and the money divided.

The developer wanted the whole thing anyway. When he signed the piece of paper for whatever he owned, he became a member of the family. He would not agree to any settlement. When they had the partition sale, he had someone come and outbid the rest of the family.

We're planning quarterly land workshops now so that people can learn more about how to protect their land.

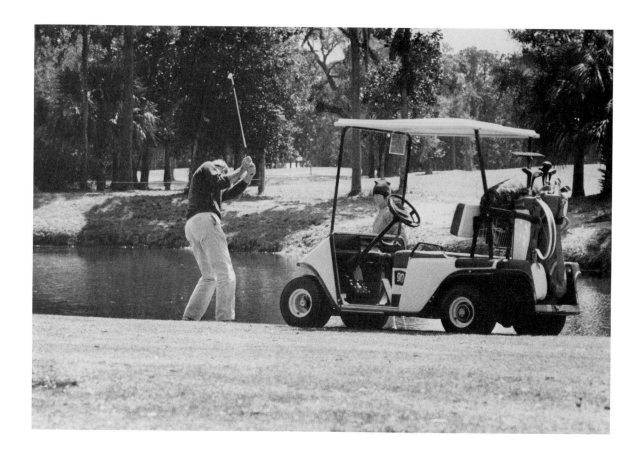

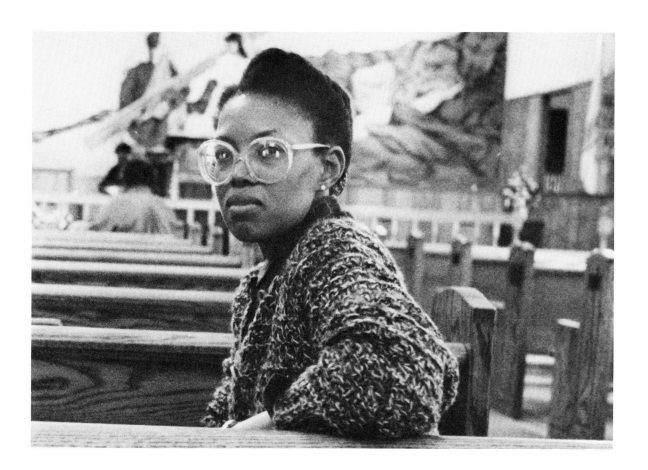

Ms. Elaine Jenkins
WE CAN HAVE SOME SAY AS TO WHAT'S
GOING TO BE DEVELOPED

We've been meeting and talking about heirs' property and how to get it cut up now so that folk don't lose all of it. There are so many people involved, all it takes is for one person to sell out. Once that one sells and some stranger gets in, he can force a partition suit, and they may end up losing a whole tract of land. What we've been trying to do is tell them how to get it partitioned among family members. So if one wants to sell, fine. He will just have that acre or so. But not the whole tract going out from under them.

I'm talking to them about taxes and the importance of paying those taxes. And we're notifying people when we see their land up for sale for nonpayment of taxes. I'm talking to them about making wills. If you don't make a will that's where all these heirs come in. It's just so much to keep up with.

Being a lawyer is something I always knew I wanted to do, from the time I can remember. And my intentions were always to return to Charleston and Johns Island. This is where I wanted to be. I love this place.

We can have some say as to what's going to be developed—what's going to go up and where it's going to go up. That's still open to us.

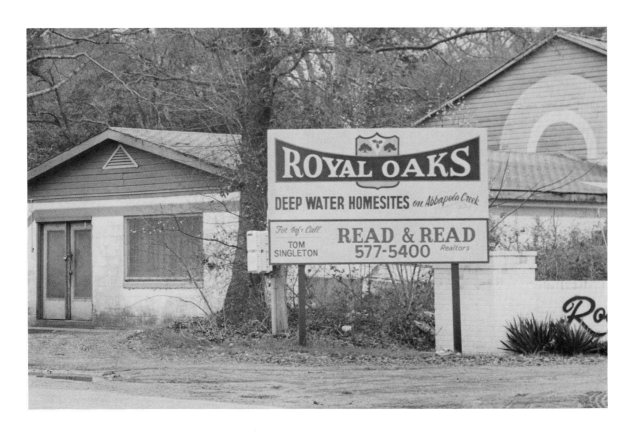

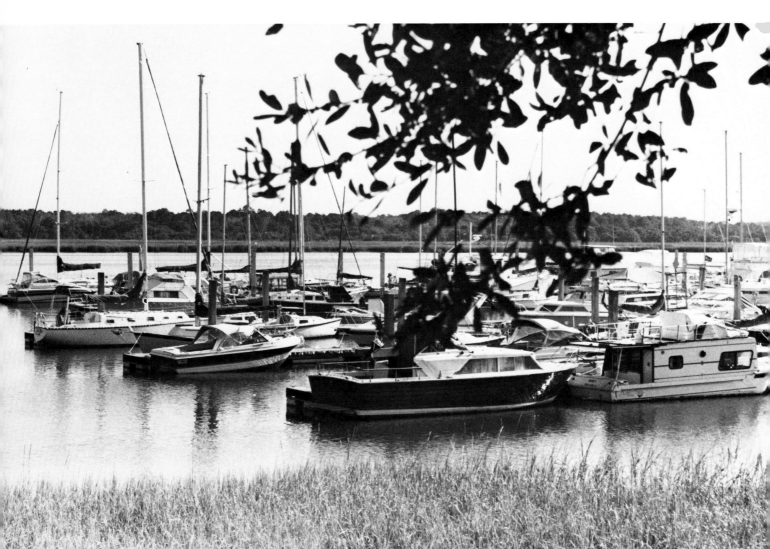

Mr. William Saunders
WHAT I TALK TO PEOPLE ON THE ISLAND ABOUT IS POOLING OUR RESOURCES

There's no way that the island can stay unchanged. It's already changed. There was a time when I knew everybody on the island. I can't say that anymore. There's been such an influx of new people in the last ten years. There's a real new sense of direction there. The new people can always take advantage of the older people. Hopefully, we can control some of the change.

For the first time in my lifetime, the white and black communities have come together. Some of the whites who hated my guts back when you guys were there now are using me sometimes as spokesman to the county government. Some of them who would never have spoken to me, I've been in meetings with them and they'll say, "Let Mr. Saunders explain that." There's a Johns Island planning committee to look at what needs to be changed. I think we might be able to maintain our roads—if we could get some cutoffs on the roads, where those big farm vehicles or the school bus can pull over for the traffic—and if we can do it *and* save the big trees.

I wish I was in a position to get a group of people together to buy up a good bit of the land that is for sale on Johns Island. Some of it I would like to just sit. Some of it you could build the things that need to be done. I would like to see a nice Holiday Inn–type motel over there. There are so many people from the island that are living away from here that come home and their family don't have a house large enough for them to stay in. And they don't want to stay in the city, so they just crowd in together. But if you had a real nice hotel and just a nice restaurant, you could make money on it. There are so many things that could be done.

What I talk to people on the island about is pooling our resources to build the things that will be built on Johns Island. It can be done, but we would have to trust each other.

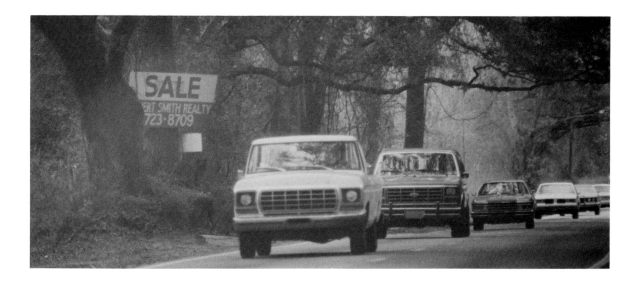

Mr. Abraham Jenkins
PEOPLE DON'T SEE THAT "BIG SANTA CLAUS" THEY ONCE THOUGHT OF

People saw what happened when all that money came in with Kiawah and yet no one that I know got in any of those administrative positions out there. You find a few people got into the more menial jobs. Ninety percent of the jobs are in the lowest level, and then maybe five to ten percent are in a higher bracket, but not up in the really well-paid bracket. So people don't see that "big Santa Claus" they once thought of.

Mr. William Saunders
THEY WERE NEVER CONCERNED ABOUT THE PEOPLE THAT LIVE ON THOSE ISLANDS

I get pretty upset about things. There was a million dollars spent on turtles on Kiawah, because these people were concerned about the turtles. But they were never concerned about the people that live on those islands.

Still, as long as I can get some help from those people, then I don't have any problem with their lives. The moment all those rich people begin staying on Kiawah and Seabrook, they begin to improve the roads. Although it was built for them, I use it. It's accessible to everyone. And the people on Kiawah and Seabrook are pretty much conservationists, so they back most anything leaving things the way they are.

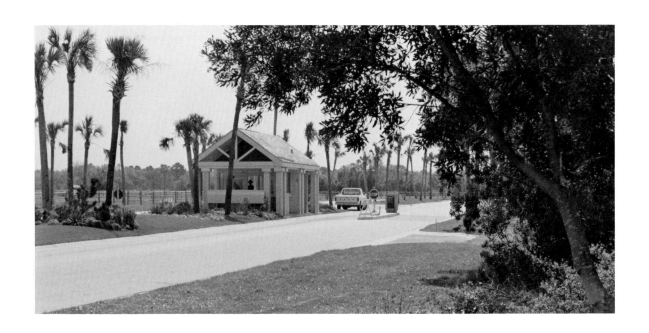

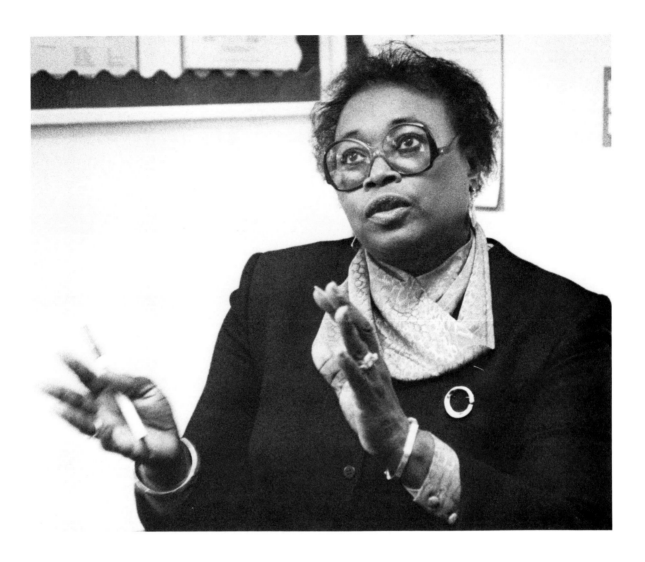

Mrs. Ethel Grimball
THAT IS GREAT PROGRESS

When I walk on Johns Island and I stand in the yard and look at the nursing home, look at the lab, look at the clinic, and look across the street at the housing project, I feel like that is great progress. I'm sure that the low cost housing project added ten to twenty years to the life span of a lot of those people who live there because of the living conditions they had prior to that. They feel comfortable, they feel more secure, and they feel good about themselves. And then if anyone gets sick or doesn't feel well, all they have to do is walk across the street to the clinic. And that is great progress.

There's a fight right now to keep it going, because of political reasons, but it's still great progress. That was one of the things my father spoke about—the health care on these islands. I wish he were here to see it.*

*Mrs. Grimball is the daughter of Esau Jenkins.

181

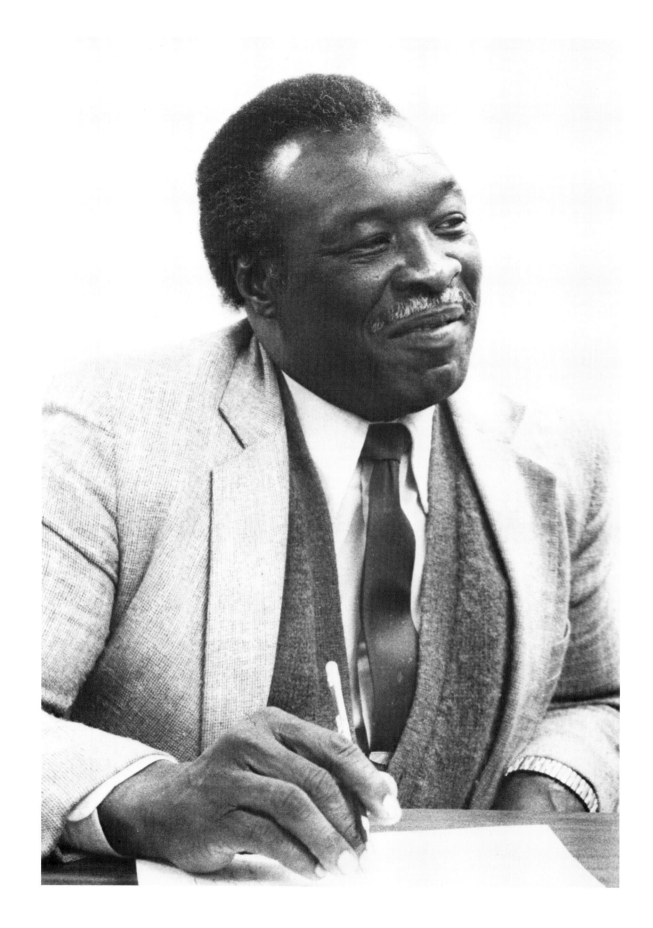

Mr. Abraham Jenkins
THE PEOPLE WERE TREATED SO BADLY

Prior to the establishment of the Sea Island Comprehensive Health Care Corporation there was no medical care on the islands and everybody had to go to the emergency room in Charleston. The people were treated so badly by the nurses and sometimes the physicians. It was segregated there. And many people died trying to get to medical care waiting on the bridges to open and close.

My father was a fighter. In my case, I retired as a major in the air force in 1971 and moved back home. I figured I'd come back to give my daddy help. I was in a position to help him do some things. I grew up around this work and I guess I would have come back eventually. I spoke to my daddy. He never said I should come back, but just the way he spoke, I knew I should. After talking to some other people, I knew the work needed to be done. When I looked at the groundwork that had been laid by these people, and saw the intensity of their effort and how much sacrifice had been made, I know I said to myself, "I gave the military twenty years, I can give Sea Island twenty." Several of us started trying to put a health program together for the islands.

Mr. Abraham Jenkins
PEOPLE STARTED SEEING
THE BIGGER PICTURE

Our community consists of the sea islands west and south of Charleston—five islands altogether. So when we started looking at the needs of the people, we tried to organize a local health council on each of these islands. Either we created or we got to be a part of an existing organization on each island. We started getting input from all of the islands and we started trying to meet their needs. We eventually started dealing with environmental issues, social work, health education, and nutrition.

When some people became interested in the problems of migrant workers on the islands, Rev. Goodwin, my daddy, Bill Saunders, McKinley Washington, and others said, "Well, it's all right to be doing something for the migrants, but whatever the migrants are experiencing for six or eight weeks, the people on the islands are experiencing for the whole year. So whatever we do, it should not be limited just to the migrants." Some of the first issues that were identified were health issues.

They decided they needed to form a rural organization that would deal with these problems the people were having. That was the beginning of Rural Missions, Inc. It started out of the Progressive Club and was formed to address local issues on Johns Island. But then people started seeing the bigger picture and the similarity of the situation on the other islands.

Mr. William Saunders
THE SEA ISLAND HEALTH CARE CORPORATION WAS A POWER BASE

I think the housing, the health care facility, you have to look at it as an elevation, an improvement. We had the foresight with the health center to add the nursing home and the home for the elderly, so even when they took our health center grant away from us, we owned the building and we owned the property. The health center is now being run by the City of Charleston. The taking over was really a political party fight. In 1980 the Republican party needed to be able to say that they got something going on in the community, so what they did, they found problems with a lot of stuff that was already there—got rid of the Board, got a new Board, and allowed it to function.

Anytime you're talking about being able to control something, anytime you're talking about power, then you're talking about something real that was done. The Sea Island Health Care Corporation was a power base that we put together that exists. It really exists today. We've got forty acres of very choice land. The city now wants twelve acres of it. That's the kind of thing where Esau and others were thinking ahead and did things in advance, and we planned that one way ahead of everybody. And it's there. We've got control of the nursing home and the housing.

Mr. William Saunders
THERE'S A LOT OF RELATIONSHIP BETWEEN HEALTH AND POVERTY

Our goal for the Comprehensive Health Center was that it would serve everybody on the islands and would be totally independent. The first director, Jim Martin, was a real strategist. He and I used to spend hours dreaming and scheming about what could be, how you could work politically within the system and make things work. Jim was a past master at that.

Beyond just providing health services, for awhile the Health Care Corporation was the biggest employer on the island. We found that when people were working, they were healthier simply because they were making their own living. There's a lot of relationship between health and poverty.

We were looking to be able to sell health care to Kiawah and to Seabrook and to the other big interests on the island, which would have actually made the health center self-sufficient. You would not have needed any governmental money. We were just about there when they took it away from us. We don't have control of the daily operation of the clinic. But the people who are using it have to pay us rent. It's a good bit less service than it used to be. But it could come back. The whole facility is there, so the possibilities are unlimited.

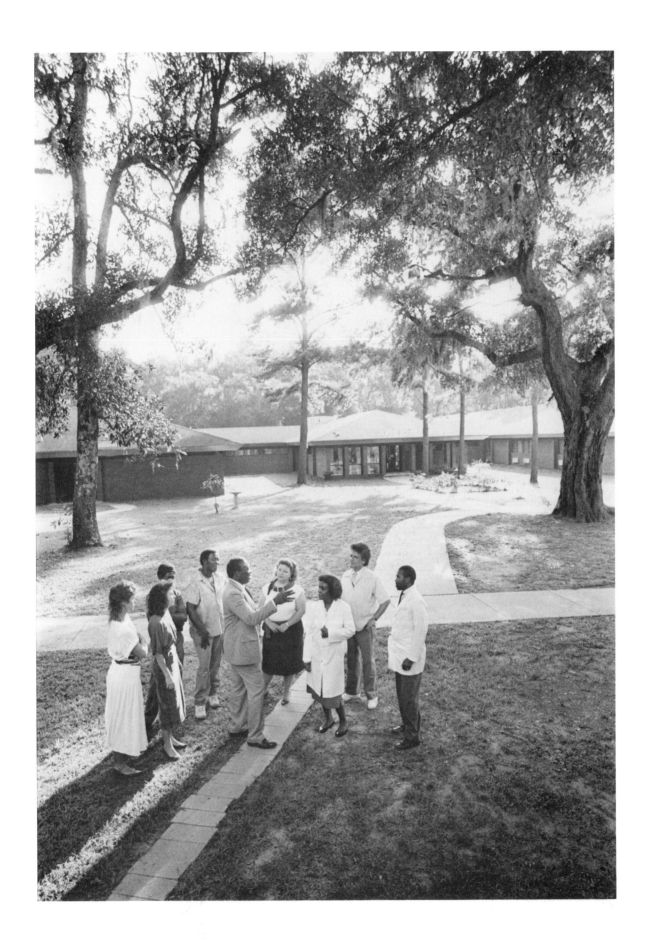

Mr. Abraham Jenkins

I'LL GIVE YOU AN EXAMPLE OF PEOPLE
WHO REALLY MADE A DIFFERENCE
IN THESE ISLANDS

Sometimes people don't recognize the hard work of people behind the scenes. I'll give you an example of people who really made a difference in these islands. Mrs. Alleen Brewer Wood came to Johns Island in 1929. Her husband, Rev. Brewer, was the pastor of two churches on the island. She was quite a community person. She would help with anything that needed doing. These were the days when people depended on root medicine and midwifery, what I call indirect health care. It was not the approved method of health care, but people had their own methods for taking care of problems. Mrs. Wood was around in that time when we were trying to get people to feel better about themselves, and trying to teach them about self-respect. She was one of the persons that we call the "grandmoms of the islands," instrumental in so many little things that you don't hear that much about. She helped lay down some of the foundation for the projects that came to Johns Island. Later on she taught the Citizenship School classes on Edisto.

Rev. McKinley Washington was one of those people that my daddy really relied on. He would call him up every Sunday morning before church and talk over with him the things he would like to see discussed in church—voter registration or whatever the issue was. He was just a young minister in those days, right out of school. He started the NAACP here. And later they formed a group from the Presbyterian church called the Self-Development of People to deal with the needs of people on Edisto. They bought an old school building (used to be the school for the white kids) and used it as a community building.

When Esau was working through the Charleston Citizens' Committee, which took in all of the sea islands, Rev. Washington was his connection for Edisto and Yonges islands. People were always reluctant about how fast to move to bring about change. They will go with you for awhile, but then if it looks like you're not giving up, some will want to put the brakes on. So Esau had to have people that would keep that motivation going. And McKinley was one of those people. He's a real good speaker. His voice is deep and heavy, and when he starts preaching, you have to listen to him. So my daddy used him as an inspirator.

When Rev. Willis Goodwin came to Johns Island to pastor in 1966, people just looked on the ministry as church on Sunday. When Rev. Goodwin got here he changed all that. His ministry was seven days per week. He would go around to the people who were sick or were in need—and everybody was in

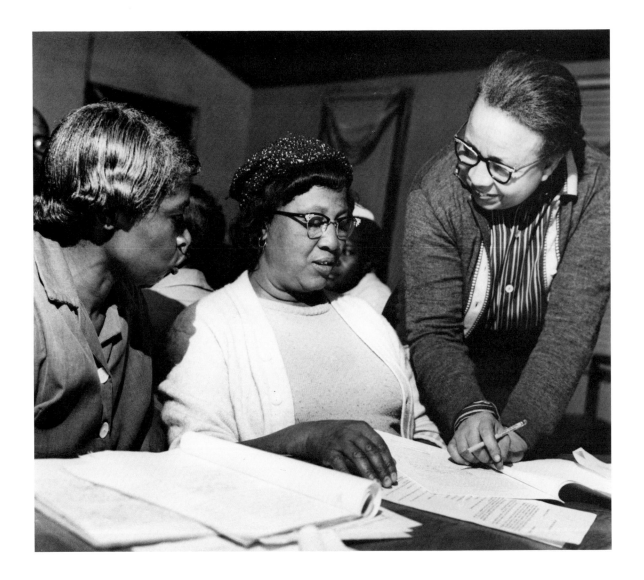

need for something. He tried to find out what he could do to help. He would go around to the piccolo joints and talk to people, and go down to the fishermen and talk to them, go to the growers and talk to them. After awhile he didn't have to buy anything for the people. He was getting everything donated. Once people saw that they could depend on him, then he started getting into the social issues. That's when he started working with my daddy. Then they would call in McKinley and some of these other people, and they would brainstorm about the problems. To me, Rev. Goodwin did more for people on these islands, especially from the pulpit, than anyone since my daddy.

Mr. William Saunders
I'M PRETTY BITTER ABOUT THINGS
LIKE THAT

I've been thinking about Mrs. Septima Clark. Here's a person who got fired from a system after teaching over thirty years for belonging to an organization that she would not denounce (NAACP). They refused to give her even her retirement. That same system, that same power base, allows her fifteen, twenty years later to be on the school board. That same power base turns around later on and says, "You can have your retirement." And that same power base is saying, the mayor is saying, the governor is saying, "This woman is a hero." There's something wrong with that!

Those power brokers can say, "At eighty years old we can make you a hero; we can line your wall with plaques; because you're no more threat to us." And the reason we can make you a hero is that now we got to look out for Bill Saunders and them that is coming along. And they're the ones that's going to give us some trouble. And as new people come along, then some of us become worthless, so we get plaques and stuff.

When the superintendent of the school system for the state can say, on the morning that Mrs. Clark dies, that there's nothing wrong with our school system, we got a perfect school system, there's no bias, there's no problem, and that will go. And then the judge turns around and says yes, the only problem is poverty and it will take fifty to a hundred years to straighten that out, and then they say Mrs. Clark is a hero. The mayor says, "There's nobody like her. She never got loud, she never raised her voice, she's sweet, and she got things done. We loved her." I'm pretty bitter about things like that.

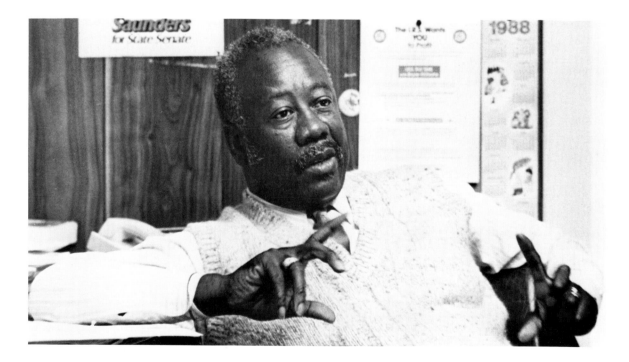

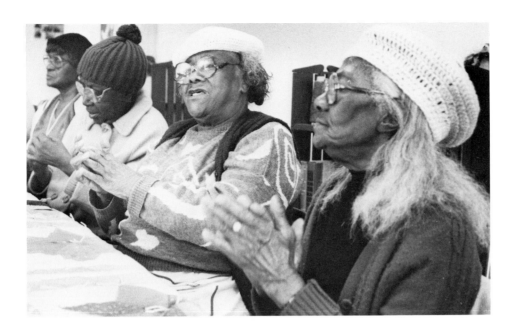

Mrs. Bernice Robinson
EVERYBODY LISTENED WHEN ESAU TALKED

Esau did not get the kind of recognition he deserved for the work he did. He spearheaded so many things: the Charleston County Citizens' Committee, the Credit Union (and it was countywide, which is very unusual), the Comprehensive Health Center on Johns Island. He would be really proud if he was alive today to know that they got the nursing home and the senior citizens' home. He fought like anything to get the health clinic on the island so they could have medical care for the people over there.

While he was living, he didn't get that much praise. But it didn't daunt his efforts at all. His children suffered a lot for him being so aggressive. They couldn't get jobs in Charleston County. But he still wouldn't let that turn him around. He continued to fight for what he thought was right for his people.

Esau didn't finish his high school education until after he'd gotten married. There were a lot of people, professionals or educators, who felt that if he changed the way he talked, it would be so much better. But I used to say, "Everybody listens when Esau talks in his same Gullah language." He was telling it like it is, and they heard what he was saying. You would think that with the exposure he had, and with him going all around the country, some of it would rub off. I don't think he wanted it to rub off. He maintained his speech as it was. So he had criticism from a lot of the educated folk, but he was saying what they needed to be saying. And he got the benefits for them.

He would have a whole lot to say about education. He would be very disappointed about how far we still have to go, but he wouldn't be bitter about it. He would be saying that we haven't accomplished yet what we need to accomplish. And he would see in what way he could work to bring it about.

Mrs. Ethel Grimball
I DON'T MIND TALKING ABOUT WHAT I SEE

The school situation is still one that really bothers me—especially St. Johns High School. The school has 660 students and seventy percent of those students are on free or reduced lunch. These are black children from Johns and Wadmalaw islands. Ten percent of the students go on to college and I'm not concerned about them, but I am concerned about the ninety percent of these black children who cannot go to college, who do not have skills to develop self-sufficiency, and who have to go through school for four years, finish high school, and then have to go right back and either do domestic work, go to Kiawah Island and make beds, go to Kiawah Island and clean yards, or go to Kiawah Island and wash dishes. It doesn't make sense.

I feel very frustrated by what's happening to our children on Johns Island today. They're saying they have to go to James Island if they want to learn a trade. I'm against that. And so that's my fight with the school system. If you have a curriculum that's not meeting the needs of these students, something is wrong.

I would like to get on the school board, but they won't put me on there. They think I'm radical. I'm not radical. I'm just very candid about what I see and I don't mind talking about what I see.

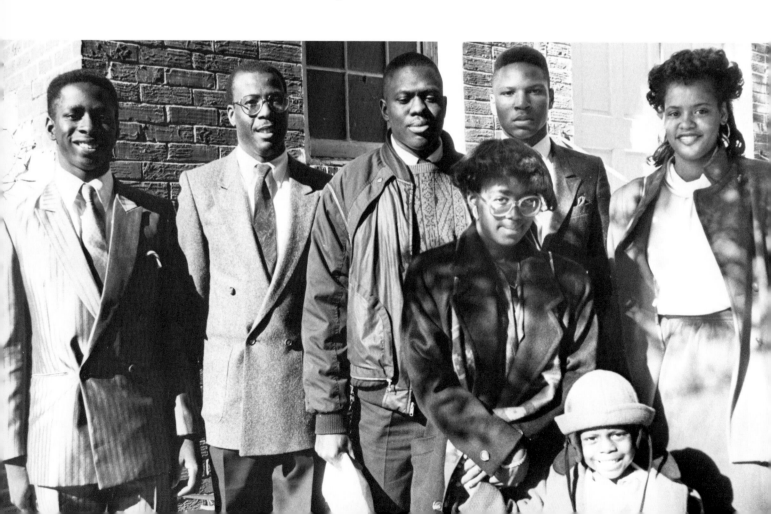

Mr. Gerald Mackey
BLACK YOUTH NEED POSITIVE ROLE MODELS

Many of the problems that young people face—substance abuse, teenage pregnancy, illiteracy, suicide attempts—are a direct result of these young people having a poor self-image and low self-esteem. So the first step in finding a solution is helping these young people to feel good about themselves. A lot of the young people are insecure. They fall prey to peer pressure because they don't feel good about themselves. They don't love themselves for one reason or another.

Black youth need positive role models. When you look at the television or read the newspapers, or the history books, blacks are rarely shown in a positive light. As a result many of the young people feel that blacks have not made any significant contribution to America. That causes them to feel negatively about themselves and about their ancestors.

I attended a segregated elementary school and a segregated high school on Johns Island. My childhood dream was to become a teacher. My black teachers were my role models and I always looked up to them. These people worked extremely hard with the boys and girls on Johns Island—giving us lots of support and encouragement. They cared enough about us to go the extra mile in spite of the limited resources that were given to black schools at that time.

The most important influence in my life was my mother, Ms. Wilhelmina Mackey, who died this year. My mother wanted her children to be educated and to "make something" of themselves. She was a stern disciplinarian. She took a no-nonsense approach to education and social behavior. Because of the Jim Crow laws of the South, and because of extenuating circumstances, she did not have the opportunity to get a high school education. She went only as far as the eighth grade, but she was a smart woman. She worked hard to have her children educated. And she also saw to it that God and religion played a very important role in our lives. My mother's strong desire to see us succeed helped me to develop self-discipline at an early age.

I would urge young people today to develop self-discipline in all aspects of life. They need the initiative to move ahead and do those things that should be done.

At Wesley, we've set up a weekly communitywide tutorial session. The response to that program has been overwhelming. We have people who have specialized in all subjects coming in to work on an individual basis with kids so that they could get the time and the attention they need.

I believe that those of us who have been blessed by God, and have been fortunate enough to be successful, have a moral responsibility to help those less fortunate than ourselves—especially the young people. We need to concentrate on working with our youth, because they are our future.

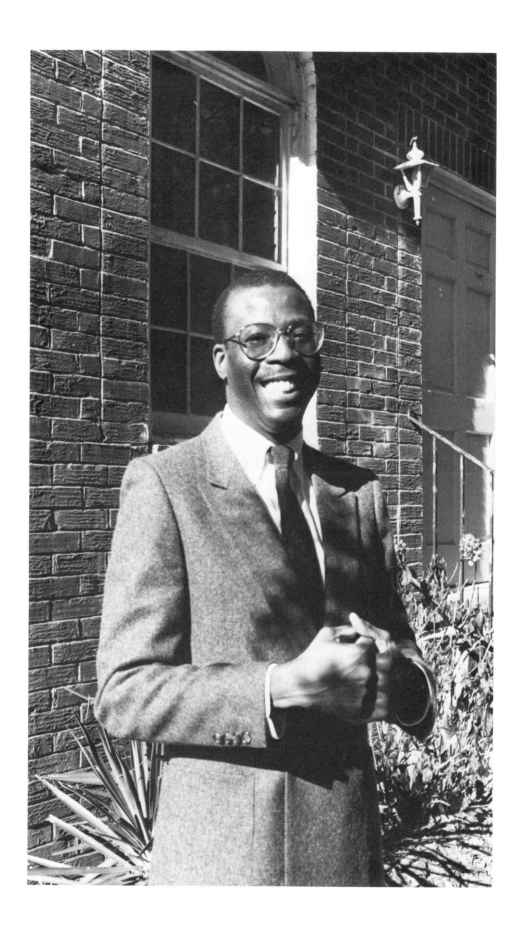

Mr. Gerald Mackey
YOU NEVER KNOW THE NUMBER OF LIVES YOU TOUCH

The employment situation for young people nationwide is extremely frustrating. I work with the division of personnel for the Charleston County School District. We have problems getting black teachers in the school system. For example, Charleston County hired approximately 224 teachers at the beginning of the school year and approximately 21 of the 224 were black. When you look at the racial composition of the district, you have more black than white students. So we have a problem with black teachers and administrators coming into the district. It's one of the reasons why the desegregation suit brought by the Justice Department and others is now going on.

In some schools in the county, we have no black teachers. In some of the larger schools, you might have two or three. There is no equity in student-teacher ratio in terms of black and white. So the kids have very few black role models in terms of teachers. That's a very sad indictment on a system when kids come up from kindergarten through high school and not see a black teacher. Another argument that we make in the county is that blacks are not going into teaching. They're considering other options like science or math, and they're going into the industries. They're studying computer science and engineering and medicine, and they're not going into teaching. But it's going to be sad again for the kids.

I wouldn't trade my experience of being a classroom teacher for anything in the world. You never know the number of lives you touch. Teaching is very rewarding.

Mr. Abraham Jenkins
I THINK THAT'S A STEP IN THE RIGHT DIRECTION

With the Sea Island Health Care Corporation, the Citizens' Committee, the Ministerial Alliance, Johns Island's going to be a better place to live. With the dedication we have now we have turned that exodus of young people leaving the island around. We have seen some engineers and attorneys and professional people coming back home to live. And if they're not living here, they're still making a contribution by coming back periodically, making their presence known, sharing their knowledge, or making a financial contribution. There's much more of that now than there was ten years ago. I think that's a step in the right direction.

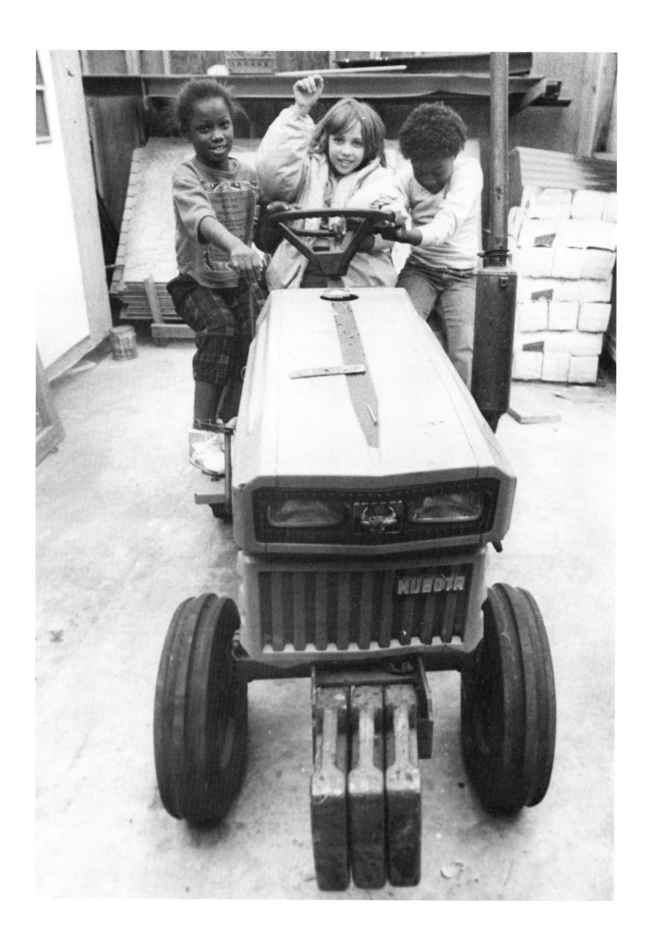

Mrs. Alice Wine
KEEP YOUR EYES ON THE PRIZE

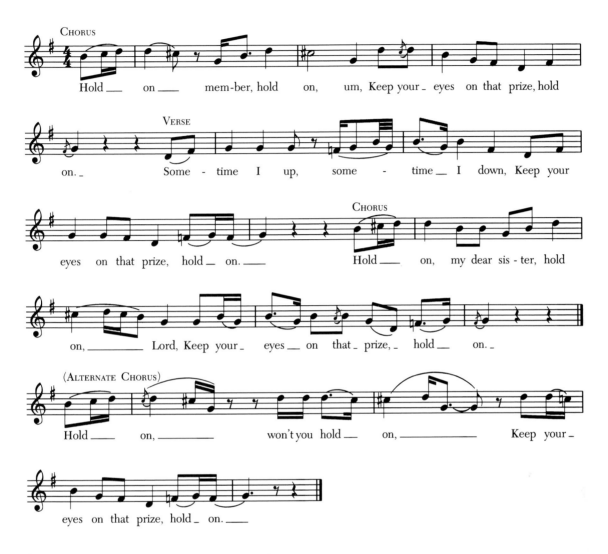

♩=54 (represents a composite tempo)

(CHORUS)
Hold on, member, hold on,
Keep your eyes on that prize, hold on.

(VERSE)
Sometime I up, sometime I down,
Keep your eyes on that prize, hold on.

(CHORUS)
Hold on, my dear sister, hold on, Lord,
Keep your eyes on that prize, hold on.

This song has an interesting history. When Guy first spent time on Johns Island and sang a version of "Keep Your Hand on the Plow," which he had learned from Pete Seeger in the 1950s, Mrs. Wine said, "Oh, I know a different echo to that," and sang, "Keep your eyes on the prize." Guy later passed these words on to the young people then involved in the civil rights movement. Those words became the ones sung all across the South as part of the movement.

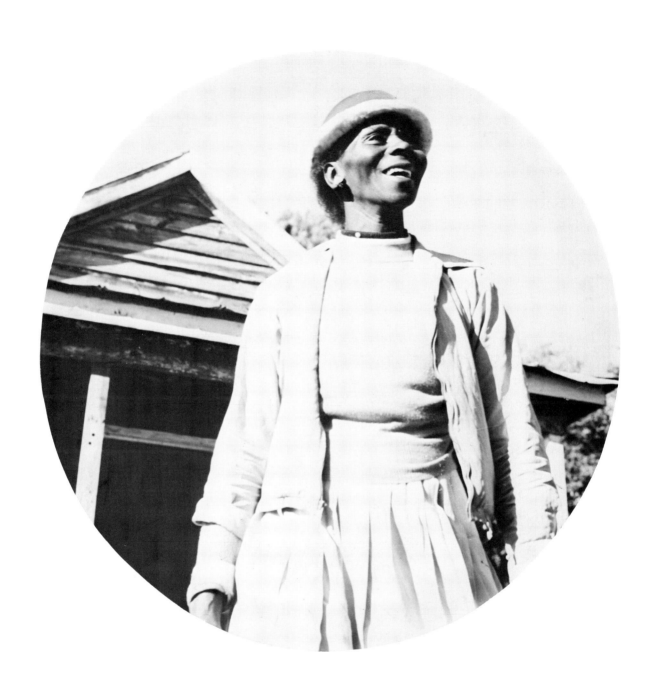

8. WE WILL OVERCOME

LAYING THE GROUNDWORK IN THE 1950s

Mr. Myles Horton*
THE PEOPLE OF JOHNS ISLAND
DESERVE TRIBUTE

The citizenship schools were inspired by Esau Jenkins who was trying to teach his Johns Island bus passengers to pass the South Carolina literacy test required for voting. In a 1955 Highlander Folk School workshop he had asked for help. In an effort to respond, we spent the next two years acquainting ourselves with the culture of the island and with the people. We found out by living and working with them what their problems were and that they wanted to be voting citizens.

Bernice Robinson was chosen to teach the first citizenship school because she respected the people and, having had no teaching experience, would be nonjudgmental and experimental. She began the first class in the back room of a cooperative store by saying, "I am not a teacher; we are here to learn together. You're going to teach me as much as I am going to teach you."

The curriculum was developed day by day. They learned to write letters, to order from catalogs, and fill out money orders. They made stories about the vegetables they grew and the tools they used, the chairs and tables in the room. They moved on to reading the Declaration of Human Rights, which hung on the wall, and the South Carolina constitution, which was a prerequisite of becoming a voter.

Music and singing familiar songs livened up the long evenings and blended with the joy of learning. Singing sea island folk songs, spirituals, and protest songs helped build the group's consciousness and boosted morale as together they tackled the difficult task of learning to read and write.

This pioneer citizenship school, which met biweekly for three months, grew from fourteen to thirty-seven students. It was soon followed by a second school. Out of the first two schools, sixty people, two-thirds the total enrollment, passed the literacy test for voting. That is, they "graduated."

Esau Jenkins had an explanation for this accomplishment. He said, "No one wants anything more than to be a first-class citizen. That is what makes you learn what you have to learn." Their motivation was for an achievable goal rooted in their culture. Although each individual had to learn to read for him or herself, they studied as a group, they supported and encouraged each other as they painfully struggled to read. As they took the first steps in learning to read and write, they made use of what they had learned without delay. The process that evolved was simple and easy to explain and could easily be adopted elsewhere, making the multiplying process easy.

The enthusiastic new voters immediately spread the word to neighboring South Carolina and Georgia sea islands. Soon the citizenship schools were started on Edisto and Wadmalaw islands, and before the three months period ended, half those enrolled had learned to read and write well enough to pass

*Founder and former director of the Highlander Folk School.

198

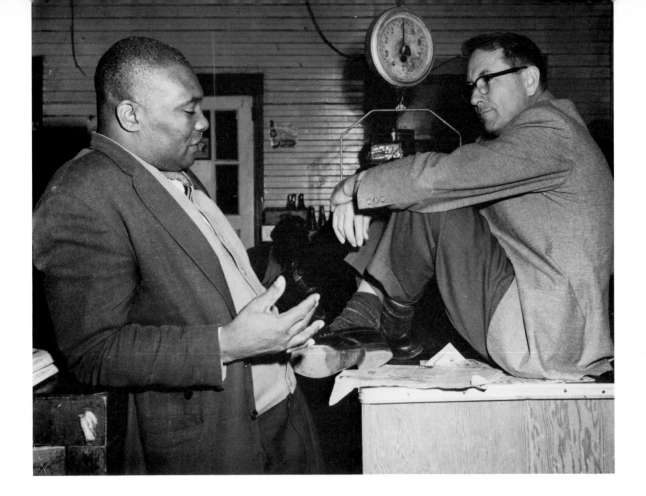

the literacy test and become registered voters. Some had organized their community for discussions of civic issues and voter registration campaigns. Later, as on Johns Island, they would run for public office and provide leadership in the emerging civil rights movement.

In 1961 the citizenship school program was transferred from Highlander to the Southern Christian Leadership Conference. In the meantime Septima Clark and Bernice Robinson had developed a residential program for training volunteers who wanted to be citizenship school teachers.

Before becoming the educational arm of the SCLC, the number of teachers trained were counted in the hundreds, but after the transfer, Septima Clark reported that they were counted in the thousands. More impressive than these figures was the vitality of the educational process which set in motion a liberating force that gave dignity and collective power to thousands of black people throughout the South.

The people of Johns Island deserve tribute for the role they played in the origin and development of a citizenship/literacy movement that became a vital part of the civil rights movement and has achieved international recognition. Special tribute is due to the first pioneer citizenship school, created by a teacher who had never taught before and her students who had never been to school; and to the coordinator Septima Clark and especially to Esau Jenkins whose idea it was in the first place.

Mrs. Septima Clark
AFTER I CAME BACK FROM HIGHLANDER,
I DECIDED I SHOULD GET ESAU TO GO

I knew Esau Jenkins when he was a boy of fourteen and came to my school to learn how to read. All his life Esau devoted himself to improving conditions on Johns Island.

Esau had a bus that he drove from Johns Island to Charleston and back, carrying tobacco workers and longshoremen to work. One morning one of the women on the bus made Esau a proposal. "I don't have much schooling, Esau," she said to him. "But I would like to be somebody. I'd like to hold up my head with other people; I'd like to be able to vote. Esau, if you'll help me a little when you have the time, I'll be glad to learn the laws and get qualified to vote. If I do, I promise you I'll register and I'll vote."

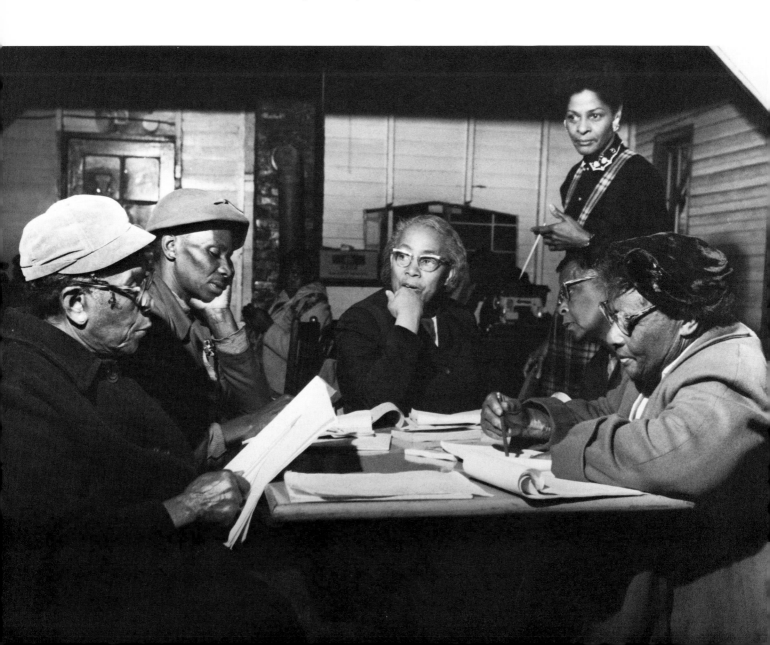

That appealed to Esau, and he agreed to help her. He had a portion of the South Carolina laws typed up, those that pertained to registration and voting, and he passed them out to the people who rode his bus. To those who couldn't read or couldn't understand the language of the law, he patiently explained the requirements. When he was waiting for his passengers to assemble or when his bus arrived in town a few minutes early, he would discuss those laws with them.

The woman who asked Esau for help was Mrs. Alice Wine. She had a marvelous ability to memorize; she memorized the whole section of the constitution that they were studying. Soon she was ready to go and be registered.

While she was standing in line awaiting her turn, one of the women ahead of her, in reading a section of the constitution, mispronounced the word "miscegenation." Immediately Mrs. Wine pronounced it correctly. The registrar spoke out sharply, "No coaching, please!" When it came her time, Mrs. Wine "read" every word perfectly by reciting from memory. She was given her registration certificate, and she was one happy soul.

But Mrs. Wine wasn't satisfied. She really wanted to know how to read. She asked Esau if there was any kind of school where she could learn to read and write.

After I came back from going to Highlander the first time, I decided that I should get Esau to go. We went up there and found out that many people could talk to him and give him help.

Myles Horton had been into Charleston to try to get people to come up to Highlander. Now, through Esau, he had a way to reach people. One Christmas Myles went down there with his children and spent the whole Christmas season just walking around the island and talking. He stayed in Esau's house, and the people really enjoyed him. Myles had a way of speaking to people that made them become endeared to him.

Myles always told people about the injustices that were there, that they had not seen. He said, "Now, you know, any day I can go back with my own people and not have to endure these things, but you have to live with them always. I want you to see if you can get to the place where you can register and vote. You need to think about what you can do for these children that are coming along."

Septima's words are from her autobiographical book *Ready from Within: Septima Clark and the Civil Rights Movement*, written with Cynthia Stokes Brown and published in 1986 by Wild Trees Press, Box 378, Navarro, Calif. 95463.

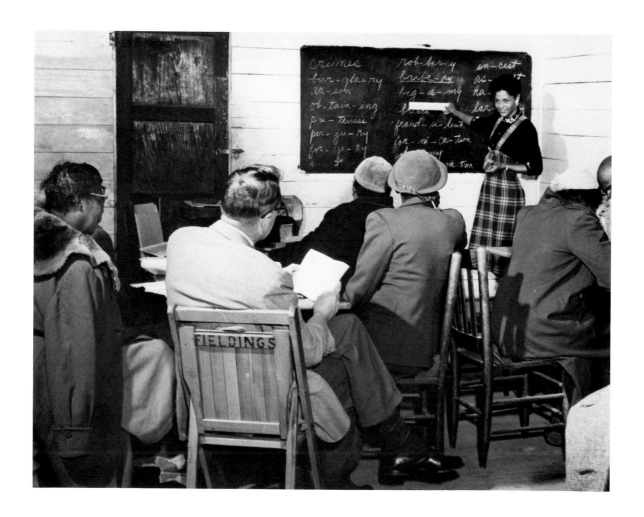

Mrs. Bernice Robinson
I STARTED TO TEACH THEM WHAT THEY WANTED TO LEARN

When they asked me to teach the course, I said I would help but I wouldn't teach because I wasn't a teacher. But Myles and Septima both said that if I didn't do it, it wouldn't be done. They wanted someone who was familiar with the philosophy of Highlander. They did not want a professional teacher to do it because they adhere to too strict a curriculum and they wouldn't listen to what the people were saying. So I accepted the challenge.

I had this material from my sister-in-law and she taught from the first to the third grade. That's all the material I had, plus the voter registration material and the Declaration of Human Rights. As soon as I walked in there and started talking with the people, I realized that her material was too juvenile. They were adults and I had to teach them on their level the things that they needed to know.

I had each one of them come up that first night and talk with me about some of the things they would like to learn. I had a little article for them to read and to sign their name. And they would say quietly, "I can't write" or "I can't read that well," and that's how I found out where each one of those students was on that first night.

The people we worked with were denied an education and so we had to teach them how to read and write. I don't remember when they got a full nine months elementary school on Johns Island. They didn't have anything but a little four-month school when Septima was teaching over there. When the people needed them to work in the fields, the farmers just went and knocked on the school house and the kids had to come out. So they didn't even get a full four-month education.

And then they told me the things they wanted to learn, which was to be able to write letters to their relatives that live elsewhere and read letters from them, rather than have to carry them to the white people they worked for to read them for them. They wanted to know how to do money orders. So then I started to teach them what they wanted to learn.

And of course they were conscious of the voting process because Esau had run for school board in 1954. He didn't win because he didn't have enough blacks registered on the island to put him in. They had three positions open and he came in fourth. Well, after that election they started appointing the school board members. Therefore, the students knew the importance of getting registered to vote. So it wasn't hard to sell them that idea. But like I said, I worked with them on the things they wanted to know first.

We had no idea of the school spreading. We were just doing what Esau asked us to do for his people on Johns Island. Well, they started registering to vote, and then they encouraged other people to go and register to vote. People on Johns Island were registering to vote so fast that people on Wadmalaw wanted it. Then Edisto wanted it. Then we wound up in the north area of Charleston with two classes.

Mrs. Bernice Robinson
THE PROGRAM WAS TRANSFERRED TO THE SOUTHERN CHRISTIAN LEADERSHIP CONFERENCE

By 1961 so many people were asking for the program from all around the South. Myles felt it was getting to the point where we were spreading ourselves too thin. The best thing for us to do was to contact organizations and have them send people in to Highlander to be trained as teachers. We would work with them for one week and train them as teachers. Then they could go back and set up classes.

And then we talked about second-stage classes—political education. Our classes didn't just stick to reading and writing to register to vote. We talked about the power that was in the hands of the people if they know the set-up of the government. So we talked about the set-up and who you go to for what.

We always told the teachers that if there wasn't an organization in their community, organize that first class into a community organization so that they would meet once a month and could get information about what was going on in their community, what they needed to do, how they needed to pressure their local government about certain things, what they could get from the federal government. And to always try to bring someone in who had some information in those fields, so that it would be a continuing, educating process.

In the summer of 1961 the program was transferred to the Southern Christian Leadership Conference. SCLC continued to do what we had started to do when we had the program at Highlander and that was have organizations send representation to them for a one-week workshop—for teacher training. Then they would go back into their areas. They came from Georgia, South Carolina, North Carolina, Alabama, Tennessee, Mississippi.

Mrs. Septima Clark
THE CITIZENSHIP SCHOOLS WERE THE BASE ON WHICH THE CIVIL RIGHTS MOVEMENT WAS BUILT

We were trying to make teachers out of people who could barely read and write. But they could teach. The people who left these training sessions went home to teach and to work in voter registration drives. They went home, and they didn't take it anymore. They started their own citizenship classes, discussing the problems in their own towns. "How come the pavement stops where the black section begins?" Asking questions like that, and then knowing who to go to to talk about that or where to protest it.

One time I heard Andy Young say that the citizenship schools were the base on which the whole civil rights movement was built. And that's probably very much true.

It's true because the citizenship schools made people aware of the political situation in their area. We recruited the wise leaders of their communities, like Fannie Lou Hamer in Mississippi. Hosea Williams started out as a citizenship school supervisor. The citizenship school classes formed the grassroot basis of new statewide political organizations in South Carolina, Georgia, and Mississippi. From one end of the South to the other, if you look at the black elected officials and the political leaders, you find people who had their first involvement in the training program of the citizenship school.

It was 1962 before the major civil rights groups were ready to do something about voter registration. But we had developed the ideas of the citizenship schools between 1957 and 1961. So all the civil rights groups could use our kind of approach because by then we knew it worked.

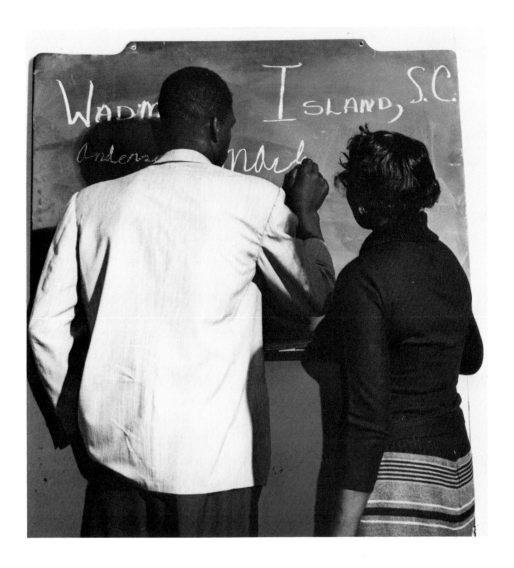

Mrs. Bernice Robinson

I DON'T THINK PEOPLE ON JOHNS ISLAND
KNOW WHAT AN IMPACT THE PROGRAM HAD

There were tens of thousands of teachers and students who went through that program. It lasted until 1970, and I think that what happened is that foundations thought that we had achieved what we were working for. We had the Voting Rights Bill and we had accomplished desegregation and we had gotten blacks elected to office in all these different states, so the money started drying up for the program.

The curriculum we developed on Johns Island became the curriculum that went all across the South. It was all the things the people had said they wanted to know and learn. I don't think the people on Johns Island know what an impact the program they were involved in had—how it went so far and so wide.

Mrs. Bernice Robinson
ALL THIS IS AN OUTGROWTH OF PEOPLE FEELING EMPOWERED

On Johns Island you see the results now really, the aggressiveness of the people and the confidence they had in moving forward, when you look at the sea island clinic, and you look at the senior citizen center and the nursing home and the housing project for senior citizens. All this is an outgrowth of people feeling empowered by being able to read and write and understanding how to go about pressing for things like that. They became very active in the PTA and things that they didn't bother with before because they couldn't read or they couldn't understand what was going down. Before they had a high school on the island, a lot of people who had relatives over here in the city would send the children over here to go to school, to try to get an education. And they had to do that for a long time before they got the high school.

But all these things that finally came about, came about from these same people that learned how to read and write and fight for their kids to get a decent education right in their own home rather than having to cross the bridge to come into town to get an education.

Mrs. Ethel Grimball
WE'RE GOING TO VOTE FOR THE CANDIDATES WE WANT

People are still voting today. Blacks now rule Wadmalaw Island for the Democratic party. Before this, the white people in the Democratic party brought a slate in and then they immediately passed that slate. My father and others said, "We're not going to go along with a slate that they bring in. We're going to vote for the candidates we want." And that's how we changed that situation on Wadmalaw Island. After the voter registration drives, the people got more interested in the importance of voting. Therefore, we got a lot of people on the books. Eighty-five percent of the population on Wadmalaw is black. Most of the whites left the Democratic party when the blacks got control of it. Before that the whites ruled everything on Wadmalaw Island. It was the tradition.

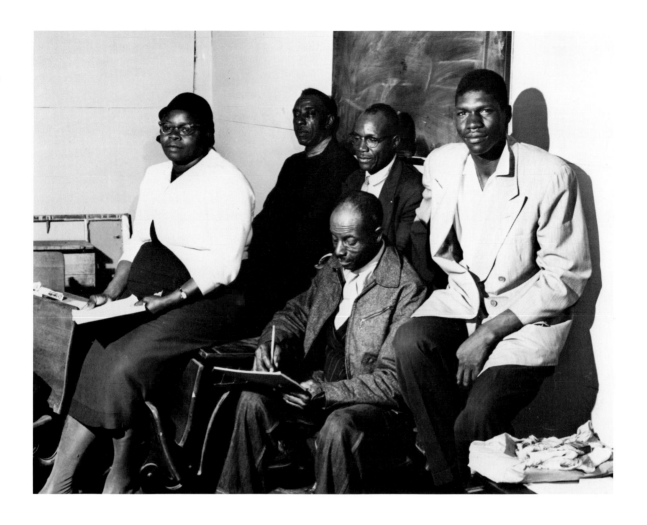

Mrs. Alice Wine
EVERYTHING IS CHANGED NOW

I still vote. I want to vote for right, but I don't get it. My mother always told me, "You see somebody that jump, you jump too. Cause you, one, can't do nothing. Among the majority, your word just go for nothing." But the people gave us our right, seems like they take our right from us. But it don't stop me from vote. I still vote for the President.

And everything is changed now. The world so tough today.

The older people sang "I Will Overcome" because they had a hard time. They had to row boat to go to the city and carry their peas and corn and potatoes, rice and things. They had a hard time, living and raising their children. Them people had to work with their children on their back. Rebeltime people were mean. But God changed those people. That's a just God. He don't walk knock-kneed. Those oldtime foreparents was something else, I tell you. And one of these days they were able to overcome. They were able to buy the land. Money was scarce, but they had a chance to pay a dollar or two dollars for a piece of ground.

Mrs. Alice Wine

I WILL OVERCOME

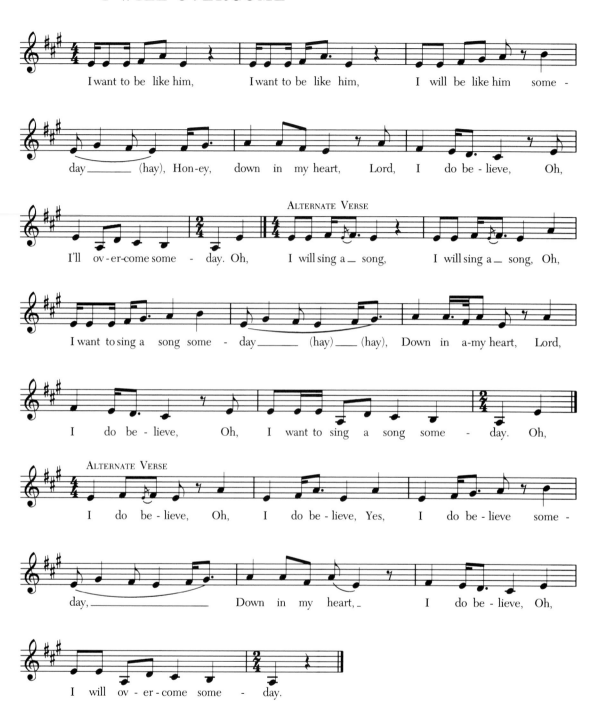

I want to be like him . . . etc.

I will sing a song . . . etc.

I want to walk like him . . . etc.

I want to pray like him . . . etc.

I'll see the king . . . etc.

Oh, I will overcome, I will overcome, I will overcome someday,
Lordy, down in my heart, I do believe, I will overcome someday.

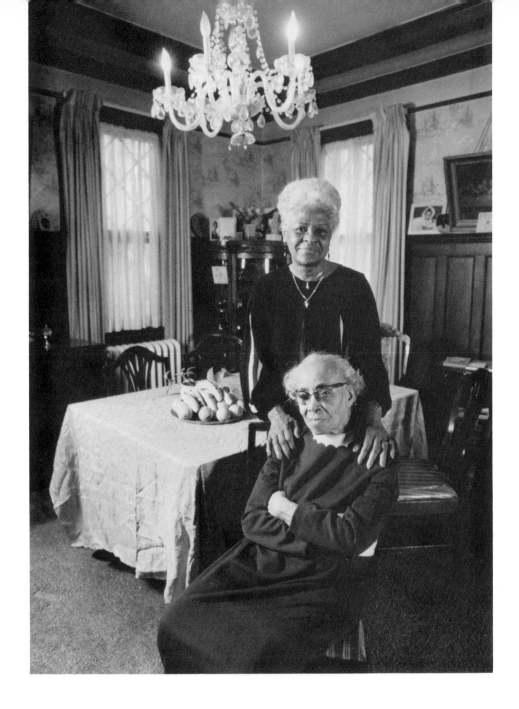

The story of how "I Will Overcome" became "We Shall Overcome" is a fascinating one, and much of the history is in the South Carolina lowcountry area. "I Will Overcome" was widely known in black churches throughout the South. The first time it was used in an organized protest situation was in Charleston in 1945, when the Food and Tobacco Workers were out on strike for five months and had a daily picket line. The striking workers, mainly black women, began to adapt the song to fit their situation. They changed the *I* to *we* and sang, "We will win our rights" and "We will organize" and "The Lord will see us through." Workers from the Charleston situation took the song to Highlander where it became the unofficial theme song for years and was carried to many other picket lines by Zilphia Horton of the Highlander staff. Pete Seeger learned it from Zilphia and began introducing it to northern gatherings and northern audiences. Guy Carawan heard it from Pete and others, and through his work at Highlander, helped pass it back into the southern freedom movement in the early 1960s. From there it went around the world.

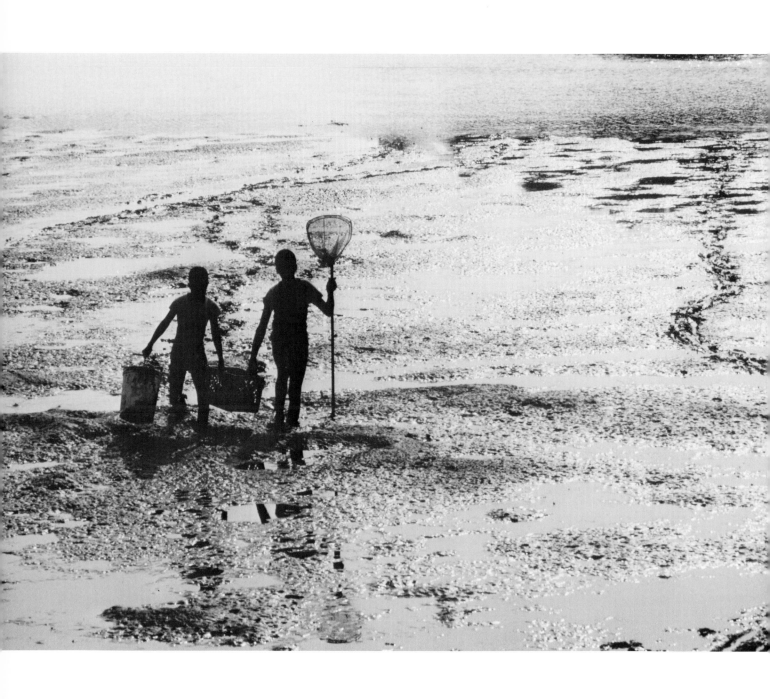

9. HONEY IN THE ROCK

PASSING ON THE CULTURAL TRADITIONS

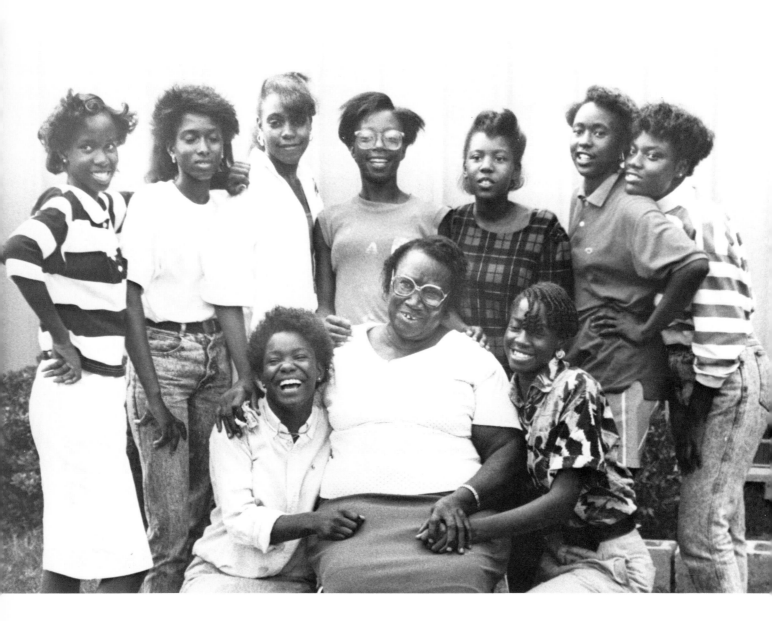

Mrs. Idell Smalls
I WANT THE YOUTH TO BE PROUD
OF WHO WE ARE AND WHERE WE'RE FROM

I was born on Yonges Island. My mother was a farm worker, my father an oyster picker. I attended elementary and high school here on the island, but my family could not afford to send me to college. Instead I worked on the farm and restaurants to help my mother raise six children. I married and lived for a time in Washington, D.C. I returned to the island for a visit and decided it was time to move home.

In 1985 I had the opportunity to go to Nairobi, Kenya. I had an experience that is hard to put into words. Being there, I could feel, smell, and relive my childhood through tradition, dialect, customs, and being able to look at my people there in Nairobi and see my family in South Carolina in their faces. On returning home I wanted to instill in the youth and adults the importance of holding onto our heritage and African customs, because not many of us will ever get to Africa to experience what I did. I wanted the youth to be proud of who we are and where we're from.

The trip helped me address some of the problems our teens were having, such as being teased about the Gullah dialect, which is a mixture of African and American speech. We began to develop a play called "In Celebration of Us." Each teen adopted a senior at the senior center and began interviewing her about her life. The teens wrote and produced the play.

We're focusing on changing images and instilling self-respect in the young adults of the sea islands through economic and cultural survival development.

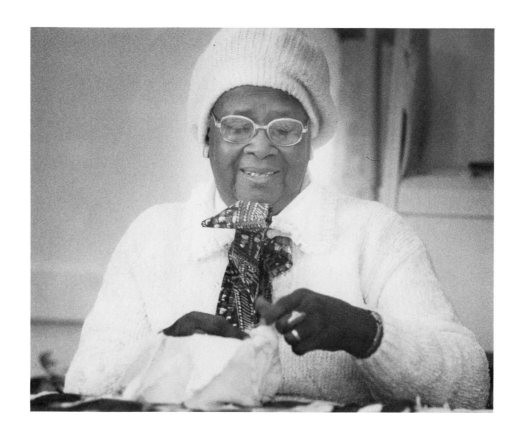

Ms. Elaine Jenkins
I GET MY STRENGTH FROM THE OLDER PEOPLE ON THESE ISLANDS

I don't know how other young people feel, but I get my strength from the older people on these islands. My mother is one of them. I like to talk to my mother and her friends. When we get together, we always go back to the old days. And those days were hard days.

The songs at Wesley, I mean the songs that the older people raise from the floor, those things do something for me. The music is a vital part of that service. There's almost a song for every feeling and mood. I can only talk about Wesley, but I don't think there's any danger of the older songs dying out there. Those songs are being passed down from the old people. Like Mrs. Hunter—Mrs. Hunter's children and her grandchildren. And then I hear them, and I'm sure other people hear them, and you write down the words.

My brother Bill has been doing a lot of videotaping and the folk don't mind. We hope to just hold onto those things and put them aside for safe-keeping for the others who'll be coming along. Talking to the older people about the old days when there was really no connection to the city, they had to be self-sufficient. I don't think any of those things will ever be lost.

Mrs. Janie Hunter
WHAT I KNOW I TRY TO TEACH MY CHILDREN

When I come up, my parents sat us down on Sunday afternoon after church and taught us stories, and their life stories—how they came up. Some of my great-grandparents came up in slavery times, and all these stories and folktales that I tell are from way back in the history of slavery times.

And what I know I try to teach my children—my seven daughters and six sons, and ninety-five grandchildren, and twenty-four great-grands, so as the generations go on, it won't die out. I think the past is very important for them to understand. We don't know what the future will bring. So maybe the future will bring back the past. There's a lot of people on this island, older than I am, they know all about the past, but they feel so embarrassed to explain about it. They figure people are going to look down on them as nothing. But I always say, "I am just what I am." And what I want my children to know that when I'm gone, my children can teach their children.

So I have over thirty head of children come to my home on Sunday afternoons and I teach them different things that it's important for them to know. They rather hear stories and folktales. I think if all the mothers would teach what they know, they would keep their children out of trouble. They would have something to build upon. They'd have something to look forward to. But to just turn them loose and not let them know what to expect, that's why children be in so much shock when things happen to them. It's our parents' task to teach our children.

The songs tell stories too—the religious songs and the blues songs. Those songs gave us a feeling to go on. That's all we had to live by. We sang and the games we played. We didn't go to piccolo or none of that—there wasn't any of that in those times. We take a tub and washboard and make our own music. On Sunday evening my father's house was full up. We sing and shout and feel good about it. We had a good time. We didn't be sick. We didn't get in no trouble. Everybody loved one another. And we still love to sing. That is our talent God bless us with. We love to sing and we love people. We love to get along with everybody. We was brought up like that.

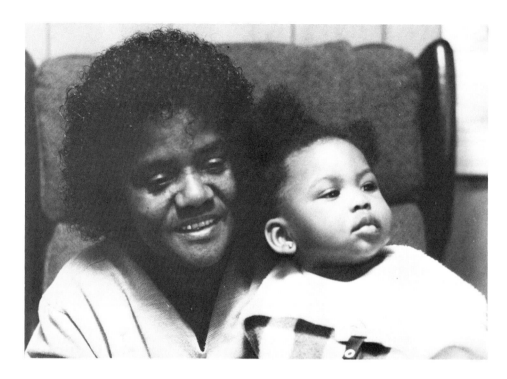

Mrs. Ruth Bligen
I LIKE TO BE ME. I DON'T LIKE TO PRETEND

At first I thought people won't want to hear this kind of song. But after I went to Atlanta, Georgia, I was very pleased. I was happy. Everybody was so nice. And I enjoyed myself. That's the first time I ever leave Johns Island to go sing.

Going off, it made me learn a lot. You see a lot of people. You enjoy yourself. People treat you so nice. They really make me feel like I'm something special. That time we went to Seabrook, my picture was in the paper. The lady I work for daughter, she get the picture. She call and say, "Tootsie, you're a celebrity. Your picture's in the paper."

You know, I like to be me. I don't like to pretend. If I go off, I'm not going to pretend that I'm somebody else. I'm going to be me! My children and grandchildren are happy. They're happy to know that their grandmommy go off and sing and picture been in the paper. So I'm happy, too. I didn't realize days past and gone that things was going to work out like that.

The best trip I had was when a busload went to Washington from Wesley Church. Rev. Goodwin went and everyone was like one big family. The bus driver took us around and showed us different places. We had a good time. On Sunday morning, we did a church service at the festival.

I really wish we could get some more programs off from here. That's something I been looking forward to. If just once a year, you just get away on some kind of program. I like to see friends I've made in different places. And when I go, I don't want to rush off. After we sing, I want to sit around and listen to other people sing.

Mrs. Janie Hunter
I FOUND OUT I HAD SOMETHING I DIDN'T KNOW I HAD MYSELF

When we started to travel, we had a lot of criticism. Everyone didn't like it, but that didn't stop me. They didn't understand. I try to let them know that when we're doing these different programs, it really establish Johns Island. We put Johns Island on the map.

And I was carrying my children since they was six and seven years old. My children hardly be bashful. They really experienced something and they learned a lot. They went to Rhode Island twice; they went to New York. And several times to the Smithsonian in Washington. They learned to face people and be what you are.

I enjoyed every bit of it. The travel taught me a lot. I saw places I wished for many years I could see. My dream did come true. When I was young I hoped I could travel and see something, and I did. I learned something in traveling that I never learned in school. You couldn't tell if we were black or white from the treatment we got. That means a lot. Treatment is what cause love.

So I feel good about it because I could show somebody something that they didn't know. Although they finished college and have education, I feel like I have something that they wanted. I found out I had something I didn't know I had myself. And that makes me feel like going on with it. And if there's anything I can do to help somebody learn something they don't know, I'll be glad to do it.

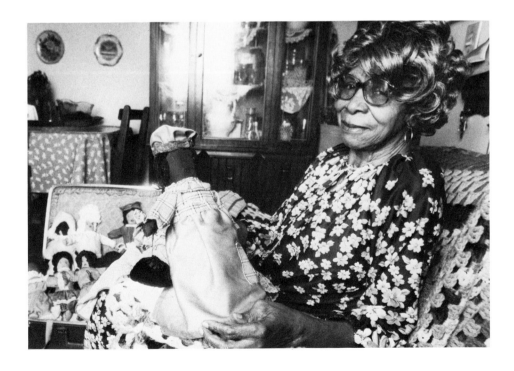

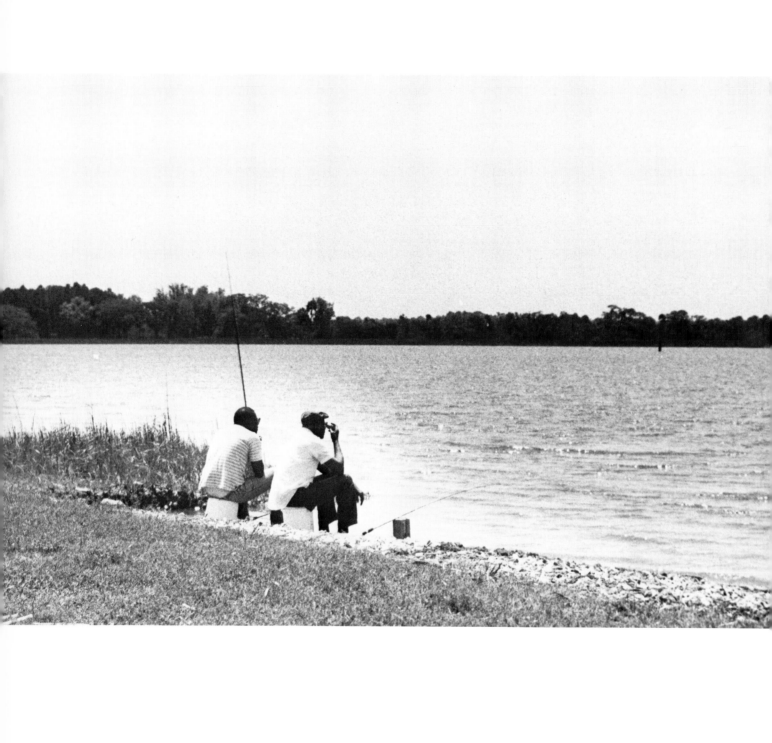

Mr. Benjamin Bligen
I FIND NO FAULT LIVING HERE
ON THE ISLAND

Johns Island is my home. I was born and raised here and it's peaceful. I've traveled across different parts of the world and I love different places, but I love Johns Island the best. There's peace and quiet here and nice places to go if you feel like travel. You can go in the river. You can go swimming if you want to. You can go fishing if you want to. You can go crabbing if you want to do that. You can go and sing and shout if you want to; no one to stop you. I find no fault living here on the island. I love it here. I make up my mind to be here until the Lord make a change in my life, to take me on home.

The singing brings joy to your soul. Regardless of how much you feel down and you feel like you can't move, you start singing one of those songs and it brings joy to your soul and lifts you up. You start thinking about the good things, and we realize we've got somebody on our side. We're trying to pass it on to the younger folks so they can carry the old traditions on. Our old folks taught us these songs and they would like for we to carry it on through and they would like for we to pass it on to the young generation so they can keep it up. And I hope that many and many that come to our different churches will hear these songs and sing these songs and will be able to carry it on when the older ones have passed on out of this world.

It's a different time now than when I was growing up. It's harder now to get the young people to come on the old side. My family had a strong religion. I try to keep on the road that they was traveling on and do the things they want me to do. Hopefully, I will be able to teach the young people the way that my old folks taught me, that they will have something that will stand by them when trouble rise. Whatever comes up against them in life they will have something to hold onto, something that will deliver them in the time of their need.

Mrs. Ruth Bligen
I LIKE TO BE ALONG WITH THE OLD PEOPLE

In church we have a lot of different choirs. But if you want to raise a song, you do that. Sometimes I'll sing. Sometimes Benji will sing. We have a good time. Our pastor is very nice. He likes singing, too. He likes singing and shouting. On Thursday nights, we have prayer meeting at the church. You express yourself and pray. It's like in the hall. The young children are not going to carry on like the old people. But I like the old people. I like to be along with the old people. And we had some wonderful times in Moving Star. I don't think the old songs will die out. We still sing it. I love the old songs.

Mr. William Saunders
IT'S THE PLACE WHERE PEOPLE SINK OR SWIM

I feel I am more fortunate than most of the people who are fighting in the arena I'm fighting in because I have a way to recharge my batteries. The religious aspect of my life is pretty real to me. It gives me a lot of strength. Wesley has been my power base. It has made me feel capable of doing anything.

It's real to me. The singing of a person like Ruth Bligen. To hear her some Sunday morning. Her voice is purer now than it's ever been. She just gets to the place that she passes out. Just knowing what she's been through, when she sings it's not a performance. You can see Benji on a Sunday morning. He's so articulate and his Gullah becomes more profound than most people because he says it so distinctly. But to see him pray and he gets to a point where he's got to stop, and somebody's got to go and take him down because of his problems.

It's the place where people sink or swim. And it's the only thing they have to turn to. And yet they're always walking with their heads held high. And that's a strength that the people had on the island that I believe is dying. That strength and the proudness is not there anymore like it used to be. Sometimes you skip a generation, for whatever reason. So maybe the cycle will come back again.

But it's a base for me. It's my power source. I come back to the city, where I can go for another six days with all of the adversities that face me.

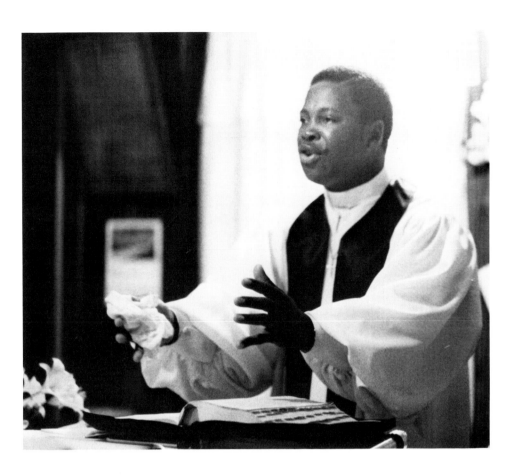

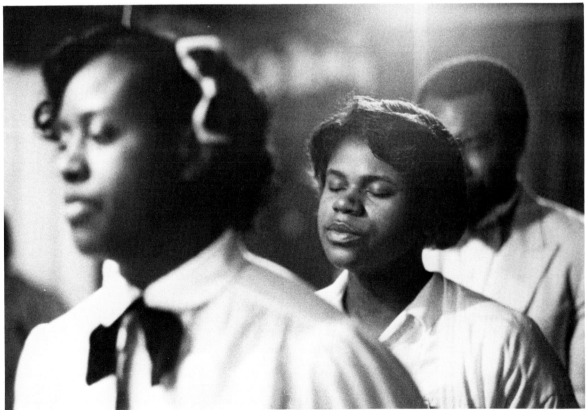

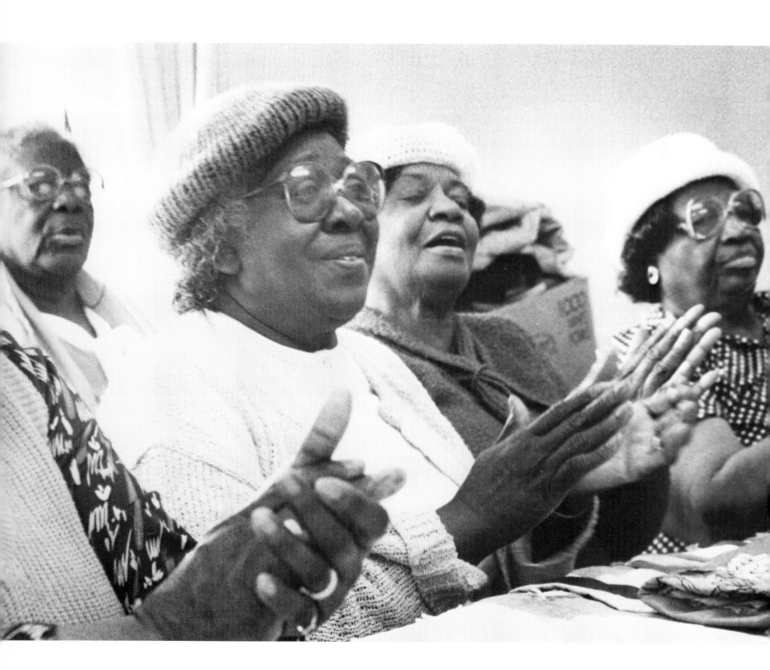

Rev. A. C. Jenkins
ANY MINISTER WHO DOESN'T TAP INTO THOSE DEEP FEELINGS WILL NOT SURVIVE HERE

I want to bring a world view into the church—a view that includes justice and liberation in Latin America and in South Africa. My challenge is to make it real to the people on Johns Island, and if it is real for them, they want to shout about it. The way I can touch those feelings is to end my sermon with the words to one of the old songs.

Any minister who doesn't tap into those deep feelings will not survive here. The people will go elsewhere. I love serving on Johns Island. Before I was here I was at an elite church in Charleston. Amens were few due to a different worship experience.

Mr. Gerald Mackey
I TAKE MY TAPE RECORDER TO CHURCH EVERY SUNDAY

I enjoy the older people. I'm always around them, and I talk with them often. I enjoy the singing. In fact I take my tape recorder to church every Sunday, hoping for one of the old spirituals raised from the floor. Then I play them all through the week on my stereo here or in my car. It's very uplifting. I don't miss any opportunity I get to hear the older people sing. To me, that's pride. I really enjoy listening to them and I think it's great that they have managed to preserve that aspect of our history.

I'm afraid that eventually after all these people are gone that the younger people will not feel as comfortable carrying on. I wish it wouldn't happen, though.

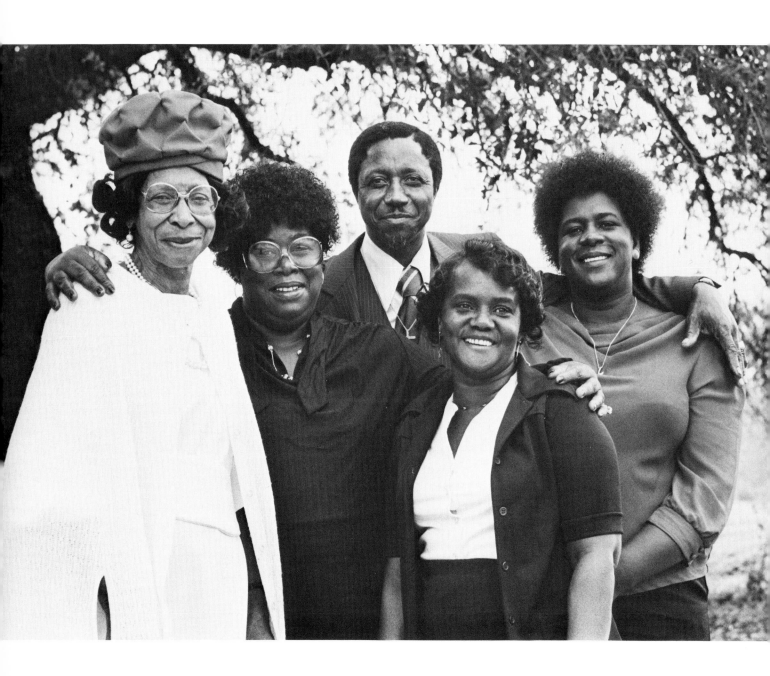

Mrs. Alice Wine
A LOT OF PEOPLE MISS IT

We don't have class meeting in the hall anymore. I miss it. We don't have it now because all these young preachers have everything to the church. What are a few people going to do in a big old church like that? If the people turn out, it never be too large. I like to go to the hall cause you can have your way. You can exercise better. You can feel yourself. You can do the same thing in the church, but the church so big.

We used to have watch meeting on Christmas night. We turn out in the hall and be there until sunrise. On New Year's, people go all night and be there til New Year roll in. We pray and sing until New Year roll in, then they go to preaching. And about five or six o'clock, then the ladies take over to testify. You don't find that now. Some people can't even say their prayers.

A lot of people miss it. These people is too funny. I can't figure how people could change so fast. Everybody go down to the church. They have watch meeting there, but they don't go but half the night. The hall go until day broad clean. Sometime people shout there until eight or nine o'clock in the morning. We have crowd from all different place—Wadmalaw and Mt. Pleasant and James Island. Ooh man, that hall is packed.

It's too dangerous now to walk to the hall at night. You don't find nobody walking this road no more. It's not the cars only, people do wicked. People will kill you and knock you down and do all kind of thing with you, no, no. When you see my door shut, it's shut. I don't come out.

The people don't have no old songs now, the people have new songs. And I don't know one of them. When they start to sing, I just shut my mouth. Nothing but new songs now. Ain't got a taste to it. Ain't got a spirit in it. But when the old people used to start to sing those old songs, and it's time to go to church, man, you run.

Mr. William Saunders
I LIKE THE HISTORY OF IT, AND TO KNOW
THAT I HAVE BEEN A PART OF IT

You might take the position that people who live in the culture recognize it as something real great. Most of the time people from outside recognize it a whole lot more than the people that live it everyday. You're talking about people who have done a lot of hard work and been through a lot of hell. But if you can come in and see it, it's so nice and quaint. "I just love to see the quaint little way that they talk," and so on. Folk don't see themselves in that way. Many folk have tried to get rid of that culture that you're talking about.

I don't miss being in Moving Star Hall at all. The way that I like to miss Moving Star Hall and some of the things of the past is to reminisce. But I would not like to be back in it. I like the history of it, and to know that I have been a part of it. I do miss that tradition when Moving Star and all the lodges used to come together on Labor Day. That was a festive time with food and a parade. They used to play flute and drums. That was really exciting.

At certain ages we used to go to Moving Star Hall, and the young people would stand outside and burn tires until almost time for them to have whatever they're going to eat and then you're going to go inside. That's the part that really used to be nice because guys would be talking so much jokes, those stories about the monkey and the baboon; people doing the dozens.

People probably do miss things like the Hall, but there is a lot of community concern and coming together still going on. I still have certain places on the island where I will go on a Thursday or a Friday night, and I'll just slip in and catch up on everything that has gone on. You just sit and all the information passes on. There's a kind of camaraderie that comes out of that.

I always believe that things just move to other levels. Another generation takes it to another level.

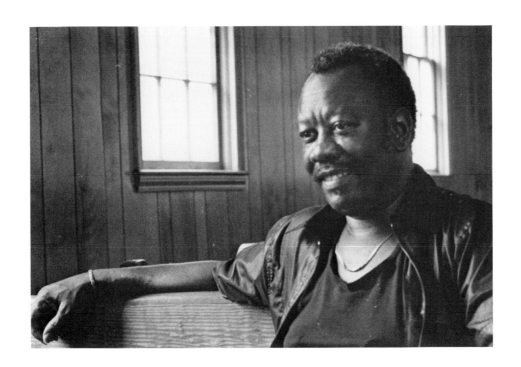

Mr. William Saunders
CULTURE IS AN INBRED THING, BUT IT NEEDS TO BE FED

I think the culture has a better chance to survive if you have some control over it. That has been my dream to try to make sure people have an economic base, and then you can go back, then you can sit around and talk about parents and grandparents. But if somebody is sitting around hungry and you're gonna tell them about some damn culture, it don't make any American sense.

So what it is that some of us have been about is you can upgrade peoples' health care, you can upgrade their housing, if you can upgrade their education, then they themselves begin to look at their own history, because they have some leisure time to look at it.

Culture is an inbred thing, it's in there, but it needs to be fed. The best way to feed it is to make sure you got some of the basic necessities to survive.

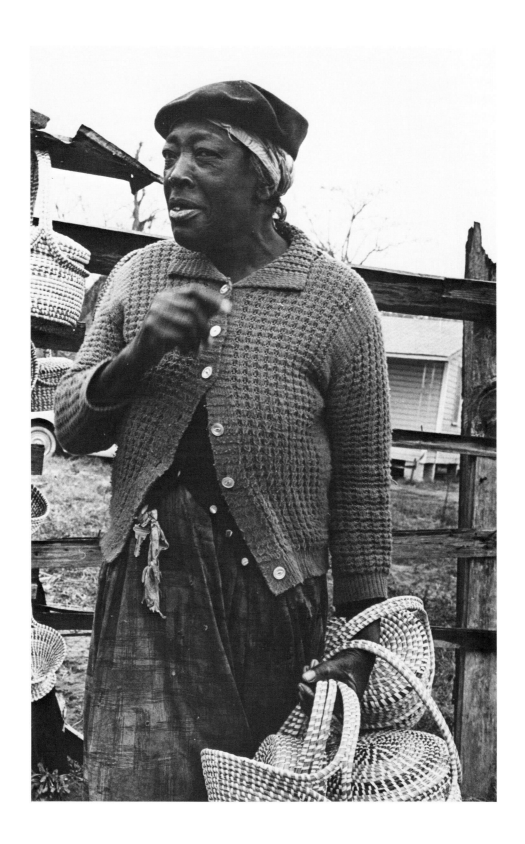

Mr. William Saunders
THE CULTURAL THING IS SOMETHING THAT CAN ALWAYS GO ON

When we had the festivals on Johns Island back in the sixties with the folk from Moving Star Hall, the Georgia sea islands, and the young freedom singers, nothing was happening in isolation. It was a time in history when a lot was going on—voter registration, awareness, blacks were about being black. Everything fit in, and the festival was like the tape that brings a lot of things together. It really kept people's spirits up, and that is what was needed at that particular time. We needed to draw on each other. The religious aspect of it was key. Most of the white community around here really don't understand the strength of something like that.

For instance, the Hospital Workers' strike just grew out of that whole thing. The same singing went on in all the things we were organizing. It never changed. It stayed the same. The song is sung according to the mood of the people that day. And very rarely the same words are used. The tempo is different depending on whether it's sad or happy. You cannot really capture that.

I think the festivals we did were really a benefit and a strength to the community itself. It was the only legitimate place that blacks and whites could get together. Everybody enjoyed themselves and it was part of our expression for that time. It would not be workable today, because all of those things are not in place anymore. You would have to have a different reason.

Now you would have it based on culture. If it were to be more than that, that thrust would have to be defined. When we did it back in the sixties, the political thrust was already there. We knew exactly who our enemy was. We didn't have any question about what was right and what was wrong.

But the cultural thing is something that can always go on. And there are so many young people that have been left out of that era. So if you do it from a historical perspective, it's workable.

Mrs. Janie Hunter
WE HAVE TO KEEP IT ALIVE

I want to see my children go on, as long as people want to hear them and they've got the voice. It means a lot to me and it means a lot to them. If they stop, it's going down. We have to keep it alive.

You've got to talk and give people an understanding about what you're talking about—the background and where it came from. That's very important. The young people don't know many of the things that happened. It takes somebody who came out of this experience to teach them and tell them the meaning of it and what it can do for them. I have the experience 'cause that's all I was doing my whole life. My parents and grandparents talked all about how they came up, and I took it in.

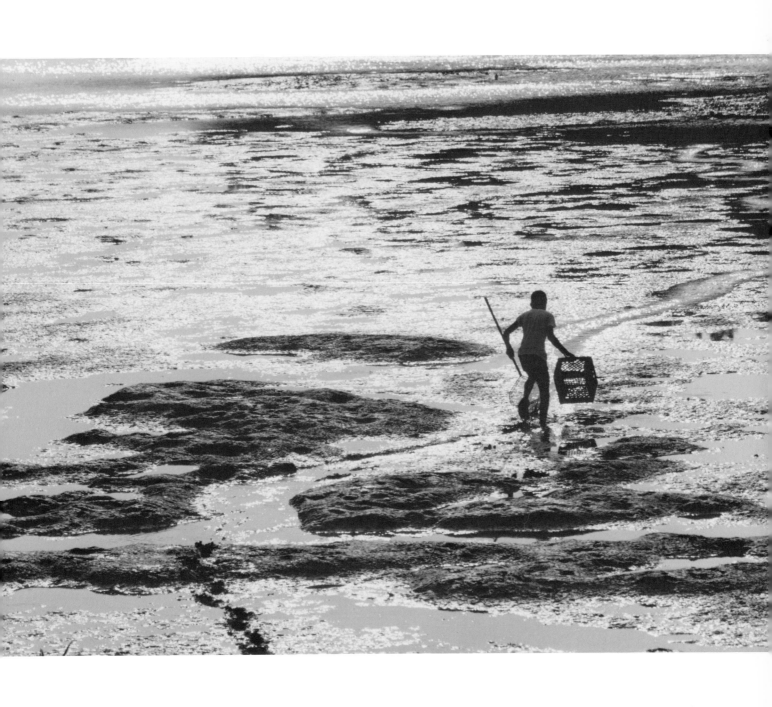

Mrs. Alice Wine
HONEY IN THE ROCK

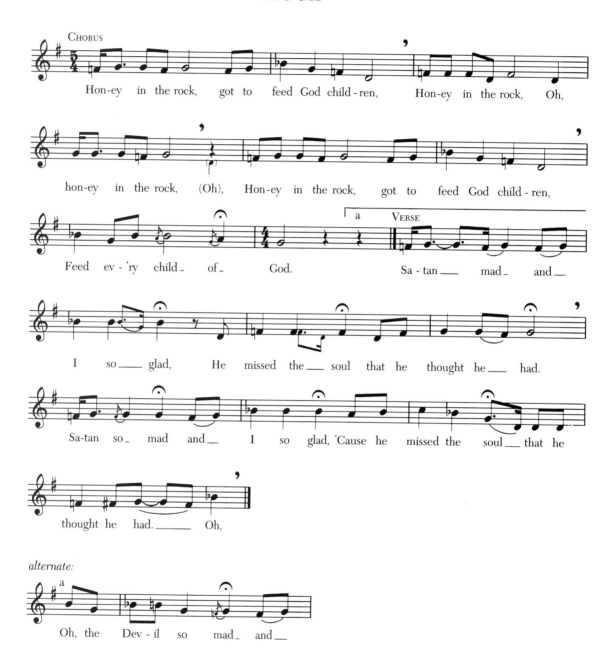

Hon-ey in the rock, got to feed God child-ren, Hon-ey in the rock, Oh,

hon-ey in the rock, (Oh), Hon-ey in the rock, got to feed God child-ren,

Feed ev-'ry child_ of_ God. Sa-tan ___ mad_ and ___

I so ___ glad, He missed the ___ soul that he thought he ___ had.

Sa-tan so_ mad and ___ I so glad, 'Cause he missed the soul ___ that he

thought he had. _____ Oh,

alternate:

Oh, the Dev-il so mad_ and ___

(CHORUS)
Honey in the rock, got to feed God children,
Honey in the rock, honey in the rock,
Honey in the rock, got to feed God children,
Feed every child of God.

Satan mad and I so glad,
He missed the soul that he thought he had.
Oh, the Devil so mad and I so glad,
He missed the soul that he thought he had.

(CHORUS)

Oh, 'member, hush little baby don't you cry,
You know that your mother is born to die.
Oh, 'member, hush little baby don't you cry,
You know that your mother is born to die.

(CHORUS)

Oh, children, one of these mornings I was walking 'long,
I saw the grapes was a-hanging down,
Lord, I pick a bunch and I suck the juice,
It's the sweetest grape that I ever taste.

(CHORUS)
Oh, honey in the rock, got to feed God children,
Honey in the rock, honey in the rock,
Honey in the rock, got to feed God children,
Feed every child of God.

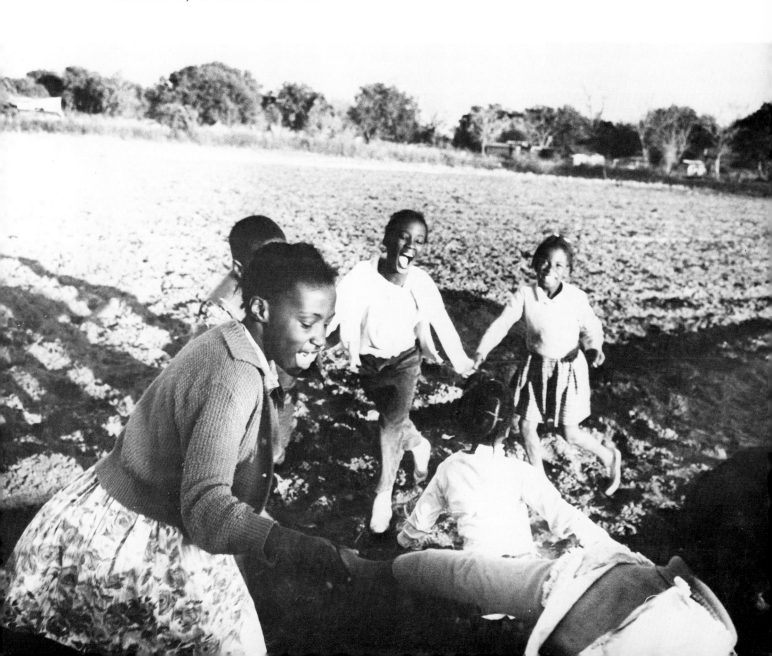

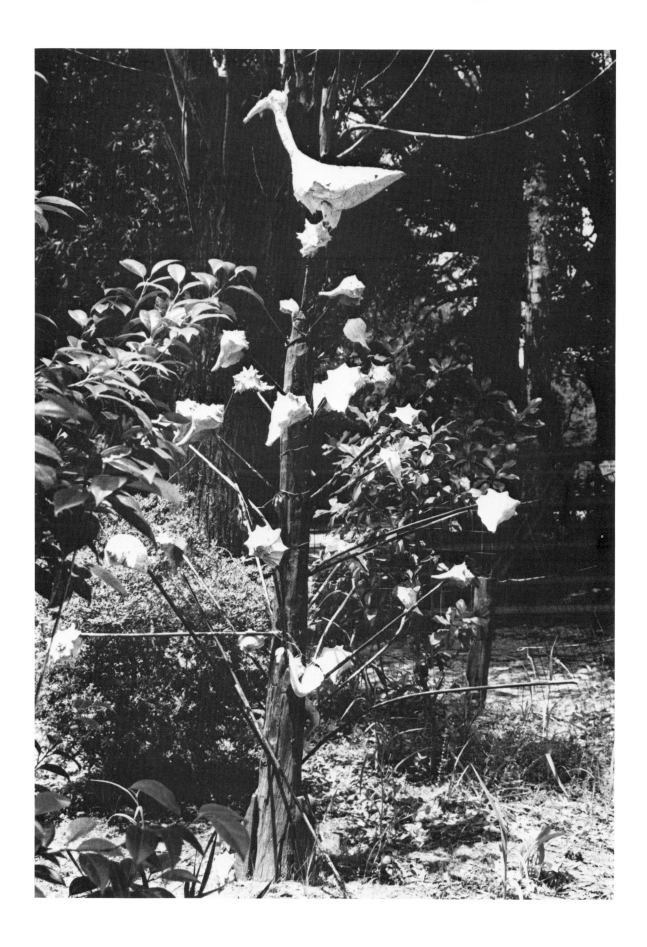

AFTERWORD

In 1961 I was one of the students driven from Albany, Georgia, to Dorchester Center in McIntosh, Georgia, for the first Citizenship Education Training School operated by the Southern Christian Leadership Conference. Andrew Young had come to Albany to describe the program, which was based on the one Septima Clark, Bernice Robinson, and Esau Jenkins had initiated on Johns Island. Many of us who made up the first class had been suspended from Albany State College for participating in demonstrations and getting arrested. The demonstrations were in support of students who had been arrested after they attempted to buy tickets from the "white only" window of the Trailways bus depot. The demonstrations and increasing arrests quickly developed into a full-blown local movement. The idea of becoming trained to run schools to teach people to register and vote seemed a worthwhile activity to us and to the leaders of the local movement.

When we arrived at Dorchester, we met our teachers—Dorothy Cotton, who came from Petersburg, Virginia, to work with SCLC; Septima Clark, who lost her job as a teacher in Charleston because of her membership in the NAACP and her work with Highlander; and Bernice Robinson, who was the first teacher of the citizenship school on Johns Island. In the classes at Dorchester we learned about the political structure of our communities as well as how to teach people to read and write. At that time I had never heard of precinct meetings and knew nothing about the local and state party systems, even though I had done well in my civics and government classes in school. But those classes had nothing to do with what I knew about Georgia. The classes that Septima Clark, Bernice Robinson, and Dorothy Cotton taught were eye-openers to a new way of looking at our community. For the next ten years, the citizenship school program trained grass roots leaders as they rose to action in the growing civil rights movement throughout the South.

At Dorchester, Cordell Reagon, a SNCC field secretary and native of the Nashville sit-ins, brought some of us together and told us that a white folk singer was coming to lead us in songs. I was also told that, though he might sound different, we were not to laugh when he sang because he was a true friend of the movement and had been tested and tried during the sit-ins in Nashville. Well, the singer was Guy Carawan, who immediately pulled out his guitar and began to play and sing. I remember hearing for the first time songs such as "Where Have All the Flowers Gone?," "Wasn't That a Time!," and hearing the name of Pete Seeger and the Weavers. I remember experiencing no feelings for the soft, flowing ballad style of "Flowers." But when Guy sang "Ol' Blue," he hit familiar territory. None of us had heard the song, but we could feel the story. We requested it over and over again.

Guy spent the rest of the week with us and accompanied us on our freedom songs. He later showed up again and again in mass meetings all over the South and asked me to help him organize several workshops that brought songleaders from the movement together with traditional singers such as Doc Reese from Texas and the Georgia Sea Island Singers from St. Simons Island with singers and song organizers from the topical and folk song revival from the North. Len Chandler, Alan Lomax, Theo Bikel, Phil Ochs, and Tom Paxton were new names we learned during this time.

Then in December 1964 Guy and his wife, Candie, invited us, the Freedom Singers from Atlanta, to a festival on Johns Island. There we met Esau Jenkins, who took us to the Progressive Club and a singing. The Georgia Sea Island Singers were there and I heard the Moving Star Hall Singers for the first time. I had never heard or seen this song style before. Led by Janie Hunter and Benjamin Bligen, the singing sounded ancient and the shouting and rhythms more complex than anything I had ever attempted myself.

I will never forget the waves of sounds sweeping into each response after a call by Benjie, or

Mrs. Hunter, or Ruth Bligen. Benjie would call, "Oh, see God's ark," and everybody would respond, "See God ark . . . Tell me how long . . . See God ark a moving." Every note had a wave to it, a curve of sound loaded with vocal power and emotion. Ruth Bligen always carried the high line and the sound of her singing reached you first, pulling the other, lower lines with her. When the chorus ended, the rhythm changed. What had been double rhythm format moved into three cross times. People rose to their feet, and their feet moved in one time, their hands crossed their foot pattern, and the melody operated at a more intense level on top of, or driven by, this multi-rhythmic activity.

Since that first visit I have returned to the island many times to work with Mrs. Hunter and also with Septima Clark and William Saunders, always guided by the work that began with Esau Jenkins' efforts to transform the lives of people of his home community and the cultural research of Guy and Candie Carawan, which went far beyond field collecting. In 1972 I returned to the island for the funeral of Esau Jenkins. I returned also to interview Mrs. Hunter, Septima Clark, and later the tobacco workers who had used "We Shall Overcome" in their union meetings and on the picket lines. On the island it was sung in their traditional song style, complete with the shout and as "I Will Overcome." While working on the Bicentennial Festival of American Folklife at the Smithsonian, I worked with Rev. Willis Goodwin to bring a congregation and a prayer band from Johns and Yonges islands to the festival during the summer of 1975.

THE WORK of Esau Jenkins lives. The work of Septima Clark lives. You can see it in the health centers. You can see it in Bill Saunders' political work and the rise in the number of registered voters. You can see it in the development of Bernice Robinson as a leader, teacher, and candidate for office. Maybe Ethel Grimball is exactly what the school board needs; maybe she is the work of Septima Clark in the eighties and nineties. Today Gerald Mackey's description of teaching in the school system is reminiscent of Septima Clark's struggles with that same system years ago.

Today Mrs. Russell talks about not being able to visit her old crabbing spot; she is kept from her homeplace by guards and gates. Ms. Elaine Jenkins straddles the old and new ways trying to show people how not to lose their land. Bill Saunders talks about development and change in a way that is based on his dreams for the indigenous people of the island community; the new developers, on the contrary, want to keep the people off the new vacation spots unless they are employed there, usually in menial jobs.

Today's Sea Island Comprehensive Health Care Corporation grew out of the Rural Mission, Inc., and the Progressive Club, begun by Esau Jenkins and nurtured by those who struggled with him to bring about change. Their efforts gave much to the local community and to the larger movement. This was the home of the first citizenship education class; "Keep Your Eyes on the Prize, Hold On" passed from Alice Wine to Guy Carawan to the Nashville sit-ins to movement communities throughout the South.

To walk through this book again is to walk through time. The first edition of the book introduced us to the old songs and the Moving Star Hall and its worship tradition. It described the islanders' yearnings and planning for change. The Carawans were beginning to share the music and culture of this community through folk festivals and programs throughout the nation. In this first book one feels the storm of change in the sound of a unique nineteenth-century black American voice.

And now we have this new edition of the book loaded with some of the same voices speaking through yet another decade; and we see and hear the voices and concerns of the children who walk and seek to extend their roads. We see the outsiders with intentions that have nothing to do with the survival of the communities they found as they moved into the islands. The questions and fears are for the youth and their future. Their voices are heard only as whispers in the minds and hearts of their parents. The questions are: Will they continue? And how and where and what of this rich legacy will they harvest to pass on?

Bernice Johnson Reagon

BIBLIOGRAPHY

In the 1966 edition of this book we gave a short list of books and albums for additional information on the sea islands. By now there are so many valuable writings, albums, films, tapes that it would be difficult to give a comprehensive list. We recommend the following sources and make note that many of the books listed have a much more complete bibliography.

OLDER SOURCES

Allen, William F., Charles P. Ware, and Lucy M. Garrison, eds. *Slave Songs of the United States.* New York: A. Simpson and Co., 1867; Freeport, New York, Reprinted Books for Library Press, 1971.

Ballanta-Taylor, N. G. J. *St. Helena Island Spirituals.* New York: Schirmer, 1925.

Georgia Writers' Project, Savannah Unit. *Drums and Shadows: Survival Studies Among the Georgia Coastal Negroes.* 1940. Reprint. Athens: University of Georgia Press, 1986.

Gordon, R. W. Chapter in *The Carolina Low Country,* compiled by the Society for the Preservation of Spirituals. New York: Macmillan, 1931.

Herskovits, Melville J. *The Myth of the Negro Past.* 1941. Reprint. Boston: Beacon Press, 1964.

Higginson, Thomas Wentworth. *Army Life in a Black Regiment.* 1869. Reprint. Boston: Beacon Press, 1962.

Johnson, Guion G. *A Social History of the Sea Islands.* Chapel Hill: University of North Carolina Press, 1930.

Johnson, Guy B. *Folk Culture on St. Helena Island, South Carolina.* Chapel Hill: University of North Carolina Press, 1930.

Parrish, Lydia. *Slave Songs of the Georgia Sea Islands.* 1942. Reprint. Hatboro, Pennsylvania, 1965.

Parsons, Elsie Clews. *Folklore of the Sea Islands, South Carolina.* New York: American Folklore Society, 1923.

Turner, Lorenzo D. *Africanisms in the Gullah Dialect.* 1949. Reprint. Arno Press and New York Times Press, 1969.

MORE RECENT SOURCES

Blockson, Charles L. "Sea Change in the Sea Islands: 'No Where to Lay Down Weary Head.'" *National Geographic,* December 1987. Photographs by Karen Kasmauski.

Carawan, Guy. "Christmas Eve Watch on Johns Island." In *Sea Island Roots: Studies in African Cultural Continuities in Georgia and South Carolina,* edited by Mary Twining and Keith Baird. Trenton: Africa World Press, 1988.

———. "The Living Heritage of the Sea Islands." *Sing Out Magazine,* Vol. 14, no. 2 (1964).

Carawan, Guy and Candie. "Keep Your Eyes on the Prize: Cultural Work in the Sea Islands." *Sing Out Magazine,* Vol. 31, no. 4 (1985).

Creel, Margaret. *A Peculiar People: Slave Religion and Community—Culture Among the Gullahs.* New York: New York University Press, 1988.

Dabbs, E. M. *Face of an Island.* New York: Grossman, 1971.

Daise, Ron. *Reminiscences of Sea Island Heritage: Legacy of Freedmen on St. Helena Island.* Orangeburg, South Carolina: Sandlapper Press, 1986.

Day, Gregory. *South Carolina Low Country Coil Baskets* (brochure). Charleston: Communication Center, 1977.

Harris, Ron. "The Gullahs: An Upside-Down World, Development Displaces Native Islanders." *Los Angeles Times,* August 28, 1988.

Highlander Center. *Cultural Activity in the Sea Islands,* Highlander Reports. New Market, Tennessee: November 1984.

Institute for Southern Studies. *Southern Exposure: Coastal Affair.* Durham, North Carolina: May–June 1982. Issue devoted to the sea islands.

Journal of Black Studies, Sage Publications. Vol. 10, no. 4 (June 1980). Issue devoted to the sea islands.

Jones, Bessie, and Bess Lomax Hawes, *Step It Down.* 1972. Reprint. Athens: University of Georgia Press, 1987.

Jones-Jackson, Patricia. *When Roots Die: Endangered Traditions on the Sea Islands.* Athens: University of Georgia Press, 1987.

Joyner, Charles. *Down by the Riverside: A South Carolina Slave Community.* Urbana: University of Illinois Press, 1984.

Lindsay, Nick. *The Life and Times of Bubberson Brown: An Oral History of Edisto Island.* Goshen, Indiana: Pinchpenny Press, 1977.

———. *Sam Gadsden Tells the Story: An Oral History of Edisto Island.* Goshen, Indiana: Pinchpenny Press, 1975.

Littlefield, Daniel C. *Rice and Slaves: Ethnicity and the Slave Trade in Colonial South Carolina.* Baton Rouge: Louisiana State University Press, 1981.

Lomax, Alan. Description of sea island festivals, *News and Courier,* Charleston, January 19, 1964.

———. *Folksongs of North America.* New York: Doubleday, 1960.

———. *Folk Song Style and Culture.* Washington, D.C.: American Association for the Advancement of Science, 1968.

Nichols, Patricia. "Linguistic Change in Gullah: Sex, Age, and Mobility," Ph.D. dissertation, Stanford University, 1976.

Raboteau, Albert J. *Slave Religion: The "Invisible Institution" in the Antebellum South.* New York: Oxford University Press, 1978.

Rosengarten, Dale. *Row upon Row: Sea Grass Baskets of the South Carolina Lowcountry.* Columbia: McKissick Museum, University of South Carolina, 1986.

Rosengarten, Theodore. *Tombee: Portrait of a Cotton Planter, with the Journal of Thomas B. Chaplin (1822–1890).* New York: William Morrow and Co., 1986.

Rozin, Skip, and Salvatore Catalano. "Time Catches Up with a Special Island" (Daufuskie Island, S.C.). *Audubon,* September 1981.

Saunders, William. "Sea Islands: Then and Now." *Journal of Black Studies* (June 1980).

Stewart, William. *Continuity and Change in American Negro Dialects.* Florida FL Reporter, 1968.

———. *Sociolinguistic Factors in the History of American Negro Dialects.* Florida FL Reporter, 1967.

Stuckey, Sterling. *Slave Culture: Nationalist Theory and the Foundations of Black America.* New York: Oxford University Press, 1987.

Twining, Mary. "Sources in the Folklore and Folklife of the Sea Islands." *Southern Folklore Quarterly* (1975).

Twining, Mary, and Keith Baird. "Introduction to Sea Island Folklife." *Journal of Black Studies* (June 1980).

———. *Sea Island Roots: Studies in African Cultural Continuities in Georgia and South Carolina.* Trenton, New Jersey: Africa World Press, 1988.

Vlach, John M. *The Afro-American Tradition in Decorative Arts.* Cleveland: Cleveland Museum of Art, 1978.

Wood, Peter H. *Black Majority: Negroes in Colonial South Carolina from 1690 Through the Stono Rebellion.* New York: Alfred A. Knopf, 1974.

SOURCES ON CITIZENSHIP EDUCATION

Clark, Septima. *Ready from Within: Septima Clark and the Civil Rights Movement.* Edited by Cynthia Brown. Navarro, California: Wild Tree Press, 1986.

Oldendorf, Sandra. "Highlander Folk School and the South Carolina Sea Island Citizenship Schools: Implications for the Social Studies." Ph.D. dissertation, University of Kentucky, 1987.

Tjerandsen, Carl. *Education for Citizenship: A Foundation's Experience.* Santa Cruz, California: Emil Schwarzhaupt Foundation, Inc., 1980.

Urban Health. *South Carolina Islands: Bringing Comprehensive Health Care to a Rural Setting.* December 1976.

ALBUMS

Folkways Records

Been in the Storm So Long: Spirituals and Shouts and Children's Games (Johns Island), FS 3842. [FS 3841 and 3842 available with accompanying booklets on real time cassettes from the Office of Folklife Programs, Smithsonian Institution, 955 L'Enfant Plaza, Suite 2600, Washington, DC 20560. Phone (202) 287-3262.]

Been in the Storm So Long: Spirituals and Shouts, Folktales and Children's Songs, FS 40031. [Available on CD, cassette, or LP from Rounder Records, 1 Camp Street, Cambridge, MA 02140.]

Johns Island: Its People and Songs, FS 3840.

McIntosh County Shouters: Slave Shout Songs from the Coast of Georgia, FS 4344.

Moving Star Hall Singers and Alan Lomax: Sea Island Folk Festival, FS 3841. [Available from Smithsonian Institution, see above.]

New World Records

Georgia Sea Island Songs, notes by Alan Lomax, NW 278.

Rounder Records

So Glad I'm Here, Bessie Jones, RR 2015.

Step It Down: Games for Children by Bessie Jones, RR 8004.

Cassette Tapes

I'm On My Way, tape by Doug and Frankie Quimby, new generation of Georgia sea island singers.

FILMS AND VIDEOTAPES

You Got to Move. Film produced by Lucy Phenix. New Market, Tenn.: Highlander Film Project, 1985.

We Shall Overcome. New York: Ginger Projections, 1988. Film giving the history of the song with segments on Johns Island and Charleston.

Yonder Come Day. Capital City Film Studios, 1976. Film of Bessie Jones and the community at St. Simons, Georgia.

Everything Change Up Now: A View of the South Carolina Sea Islands. Film produced by Gretchen Robinson. Columbia, South Carolina: South Carolina Committee for the Humanities.

Gullah Tides. Film contrasting Johns Island with Sapelo Island, Georgia. Produced by Louise Cox. Forthcoming in 1989.

Gullah Tales. Film produced by Gary Moss. Atlanta: Georgia State University, Department of Media Education, 1987.

Tales of the Unknown South. Videotapes. Part 1: *Half-pint Flask*; part 2: *Ashes*. Columbia: South Carolina Educational Television, 1986.

Northstate Public Video, Durham, North Carolina. All of the following videotapes were produced by Peter Wood and Richard Ward: *The Strength of These Arms: Black Labor—White Rice*, 1987; *Honoring the Ancestors*, 1986; *The Afro-American Tradition in Decorative Arts*, 1987; *Hand-made: Conversations About African-American Art and Artists*, 1986.

PBS DOCUMENTARIES

The Story of English, segment on Black English. New York: Lehr Productions, 1986.

The Africans, segment on Africanisms in the sea islands. 1985.

MATERIALS AT AVERY INSTITUTE

A Charge to Keep We Have, photograph exhibition.

Esau Jenkins papers and exhibit.

Field recordings made on Johns Island by Guy and Candie Carawan, 1963–65.

Photographs taken by Robert Yellin on Johns Island, 1965.

PHOTOGRAPH IDENTIFICATIONS AND CREDITS

All photographs through page 171 appeared in the 1966 edition of *Ain't You Got a Right to the Tree of Life?* and are by Robert Yellin.

Title page: Mr. Willie Hunter, Jr.
Page xxii: Mr. Joe Deas
Page 2: Mrs. Betsy Pinckney
Page 5: Mrs. Rosa Mack
Page 6: Mrs. Hester Green and Mr. Sweet
Page 12: Mrs. Belle Green
Page 19: Mrs. Isabel Simmons
Page 20: Mrs. Mary Wright, Mrs. Rena Johnson, and Mrs. Rosanne Richardson
Page 23: Mrs. Rena Johnson
Page 24: Mrs. Betsy Pinckney
Page 26: Mrs. Rosa Mack
Pages 29, 32: Mrs. Belle Green
Page 36: Mr. Willie Hunter
Page 37: Mrs. Julia Michael
Page 39: Mrs. Isabel Simmons
Page 42: Mr. Joe Deas
Page 44: Mrs. Isabel Simmons
Pages 46–47: Mr. Benjamin Bligen
Page 49: Mr. Eli Smith (top); Mr. Benjamin Bligen (bottom)
Pages 50–51: Mr. Willie Hunter
Page 52: Mrs. Janie Hunter with sons Johnny and David
Page 53: Mrs. Janie Hunter's son and grandsons
Page 55: Mr. James Mackey with grandson Leonard
Page 56: Mrs. Mary Pinckney, Mrs. Loretta Stanley with daughters
Page 57: Quintelle Hunter
Page 58: Arthur Jenkins
Page 59: Yvonne Hunter
Page 60: Mr. Willie Hunter and Mrs. Janie Hunter with family
Page 62: Mr. Willie Hunter with grandson Lennit
Page 66: Mr. John Smalls
Page 69: Mrs. Bertha Smith and Mrs. Mary Pinckney
Pages 70, 72–73: Mrs. Mary Deas
Page 74: Mrs. Mary Buncomb and Mrs. Viola Jenkins
Page 80: Mrs. Amanda Robinson
Page 82: Mr. Lee Pinckney
Page 84: Mary Buncomb, Viola Jenkins
Page 85: Mr. Willie Smith, Mrs. Bertha Wine, and Mr. Lee Pinckney

Page 88: Mr. Benjamin Bligen and Mrs. Isabel Simmons
Page 91: Mrs. Ruth Bligen
Pages 94–95: Mrs. Bertha Smith and Mrs. Isabel Simmons
Page 97: Daughter of Mr. and Mrs. Anderson Mack
Page 107: Mrs. Rose Smiley
Page 110: Miss Carol Bligen
Pages 112, 115–16: Hunter and Pinckney family children
Page 120: Mr. Joe Deas
Page 123: Mrs. Betsy Pinckney
Page 125: Mrs. Ida Walker Deas
Page 127: Mrs. Belle Green
Page 129: Mr. Lee Pinckney
Page 130: Miss Ruth Pinckney and Miss Louise Jenkins
Page 133: Michael Brown, Abraham Brown, Lee Pinckney, Frank Williams
Page 136: Mrs. Alice Wine
Pages 140, 142: Mr. Esau Jenkins
Page 148: Mrs. Alice Wine
Page 151: Joe Deas, Esau Jenkins
Page 153: Beverly Hunter, Rosalie Pinckney, and Mary Pinckney
Page 157: Mrs. Alice Wine
Page 163: Mr. Johnny Hunter
Page 169: Children of Mr. and Mrs. Anderson Mack
Pages 172, 174: Mrs. Maggie Russell, by Candie Carawan
Pages 175–76: By Gary Hamilton
Page 177: Ms. Elaine Jenkins, by Gary Hamilton
Page 178: Top, by Gary Hamilton. Bottom, by Candie Carawan
Page 179: By Gary Hamilton
Page 180: By Candie Carawan
Page 181: Mrs. Ethel Grimball, by Gary Hamilton
Page 182: Mr. Abraham Jenkins, by Gary Hamilton
Page 185: Staff members of the Sea Island Comprehensive Health Care Corporation, by Wade Spees
Page 187: Mrs. Alleen Brewer Wood (on right), by Ida Berman
Page 188: Mr. William Saunders, by Gary Hamilton
Page 189: Left to right: Albertha Wine, Lucille Walters, Laura Rivers, Fanny Walker. By Gary Hamilton
Page 190: Left to right: Matthew Sease,

Gerald Mackey, Eldred Buncomb, Herman Smith, Tamara Fisher. Small girl is Esaunta Buncomb, with Adriane Saunders. By Candie Carawan
Page 192: Mr. Gerald Mackey, by Candie Carawan
Page 194: By Gary Hamilton
Page 196: Mrs. Alice Wine, by Thorsten Horton
Page 199: Mr. Esau Jenkins and Mr. Myles Horton, by Ida Berman
Page 200: Mrs. Alice Wine (second from left), Mrs. Septima Clark (center), Mrs. Bernice Robinson (standing). By Ida Berman
Page 202: By Ida Berman
Page 205: Mrs. Ethel Grimball, by Ida Berman
Page 207: Left to right: Mary Speed, Sonny Jenkins, Frank Speed (seated), Willie Smith, and Anderson Mack. By Ida Berman
Page 209: Mrs. Bernice Robinson (standing), Mrs. Septima Clark. By Karen Kasmauski, © 1987 National Geographic Society
Page 210: By Karen Kasmauski, © 1987 National Geographic Society
Page 212: Mrs. Alma Scott, by Candie Carawan
Page 214: Mrs. Janie Jenkins, by Gary Hamilton
Page 216: Mrs. Ruth Bligen, by Gary Hamilton
Page 217: Mrs. Janie Hunter, by Gary Hamilton
Page 218: By Candie Carawan
Page 221: Rev. David Hunter (top). Both by Gary Hamilton
Page 222: Marie Ford, Maggie Russell, Christina Heyward, Mary Richards. By Gary Hamilton
Page 224: The Moving Star Hall Singers (left to right): Janie Hunter, Mary Pinckney, Benjamin Bligen, Ruth Bligen, and Loretta Stanley. By Wade Spees
Page 227: Mr. William Saunders, by Lucy Phenix
Page 228: By Robert Yellin
Page 231: By Karen Kasmauski, © 1987 National Geographic Society
Page 233: By Leonard Freed
Page 234: By Candie Carawan